# Culture, Society and Economy

# Culture, Society and Economy

## Bringing Production Back In

Don Robotham

SAGE Publications
London ● Thousand Oaks ● New Delhi

© Don Robotham 2005

First published 2005

SAGE Publications Ltd
1 Oliver's Yard
55 City Road
London EC1Y 1SP

SAGE Publications Inc.
2455 Teller Road
Thousand Oaks, California 91320

SAGE Publications India Pvt Ltd
B-42, Panchsheel Enclave
Post Box 4109
New Delhi 110 017

**British Library Cataloguing in Publication data**

A catalogue record for this book is available
from the British Library

ISBN 0 7619 4013 8
    0-7619 4014 6

**Library of Congress control number available**

Typeset by C&M Digitals (P) Ltd., Chennai, India
Printed on paper from sustainable resources
Printed and bound in Great Britain by Athenaeum Press, Gateshead

# Contents

# Contents

# Introduction

This book seeks to make seven main points. My first argument concerns the role that cultural studies have played in sidelining interest in economic questions in modern social sciences. The form in which this has been expressed is in ritual rejections of 'economism'. The examples of this discussed are the works of Stuart Hall and Paul Gilroy. While economism is certainly to be deplored, this term has been so loosely used that it has almost lost all meaning. The rejection of 'economism' has led to a decline in economic knowledge in cultural and sociological theory and a consequent weakening in the ability to develop convincing economic alternatives to capitalism and globalization. Above all, therefore, this book is an appeal for a return to the serious study of economics which sociology and anthropology once displayed in the nineteenth and twentieth centuries.

My second point is that the most important empirical and theoretical reality for ordinary people and the social sciences to grasp today is the significance of the emergence of corporate (monopoly) capital since the beginning of the twentieth century. This process has had a number of consequences which have been and continue to be fundamental for world social, economic and political development. First of all, it represents the passing of a model of liberal bourgeois society which provided (and still provides) the social, economic and political basis for traditional Anglo-Saxon notions of the individual and of liberal democracy. This is the Hobbes–Locke civil society tradition which was, of course, itself not uniform.[1]

This supersession of an economy based on medium-sized enterprises of approximately equal size competing non-monopolistically in the market (the model of Adam Smith) is a far cry from the Behemoths which today dominate national and world economies, as scholars such as Franz Neumann long ago argued.[2] Indeed, as many have pointed out, today's corporation-dominated national and global economies in some ways resemble more the mercantilist economy of the eighteenth century of which Smith was sharply critical. This change therefore is a fundamental one. It has thrown liberalism into a prolonged and irreversible crisis of unreality – the first manifestation of which was the collapse of the Liberal Party in Britain after World War I – from which it has never recovered.

The rise of monopoly in the economy has been accompanied by the emergence of large-scale organizations in other areas of society – in the state, trade unions and political parties. These changes towards the joint-stock company, trusts and cartels historically proceeded furthest in Germany and the United States but were general to all the developed capitalist economies. Today, monopoly probably has gone furthest in Japan, with its incestuous concentration of huge banks, massive manufacturing firms and vast marketing and distribution organizations which reach into the smallest recesses of economic life through the practice of 'relational contracting'.[3] Efforts at what is called in Europe 'competition policy' (anti-trust in the United States, but with no equivalent for the *keiretsu* in Japan) focus not on subordinating or breaking up large corporations but on maintaining some semblance of monopolistic competition between them. Yet the political consequences of this overwhelming power of transnational corporations is nowhere anticipated in classical liberal political theory and is ineffectually captured by contemporary liberalism.[4] This failure leaves national and international democracy as a largely formal-legal shell, substantively controlled by the power of large transnational corporations, as books such as Monbiot's make clear.[5]

Various thinkers since the beginning of the twentieth century, often from radically different viewpoints, made this collapse of liberalism and the rise to dominance of large-scale organizations, the intellectual center of their work. One only has to think of Carl Schmitt and Max Weber on the one hand, and Hilferding and Lenin, on the other – significantly, early twentieth-century contemporaries of each other.[6] From the point of view of this book, it matters little whether one understands this real transformation of the liberal economy from a Schmittian (reactionary), Weberian (liberal) or Leninist (Marxist) position. I am not here concerned with whether one perceives the process as the inescapability of 'decisionism',[7] the inexorable rise of the 'iron cage of bureaucracy' (like Weber), as the growth of 'corporate globalization', or as the rise of 'monopoly capital' and the dominance of 'finance capital' (Hilferding, Lenin), although these distinctions are clearly crucial. For my purposes, these are secondary issues. Only three issues are of concern in this work: the first concern is the recognition of the centrality of the fact that the small and medium-scale economy of the classical liberal paradigm is gone for good, never to return. Large-scale centralized organization has triumphed in the economy and social, political and even cultural life.

This reality affects capitalism as much as it affects any conceivable alternatives to it. All discussions of any feasible form of a modern economy, global justice, national or international democracy must base themselves firmly on the irreversibility of this large-scale reality and on none other. Failure to understand this fundamental reality and the yearning for a local world lost forever are at the root of the weakness of many of the alternatives to globalization put forward by the global justice movement, especially for those influenced by environmentalism and anthropology. Failure to understand the potential in this new reality leads to the sensibility that this large-scale organization is a Weberian iron cage in which one is trapped and to which, at best, one must tragically resign oneself. This is an understandable but most profound mistake. In fact, this new international division of labor, in completely different economic and political conditions, presents an unprecedented opportunity for democracy, individuality and prosperity for all peoples on a global scale.

The second concern is this: the transformation of the liberal economy has been accompanied by a process of the export of capital and the growth of a strongly integrated global economy. This means that what one is dealing with is not just monopoly capital but the rise of transnational corporations (TNCs) which includes massive financial institutions engaging daily in trillions of dollars in international currency transactions. Thus, not only national economies are dominated by large transnational corporations but also the international economy. A substantial amount of international trade today is inter-firm transfers within the same transnational corporation. This reality means that the national macroeconomic management of even highly developed economies cannot be pursued independent of the wishes of global finance capital. The third consequence therefore follows from these processes: one has to analyze modern social science problems from an international viewpoint, even when national issues are the focus of interest. These factors have radically different consequences for developed and underdeveloped capitalist economies and are the basic source of the North–South divide. They are also at the root of the most serious international economic and political inequalities and tensions which confront the world today. None of this means that nation–states are powerless in the world of today. It does mean that nation–states have to adapt to this new economic and political environment if they are to be effective.

This leads to the third point. I argue that this transformation of capitalism from its liberal to its corporate form provides a new basis for individualism which cannot now be understood on the old liberal basis. Individualism no longer rests on the private acts of purchase in the market by the formally free individual consumer of classical liberal theory.[8] It rests on a global division of labor. It is the scale and scope of this division of labor which make it possible for modern individualism to flourish. In this sense, individuality rests on large-scale global sociality and is clearly in need of being re-theorized.

The fourth point is the failure of modern civil society theory – especially the work of Anthony Giddens and his associates in the Global Civil Society group at the London School of Economics – to grapple with the collapse of real existing liberal economy in its economic, political and social dimensions.[9] I argue that while this group is right to emphasize the overwhelming significance of global social and economic relations and the need to go beyond 'methodological nationalism',[10] its principal weakness lies in its abstraction of the market from the production relations from which it arises. This results in a failure to place the rise of corporate capital and of bureaucracy at the center of its concerns. The work of this group has much to say about the emergence of a global civil society but not much about the fact that this society rests on an uncivil finance capital. In sociological terms, they have rejected Weber for Durkheim. In other words, they downplay Weberian realism – that Nietzschean tendency in Weber's work in which he stares the contradictions of capitalism in the face.[11] This fearless honesty is the quality which makes Weber appealing to Marxists and liberals alike. Weber's focus on the rationalistic transformation of capitalism from its individualistic, Protestant origins into bureaucratic collective organization – an 'iron cage of serfdom' – is a critical part of the thought of this 'class conscious bourgeois', as Weber once described himself.[12] But Giddens and his group do not focus on this aspect of Weber – the inescapable triumph of bureaucracy and its irresistible authoritarianism. They prefer Durkheimian assurances that 'organic solidarity' can be made to prevail in national and global society, profound contradictions notwithstanding. This group does not ignore the economy as is the case with the practitioners of cultural studies. But when they discuss the economy, they abstract trade from the global system of production relations – from transnational corporate dominance.[13] While important points are made about trade, this abstraction of the market from the hidden abode of production contributes little to the debate on how these Behemoths may be tamed.

This leads to the fifth main argument. Here I attempt to take up the work of the theorists of network society and of 'economies of signs and space'. The main feature of this work is the claim that the most recent economic transformations – the deployment of new production techniques, information technology and market relations – in a word, 'flexible specialization' – is creating new opportunities for overcoming the domination of the world economy by corporate capital. In other words, this school differed from the Giddens group in recognizing, if only implicitly, the dominance of 'organized capitalism' up until the early 1970s. However, it argued that this had now been replaced by a 'disorganized capitalism' and economic networks with the potential to undermine the previous economic system and to open a space for greater personal freedom, 'reflexivity' and community. I argue that this represents wishful thinking. It fails to recognize that, far from flexible specialization and Japanese production techniques 'disorganizing' global capitalism, in fact, it represented the re-organization of capitalism on an infinitely larger scale. Moreover, this view failed to appreciate that transnational corporate capitalism is inherently organizing – in so far as it strives for economies of scale and scope, and at the same time, inherently disorganizing – in so far as it remains based on private ownership of the means of production and market competition. The point is not one or the other, but that *both* prevail, leading to unprecedented volatility and unevenness in the global economy.

I then proceed to discuss the sixth key point. This is largely a critique of that tendency in the global justice movement which adopts an anti-globalization or 'localization' position. I try to show that this position is riven by contradictions and is infeasible. Where it is feasible, it has reactionary political and cultural implications which are inconsistent with the ethical and political beliefs of its adherents. I conclude this review by arguing that many of the positions in the global justice movement are seriously in need of re-thinking.

Finally, I come to the seventh and most difficult part of the argument. This is the attempt to set out what an alternative economic system to transnational corporate capitalism could possibly look like. This argument tries to show that the state-dominated, centrally planned form of Soviet socialism was not only economically disastrous and necessarily politically repressive, but that it is the very opposite of the direction to be taken. The approach adopted is similar in some respects to that argued for by David Schweickart which necessarily requires the preservation but regulation of market relations of exchange.[14] However, it is my view that there is a residual communitarianism in Schweickart's alternative economic model which underestimates the necessity for central coordination and planning of a modern economy, including central coordination on a global scale.

On the one hand, I argue that any alternative economy must be founded on large-scale economic organization and the global division of labor already achieved. On the other hand, I argue that it must be based on the free and direct exchange between socially organized producers in which 'the free development of each becomes the condition for the free development of all'. *Pace* Hilferding and Stalinism, central planning is neither the ideal nor the *differentia specifica* of a socialist economy. On the contrary, alternative economic models must recover and re-incorporate the liberal ideals of freely associating individuals involved in direct relations with each other and, over time, unsupervised and unmediated either by the state or the transnational corporation. Given the necessities of coordinating a global economy based on the international division of labor, some significant degree of centralization will be inescapable in any feasible alternative. But this centralization must be minimized and robust efforts made to maintain and enhance the democratic accountability of these undoubtedly powerful central bodies.

In recent decades such ideas have become the preserve of economic and political neo-liberalism with socialism painting itself into a statist economic and political corner. Yet, because of their support for the large transnational corporation, neo-liberals cannot consistently support direct economic relations between individuals. Socialists, however, face no such constraint. Socialism therefore has an opportunity to recover these economic and political ideals which are sharply critical of the state, envisage its steady reduction and abolition and to some extent celebrate libertarian ideals. Without this auto-critique and re-orientation to democracy and the individual, it is difficult to see how socialism will regain broad public support.

Taken separately, each of the seven main points outlined above is unremarkable. I hope, however, that when taken together, the arguments here presented may offer some limited insight into urgent questions facing the contemporary social sciences. Only the reader can judge whether and to what extent this turns out to be the case.

# ONE Bringing the Economy Back In

The most striking feature of modern social and cultural theory is its relative lack of interest in and disconnection from the economic system of society, in the sense of the system of production. Contemporary cultural or sociological theories – cultural studies, postmodernism, risk society theory – have spent much time and effort inveighing against 'economism' and in declaring their independence from economics.[1] Where a connection with economics is established – as in network society or multiple modernity theory – this is an economics reduced to the status of a mechanism, usually a technological mechanism. In the case of risk society theory, the basic configuration of national and global economies is re-affirmed but this is a notion of the economy purely as exchange relationships. Concern is with managing the margins – the social and other 'risks' which arise from the operations of the market.[2] The consequence of this is the more or less explicit affirmation of the existing economic relations which arise from the system of production.

One consequence of this sundering of the relationship between cultural and social theory and the 'hidden abode' of the economy, or, of the affirmation of the existing set of economic relationships, has been that these theories have been unable to develop convincing critiques of modern global capitalist society. The failures of this society can be and are often acknowledged and lamented but no convincing alternatives are developed. The result is that those who experience the economic problems of the existing social systems as going way beyond a matter of managing risks find themselves alienated from this contemporary reformulation of social democracy – indeed, the political process as a whole. It seems to them determined not to address their fundamental concerns. On the other hand, those who are drawn to radical solutions continue to neglect economics and to formulate their positions in largely cultural-political terms.[3] The upshot of these failures is either a continuous string of mass mobilizations which seem to lead nowhere, or apathy, or even explicit support for the Right which – whatever may be said in criticism of right-wing views – has a program, however tendentious (law and order, immigration control, free markets combined with cultural conservatism and religiosity), which seeks to address the issues of everyday political concern.

Perhaps the most striking feature of this bracketing of production relations is its effect on those who oppose globalization. It is increasingly clear that there is a crisis here. Those who oppose globalization remain permanently locked into oppositional mode, increasingly driven to acts of anarchist rage, partly because of their inability to propose convincing alternative reforms in the sphere of the economy. Especially since the widespread failure of standard socialist and social democratic economic solutions (nationalization, central planning, price controls, the welfare state), the issue of workable economic alternatives is more important than ever. In their own way, anarchist groups seem to implicitly concede the failure of traditional socialism and simply revert to the primitive idea of 'smashing the system'. But window-smashing – which will hardly 'smash' capitalism (whatever that could mean) – is not a political or economic program. This failure means that the anti-globalization movement, while able to rally hundreds of thousands, even millions of people in its support, is unable to enter the mainstream of political life since it is unable to connect the movement to the solution of the everyday economic, social and political problems facing ordinary people.

Yet this may soon change. With concern growing for the increasing export of high-paying, high-skilled jobs to Asia, the anti-globalization movement may have new, but quite different recruits from suburbia and Middle America. This makes it all the more urgent for social and cultural theory to articulate a convincing and workable critique of the current form of globalization, *but on the basis of the extension of global economic and social relations*. Otherwise these groups are likely to revert to a narrowly nationalistic rejection of increased global integration.

However, it is one thing to criticize globalization in the sense of free trade, environmental abuse and other inequities – as a distorted and unregulated form of internationalization and sociality – and a totally different matter to reject it in its entirety on principle, with a view to some kind of romantic 'return'. For some time it has been clear that globalization in its current form of unregulated free trade is undesirable and unviable – economically, environmentally, socially and politically. When the negative effects of the current approach were confined to developing countries or to displaced blue-collar groups in the developed countries, this discomfited the powers that be but did not become a central policy issue. Now, to the surprise of many, the effect is much broader. 'Distant sites' are suddenly alive with productive economic activity, receiving prodigious amounts of western investment as well as investment from each other and exporting vast quantities of goods and services to each other as well as to the West. At first it was thought that this global extension of the division of labor and corresponding global extension of the market represented simply the transfer of relatively low-end (low-skill and low-paying) manufacturing jobs to the developing world – especially to China, Malaysia and India. The high-end and high-paying service jobs would remain in the West which would in fact allow as many of the fruits of this new international division of labor to be imported and consumed at will by the West. The Western standard of living would be preserved. The Western cost of living would remain low. This immense productivity of the East of a mass of cheap but high quality manufactured goods would make this possible for the West.

Of late, however, this has turned out to be not quite so simple. For report after report indicates that the very high-level service jobs which were supposed to remain in the West – the treasured 'symbolic analysts' themselves – now are being shifted overseas in significant and growing numbers.[4] The layoff of relatively highly-paid service-sector employees in the United States (computer programmers, financial analysts, engineers) who are then required to train the Asian employees to whom their jobs have been outsourced, is only the latest manifestation of the new realities of the international division of labor. If, as reported in the American press, an American Ph.D earns $80,000 per annum while an Indian earns $12,000, then the economic consequences of such disparities speak for themselves. How long this will continue in the United States without an enormous political and economic backlash remains to be seen.

This process is impacting on the job security and life chances of broad strata of middle and upper middle-class professionals in a most profound manner. These groups are becoming more and more skeptical and alienated from globalization in its current form. The awakening of these hitherto complaisant social strata to free trade presents a golden opportunity to the anti-globalization movement, if they will but grasp it. This is the opportunity of moving the movement into the mainstream of public life from its present position of being a large but still marginal activity of the Left. But this opportunity cannot be grasped from within the dominant mindset of the existing anti-globalization movement. Software engineers and financial analysts whose jobs flee to Asia are not going to be mobilized by window smashing. Feasible economic alternatives will be the decisive factor for this group. What is more, the entry of this mainstream stratum into the anti-globalization movement will radically transform its character in a direction of which some current anti-globalization activists may not approve.

Recognition of the social substance of globalization is altogether a different matter from an acceptance of free trade neo-liberalism. For some time now it has become apparent that globalization is in desperate need of regulation, at the national and especially at the international levels. Arrangements need to be made to assist weaker and smaller economies and to compensate social groups harmed by the process. There needs, for example, to be a new pool of social adjustment funds which will provide grants and low-interest loans where needed in the manner of the social and other support funds which flow from the wealthy to the less wealthy European Union nations. The restructuring and democratization of international economic institutions such as the International Monetary Fund and the World Bank are long overdue. Special consideration has to be given to African economies, to assist them to contribute to the global production process on an equal footing. Making such measures a reality will not be easy and will require a long political struggle nationally and internationally.

I attribute part of the weakness in articulating convincing critiques of globalization to the triumph of cultural and social theories which have as their central principle the basic independence of culture and society from what I regard as their economic foundation. It is also a result of the tendency of the Left to focus on the (ideological, organizational, political) challenges of winning political power and not on the economic challenges which arise *after power is won*. In fact, as will be discussed in the following chapter, the critique of 'economism' by writers on the Left focuses almost entirely on the negative consequences (passivity, lack of audacity and political will) of 'economism' in the struggle for political power. They seldom raise, much less discuss, the vital question of what happens if and when power is won – practical alternative economic policies to construct a different way or life – 'economism' in that sense.

But critiques of 'economism' by thinkers such as Gramsci took place before or in the process of attempts to develop a socialist economic alternative. And, as we shall see in the following chapter, Gramsci strongly supported a focus on the economy, during the post-revolutionary period of 'socialist construction'. By and large the downplaying of the economic leads to the erroneous view that methods which may be appropriate to the ideological or political struggle can simply be transferred to the economy. Yet one of the most important facts of political life that anyone espousing a progressive view has to contend with today is the dismal history of over 70 years of failure of many standard socialist economic remedies. The view that socialist economic policies simply do not work in practice – whatever one may think of them ethically – is deeply embedded in popular consciousness and is a political fact of the first order. It constitutes a powerful base of passive support for existing economic arrangements. Any constructive approach to the manifest injustices of the modern world therefore requires a confrontation with these failures and a deep understanding of modern production relations.

This work is, therefore, devoted to critiquing the theories which have encouraged the rupture with the abode of production. The aim is to bring production relations back into cultural and social theory without dismissing the value of cultural critique and the insights of sociological theories. My contention is that far from this 'productionism' nullifying the role of culture, consciousness and politics, it in fact encourages a strong role for intellectual and political work. This is because it requires intense intellectual and political effort in order for the tendencies underway in the economy to be unearthed and to be brought before public consciousness in a comprehensible and convincing manner. At the same time, one should not lose sight of the simple materialist fact that what makes doctrines convincing to masses of people is only partially their logical, emotional and cultural force. The decisive element in developing a broad-based conviction in an ideology is the extent to which this ideology proves in practice to be able to deal effectively with the challenges facing people in society. It is praxis – the unity of theory and practice – which is decisive, not rhetoric, not abstract logical consistency.

It should be stated immediately that in returning to an emphasis on the system of production, I do not conceive of the economy as a 'base' or a 'mechanism' or any other metaphor which reifies and removes it from the sphere of human agency. As with any other sphere of social life, the economy is an arena of personal and social agency in which millions of individuals in definite and changing social relations act to invest, produce, circulate, distribute, exchange, speculate on and, on occasion, to destroy wealth. But, as Marx pointed out, they do not exercise this agency as they wish. Their own political and economic actions have created a mode of production which has definite characteristics and which allows for some possibilities and not others. All agency is constrained by these objective factors and is not simply a matter of voluntaristic will. In the most general sense this wide-ranging economic activity is no different from activity in politics, the arts or the sciences: they are all forms of more or less conscious human activity. What is distinctive is the sphere in which this human agency is exercised – the production, distribution and exchange of the material basis for human existence.

If one takes this point of view, then the hoary issue of economic determinism or of 'structure' versus 'agency' or of 'base' versus 'superstructure' takes on a different character. For the issue now turns out to be one of the primacy not of base or structure or of something called 'the economy' but of one sphere of human activity over another. The real question that we have to consider is not whether 'base' determines 'superstructure' or 'structure' governs 'agency' but whether agency in the field of the economy takes precedence over agency in the sphere of politics or over intellectual agency – how these different but connected spheres of agency inter-relate.

Do the activities of workers, bankers, stockbrokers, financiers, manufacturers, wholesalers, retailers, marketers *qua* workers, bankers, stockbrokers, financiers, manufacturers, wholesalers, retailers, marketers when taken as a whole and operating within the logic of a capitalist mode of production at a particular stage of its development, determine the course of social, political and intellectual life? Or is it the mental and cultural activities of intellectuals – artists, academics, novelists, scientists and the like – which is determining? Is there a dominant form of agency and, if so, which is it – economic, political or intellectual or some form as yet unknown? My argument is that action in the sphere of the economy – perhaps the most complex and many-sided form of action in the world today – is the central force in our social, political and cultural life and that any cultural and social theory which aspires to effectiveness must therefore re-connect with the economic. But again and again it must be affirmed that this action does not operate in a vacuum and as it wills: it operates on the basis of the real existing capitalist mode of production with its own systemic logic.

Some will, of course, observe that economic activity, like any other, requires intellectual effort and also involves much politics. This, however, is hardly the momentous objection that some may think. For it is quite clear that notwithstanding that fact, any person can clearly distinguish the economic from the other spheres of life and these distinctions are in fact too commonplace to dwell on. This does not gainsay the point that economic agency (which includes intellectual effort devoted to the economic sphere) is a very complex and sophisticated form of human activity in a particular sphere of social life. Agency in this arena is as creative, if not more so, as it is in any other area of human life. It is not in any sense a non-human sphere – a mechanical 'base' or a 'technology'.

None of this means that political agency and cultural critique are not of the utmost importance. In fact, it is impossible to change and transform one mode of production into another without political action. Political relationships and forces entrench a particular social system of production, distribution and exchange as the dominant and legitimate system, upholding it by means of law backed up by force. Especially today, when the media and culture industries have gained such immense global power, cultural and ideological critiques are more important than ever in the battle to undermine the legitimacy of the dominant social system and to weaken the psychological and mental hold it has on the minds of millions of persons. But such critiques are weakened as critiques when conducted largely in terms of cultural politics, neglecting the economic foundation (in the broadest sense) on which these cultural phenomena rest. Nor should one conclude that the relationship between economic, political or intellectual agency is a simple mechanical one of automaticity or reflection. Such a view has more in common with empiricism than with Marxism. I adhere very strongly to the view that the tendencies and relationships in the economy are extremely complex, dynamic and self-obscuring and are by no means obvious to either popular or scholarly consciousness. At least from the time of Kant and especially Hegel, it became perfectly clear that, *pace* Baconian empiricism, 'experience' did not immediately serve up truth on a platter to consciousness, popular or otherwise. On the contrary, the deceptive nature of appearances became proverbial. Difficult and intense intellectual and political effort by innumerable persons – a social effort – is required to understand the relationships and tendencies – obscured by experience itself – to accurately penetrate to their inner core. Politics often lags behind economics, as, for example, in the development of political parties and legal systems which entrench the rights of the individual and democracy some time after a capitalist economy has developed. Intellectual work often anticipates economic life, as in the case of eighteenth-century Enlightenment thought.

There is, therefore, no sense in conflating these different spheres of social life, nor of portraying one as the other in disguise by means of a simple reductionism. Intellectual work is intellectual work is intellectual work. It is not economic activity or politics in disguise although it may bring economic rewards and have political implications. It is not necessarily motivated by economics although it may be, and clearly there is an enormously important publishing economy, unapologetically governed by the profit motive. It is absurd and misleading, for example, to portray the development of postmodernism as a reflection of the development of flexible specialization in the economy. The truth is, in fact, quite the contrary. Like the modernism which preceded it, postmodernism is not a simple affirmation of the consumerist plenitude or flexible production systems of contemporary capitalism. It in fact represents a deep alienation from capitalism (not to mention socialism) which seems to this form of consciousness to have lost all logic and purpose – flexible or otherwise – and to have become a vale of meaningless confusion and vacuous subjectivities. The root of this anti-capitalist alienation – frequently echoed in both postmodernism and contemporary Marxism and especially prevalent in anthropology – goes back to early nineteenth-century Europe, especially to late-developing Germany. It represents a yearning, bizarre or parodic, sentimental or menacing, farcical or tragic, for a pre-capitalist past – a sense, often vaguely felt even among the beneficiaries of capitalism – that the capitalist trajectory is somehow deeply inimical to their existence and personal well-being.

Specific forms of popular and academic consciousness are not to be linked in a mechanistic fashion to or explained by specific features of the economy. The relationship is at one and the same time broader and more profound. Consciousness responds spontaneously (with greater or lesser insight) to the whole range of economic, social, political and cultural experience (a whole way of life as a historical process) – more or less the surface of life. The cultural, artistic and psychological edifice of modern life is a different thing from the economic foundation on which it is built. The economic activities and relationships which underlie these experiences are often confined to a hidden abode. The journey from the one to the other is circuitous and arduous. Consciousness often leaps ahead of current experience – via imagination and foresight. The convoluted and complex nature of economic and social reality often leads consciousness astray – to draw the opposite conclusions from what really is the case. And this 'leading astray' is not an intellectual failure but a result of what, shamelessly borrowing from Hegel, I call the 'cunning of reality'. The distinctive feature of consciousness remains the capacity to see beneath surfaces, to see beyond the current and to detect relationships and processes not immediately and spontaneously apparent at first glance. But in so doing it has to outwit reality at its own game of deception.

A classic example of this issue of the relationship of social consciousness to social being is the growing individuation and emphasis on the self in the modern Western world. A central tenet of both neo-liberalism and risk society theory is precisely the claim that a defining feature of the modern or postmodern West (but perhaps not modern Asia) is an enhancement of individuality and reflexivity. A central characteristic of popular culture, especially as purveyed by the mass media, is an unrelenting focus on the individual personality, either in the form of exhibitionism or, more frequently presented simply as a perfectly natural and unself-conscious, even casual, self-centeredness. At the same time, Western intellectuals assert that the self is more important than ever. However, this is a classic case of presenting the surface of life as the reality. For this view fails to grasp precisely what needs to be understood if the basis of modern individualism is to be grasped in its distinctiveness.

The most striking feature of the modern world is the extension of sociality as the foundation for individuality. There has been and will continue to be an acceleration of the global division of labor which is the entire basis of the acceleration of global markets. This division of labor on this gigantic scale means, in effect, that the individual producer and consumer are more dependent than ever on other producers and consumers in distant places. This is by no means an original point for it was first made by Hegel in his critique of Adam Smith more than 190 years ago. Writing about the emergence of civil society and its peculiarities, Hegel stated:

> In the course of the actual establishment of selfish ends – an attainment conditioned in this way by universality – there is formed a system of complete interdependence, wherein the livelihood, happiness, and legal status of one man is interwoven with the livelihood, happiness and rights of all. On this system, individual happiness, & c., depend, and only in this connected system are they actualized and secured.[5]

There is abroad in the modern world enormously powerful economic forces driving and restructuring the international division of labor on an immensely global scale. This interdependent system of global finance, production, distribution and exchange represents, when looked at as a whole, a complex and contradictory system of sociality. In fact, the range and peculiarity of one's pattern of consumption at the individual level are only possible because of this unprecedented sociality. It is this global division of labor which creates and presents this cornucopia to consumers all over the world. But the crux of the matter is not consumerism. As Marx argued, consumption provides 'the finishing touch' to production.[6] The object of production is consumption. Consumption is an essential part of the production process. The global producer consumes globally in order to produce globally. It is the unprecedented global demand which presents challenges to the producer and stimulates hitherto unheard-of creativity and innovation by individuals and enterprises in their capacity as producers. This is so whether the producers are working in a small service enterprise or a large transnational corporation. The source of this new sociality is not, as older Marxist theory often implied, the size of the enterprise for which one worked. That was and is an altogether too narrow and local notion of the social. It is the scale of the international division of labor which is the crux of the matter. Without this global sociality, two things become immediately impossible, indeed, inconceivable: first, the individual in the world today could not consume the range of goods which she or he does as a matter of course; second, the individual could not produce the range of goods currently produced. Either as consumer or producer, the individual's individuality is a social product. The individual exists as an aspect of the social and can have no other existence in practice, even were he or she to withdraw to a hermit world. This is true not simply for activity in the economic field. It is so for the creative social, cultural and personal life of the individual in the broadest sense.

In other words, the striking feature of present-day individualism is how much it rests completely on a shifting but immense *social* foundation – on the integration of a global division of labor. Any constriction of this global division of labor would therefore have the inevitable effect of narrowing the individuality of the individual.[7] You would no longer be You nor Me, Me. This is the paradox of our times which Marx pointed to in the *Grundrisse* of 1857. Modern-day individualism rests on a profoundly different foundation from the liberal individualism of someone like Adam Smith or even Mill. Marx long ago pointed out that Adam Smith envisages an economy in which there is still considerable subsistence production as well as local production for local consumption with only the surplus being traded – an economy of limited commodification and restricted exchange – limited local, national and international markets.[8] In such a context, individualism did have a considerable individual and local foundation and one's personal culture necessarily had a limited local and national horizon. Indeed, nationalism, when it first arose, often represented a broadening of personal and social horizons from the purely ethnic or local.

Today, however, the extension of production on a global scale means that in nearly every corner of the globe the market and commodity production prevails. A global interdependence mediated by the global market as well as by global inter-state and inter-firm relations is emerging, albeit in its early stages and very unevenly and unjustly. This necessarily undermines the local and the national, and offers, very unevenly and unequally, new opportunities for the development of a genuinely human culture which supersedes narrow local and national loyalties. This is why those, such as Gray, who have deep conservative attachments to the local or national so strongly assail globalization.[9] This is also why many who oppose globalization put forward alternatives to globalization which emphasize 'localization' of the economy, including immigration control. They understand very well that it is this very international division of labor itself which is the basis of globalization. This 'localization' model will be critiqued in a later chapter as completely unworkable, indeed, undesirable.

One should note that these ideas are in the same tradition as the Durkheimian concern for the reconciliation of individuality with sociality. To Durkheim this contradiction is overcome by the solidarity generated by the mutual dependences of the division of labor.[10] The basic weakness of his argument – as that of many Left Liberals and Social Democrats – is the idea that this can be achieved within the framework of private ownership of the means of production and without a fundamental transformation of society and the political system. Marx's entire argument is that the contradiction between individuality and sociality rests on the contradiction between private and social property – ultimately on the development of the forces of production as expressed in the division of labour. This contradiction has to be overcome if individuality is to be in harmony with its social foundation. Moreover, Marx's conception of individuality goes further than that of Durkheim. Durkheim still retains notions of self-subsistent individuals brought into inter-dependence by the social division of labor. Marx's point, however, and the reality of the modern global world is that sociality enters into the very constitution of the individual, whether such a person is self-consciously cosmopolitan or not. It is not a taste for the exotic or a self-conscious cosmopolitanism – 'cut-and-mix' – which makes persons 'hybrid'. Hybridity is really located in the most mundane and everyday processes which bear not the slightest imprint of the exotic and of which most individuals have little awareness. A much deeper and broader analysis of the issue of what has been mistakenly labeled 'hybridity' or sometimes, 'cosmopolitanism', is called for.

In other words, if one is what one consumes and produces, one could say that persons living in the United States may already be about 10 percent 'Chinese' by virtue of the substantial consumption of goods imported from China into the United States. According to its own estimates, the US retail giant Wal-Mart alone imported $15 billion worth of goods from China into the United States in 2003. Of the 6,000 factories worldwide which supply Wal-Mart, 80 percent are in China.[11] However, since China also imports vast quantities of both consumer and producer goods and services from other countries of the world, though not so much from the

United States, these goods assembled in China and imported into the United States are by no means unequivocally 'Chinese' in any simple sense. The label 'American' and the label 'Chinese' no longer refer to sealed, self-subsistent realms as in the past. Tradition-minded Americans and Chinese experience the erosion of these old securities and do not like it. If one extends this example around the world, then what we realize is that the individual is already constituted by a global sociality in his or her inner-most self. This sociality is the distinctive feature of the modern self and is the secret of its enhanced capacity for life as well of the unfulfilment of this promise. Truncate and distort this sociality and it is the individual who inevitably is truncated and distorted. There can be little doubt that this sociality will only grow and become deeper as the global division of labor itself grows. This new kind of socially-rooted individuality has enormous implications for liberal democracy and notions of the absolute autonomy of the individual on which it is based.

Neo-liberals write as if the market – any market – *per se* creates choice. Actually the market is not the source of choice as such, only the mechanism through which choice is exercised by those who have money to buy the goods and services available. It is a truism which bears repeating that before goods can be exchanged, they first have to be produced. And not produced in any old fashion but in an increasingly sophisticated system of the global division of labor in which outsourcing is growing in scale and complexity.[12] The actually vast existing range of product choice is thus far from being the creation of the market. It is the fruit of this inter-nationally divided social labor. It is this global division of labor which creates the necessity for exchange. The overwhelming majority of this product is exchanged through the global market – creating both the pos-sibility of choice between a vast range of products and the market mech-anism through which this choice is exerted. It is a mistake to think that the global division of labor necessarily implies free trade or purely market regimes. The enormous possibilities for the development of individual talent and abilities which now exist (at least for some and in the abstract) only exist because of this variegated global specialization in production and global demand in consumption, including productive consumption. One must distinguish this process from the free market process both analytically and in practice. The capitalist form is one thing, the social substance another.

Because this enormous extension of sociality is mediated by the mar-ket, it presents itself either as consumerist plenitude or, what may well be considered another side of the same phenomenon, as an opportunity for privileged selves to expand their quantity and range of consumption.

A new cultivation of the self – cognitive or aesthetic – now becomes possible on an unprecedented scale. At heart, this is a frivolous or, if you will, a 'ludic' response to social process of historic proportions. The intellectual, like the consumer, even though he or she may notice, draws no conclusions from the fact that the goods consumed originate in a variety of countries and places. In fact, today this variety is so great and the chain of subcontracting so complex, that some furniture sold by the Swedish company IKEA, for example, carry a label explaining that their products are made from such a variety of sources that it becomes difficult to label them as made in anywhere in particular! It is only when there is a significant economic event in some other part of the world (recession in the United States, for example), which impacts on others in hitherto far-away places that this interdependence seeps into popular consciousness, usually tendentiously and demagogically. Or, when jobs, as mentioned above, and suppliers are outsourced abroad at the demand of national firms, on the perfectly sound ground that failure to do so will mean a fatal loss of global competitiveness. This process has gone so far that even military supplies of the most sophisticated kind are sourced abroad by the Pentagon. Militarists who, in a political and military context, gain renown as rabid unilateralists then turn out to be equally vigorous multilateralists in the economic sphere, when it comes to sourcing the highest quality military supplies most efficiently.[13] The firm rebuffing of 'Buy America' campaigns for military supplies has become standard policy in the Pentagon and its private sector partners among the large defense contracting firms.[14] The market, it turns out, is as much a mechanism of compulsion as it is of choice.

Global interdependence is therefore as much a reality in the military production and consumption field as it is in economic life as a whole. Global interdependence is not simply to be identified with free trade although this is a clearly a vital aspect of it. This is not simply a matter of large transnationals involved in inter-firm transactions. In practice, a substantial number of small and medium-sized firms are subcontractors to the transnationals and through this means are themselves deeply enmeshed in this new sociality, where they are not direct exporters themselves. This is particularly true of high-skills firms in the producer service sector as well as personal services firms. If their clients are not large firms directly, they are employees of such firms or of others which subcontract to them. This is why, as shall be discussed more fully in a later chapter, any program of economic 'localization' is doomed to fail. It is in fact impossible today to draw a meaningful line between small and large firms connected largely to a local or national economy in the old manner.

Attempts to draw such a line reveal a profound lack of understanding of the degree of integration of small, medium and large business into a single web of economic relationships.

Yet, instead of seeing this enormous enhancement of the underlying sociality of life, contemporary social and cultural theory simply seizes on and celebrates the opportunities for increased consumption, self-cultivation and reflexivity which this sociality presents to those with the wherewithal to consume. Consciousness, especially Western intellectual as well as popular consciousness, misses the underlying social reality which is the *differentia specifica* of our time, clings to the surface of modern life and hedonistically celebrates the self with ever greater determination. It refuses to perceive that there is a new social self which is abroad whose individuality lies in and derives from its deepened sociality. Where it perceives this new sociality, it fails to see its significance or potential. It is portrayed negatively – as a 'risk' or as a force which '"distanciates" social relationships' leading to 'a runaway world'.[15] As Lash and Urry observed, globalization is presented as a dystopia. Pessimism prevails.

In the socialist movement which developed in Europe in the second half of the nineteenth century, and, especially after the Russian Revolution of 1917, this was not how the process was supposed to unfold. The 'social' in socialism was to be realized by social revolution and the construction of national and global socialist economies under the leadership of the proletariat. For many reasons which need not detain us here, this project failed. Instead it is global capitalism which has constructed this new global social. The 'real existing sociality' of this capitalist world is not easily recognizable because it is not embodied in the old factory sociality of the industrial proletariat. That, we can now see, was a more local and national phenomenon. What we are dealing with today is a far more broad-based sociality engulfing nearly all groups in society, especially increasingly, the middle and upper middle strata. Global capitalism – transnational corporations and their network of subcontractors – has been driven to implement what, according to much of nineteenth- and twentieth-century radical theory, was supposed to have been the mandate of socialism. Because of this profoundly unexpected, unpredicted – indeed, unpredictable – turn in history, many seem not to perceive what has occurred. This consciousness does not see that this growth in global sociality and mutual dependence in fact is not simply an economic opportunity or threat. It is not simply the erosion of the old solidarities. It is at the same time laying the foundation for something new, in however contradictory and unequal a fashion. It is the beginning of the extension of human social and individual existence in the only manner which offers the real possibility for human emancipation. It is a demonstration that the contradiction between individuality and sociality is a relative not an absolute one. It is revealing that the two are deeply and organically interconnected and that the further development of individuality cannot occur without such an immense development of sociality. This is occurring on a global scale without particular regard to nations, communities and other local solidarities and ethnicities – whether white, brown or black.

Anyone who thinks of himself or herself as progressive cannot therefore simply respond to globalization with a lament for the old which is passing. In the end, such a posture of cultural conservatism must end up as political conservatism as well. One may as well call for the return of the three-field system or, for that matter, of plantation slavery. Yet modern social and cultural theory fails to emphasize or even to perceive these realities. This is because this consciousness has been content to confine itself to the surface of social, cultural and economic life, to rely mainly on 'the noisy sphere' of everyday life while avoiding 'the hidden abode' of production.

But if the hidden realities of economic and social life cannot simply be reflected in consciousness, there can be little doubt that economic realities will out. Voluntarism and illusions in the economic sphere (usually born from narrow self-interest or naïvety) are the characteristic sin of politicians and political movements of Left, Right and Center, with fatal and dreadful results. This idea – that the economic sphere does not have a logic of its own, or, if it does, it is only 'in the first instance' and to 'set limits' within which the political will can freely roam, and that public policy and politicians can either disregard or play fast and loose with the economic – is one of the most dangerous and enduring fallacies of the age. In the case of the Left, this usually takes the form of the idea that economic facts can be overcome by 'political will' – revolutionary fervor, mass demonstrations or rhetorical flourishes – 'red guard assaults on capital'. Adventurism in the economy, usually but not exclusively committed by the Left, cost millions of lives in Russia, China and Cambodia and ultimately was one cause of the collapse of socialism in Russia. It also has been a major factor in the stagnation of the Cuban economy. Theories which disregard or minimize the determining importance of the economy for society have played and continue to play a major role in this failure.

One ironical aspect of this neglect of economics on the Left is that their largely cultural theories usually fail to discuss the failures of Marxist economic theory and practice in any depth. There is a strange silence on critical issues such as the role of the market, the very real problems of central planning, of how to make sense of the labor theory

21

of value in the real world of a global economy with a highly developed division of labor – very little of these play a central role in the theoretical formulations of the Left today. Yet, a cursory look at the literature on the problems of 'real existing socialism' or of 'socialism with Chinese characteristics', or of Cuba today makes it quite clear that these are indeed fundamental issues.[16] By locating the substance of Marxism mainly in the cultural sphere, one is left with the distinct impression that in the economic sphere, Marxism is unproblematic. Yet it is precisely in the economic sphere – and in the politics which was required to buttress such economic policies – that applied Marxism has been a dismal failure, except, of late, for the controversial case of market socialism in China. The theorization of the economic therefore cannot be avoided.

# TWO Politics as Culture

## Stuart Hall

The most explicit theoretical outlook which has separated itself from economics and marked out a sphere for itself is that of Cultural Studies. Although some would argue that its moment has passed, it opened the door and set the stage for an entire line of theory, critique and political action which is still very influential, especially in the anti-globalization movement. Originating in Britain in the post-war period, this school has spread widely to the United States, Latin America and the Caribbean, to Australia and East and Southeast Asia. It therefore has many exponents. Here I shall deal with the central ideas of Stuart Hall – by common agreement, the pivotal figure in its development – and not with other extensions of cultural studies for which Hall can hardly be held responsible.

Hall's ideas are of particular interest because he has striven to maintain a critical stance to his own work throughout, himself pointing to, for example, the neglect of both race and gender as well as the only too striking 'Britishness', ethnocentrism and Eurocentrism of cultural studies.[1] Moreover, although Hall was strongly influenced by Althusser's notions of structural Marxism, by Foucault and discourse analysis, by Lacanian psychoanalysis, by Bahktin and semiotics, he has been adamant in maintaining strong ties to Marxist thinking and to radicalism in general. Whatever one may say in criticism of his ideas, no one could accuse Stuart Hall of going over to the Right. Indeed, if Hall can be criticized, it is for an inclination to a leftist populism, as we shall see. He remains as he always has been, on the side of the exploited and oppressed, whether white or black, whosoever may be the source of that oppression.

In fact, the challenge in grasping Hall's thinking lies precisely here: he refuses to reject completely the force of economics and the material. He rejects the concept of 'discourse' and insists on the concept 'ideology', for example. This is vital for understanding Hall. For we are not here confronted with a simple rejection of the economic and a construing of it as another discourse, in the manner of Foucault, although Hall repeatedly and frequently uses the word 'discourse'. Nor is Hall comfortable with the anti-humanism in Althusser and either the scientistic or irrationalistic tirades against the Enlightenment. Hall has lived too long and too deeply on the side of the oppressed to lose sight of where irrationalism leads politically and culturally. What we confront in Hall is not a rejection of the economic but its confinement to the 'first instance'.

For example, he wrote the following with reference to Foucauldian and other postmodern discourses:

> One of the consequences of this kind of revisionist work has often been to destroy altogether the *problem* of the class structuring of ideology and the ways in which ideology intervenes in social struggles. Often the approach replaces the inadequate notions of ideologies ascribed in blocks to classes with an equally unsatisfactory 'discursive' notion which implies total free floatingness of all ideological elements and discourses. The image of great, immovable class battalions having their ascribed ideological number plates on their backs, as Poulantzas once put it, is replaced here by the infinity of subtle variations through which the elements of a discourse appear spontaneously to combine and recombine with each other, without material constraints of any kind other than that provided by the discursive operations themselves.[2]

Hall rejects this 'free-floating' discursive approach which is often what one encounters in other versions of cultural studies today – for example, in Gilroy, whose work I shall discuss later. He insists on the necessity to link intellectual and cultural work to political struggles and not to pretend that these are ends in themselves which they never are. Hall's critique of Marxism is a determined attempt to de-Stalinize it – cleansing it of its authoritarian formulations and arbitrariness. He insists on the connection between theory and political practice but he wants this connection to be a flexible one which gives capacious space to intellectual, cultural and political creativity, free from diktat from without or within.

In fact, although not always obvious in his later work, there are signs in his earlier work that Hall operated implicitly from a particular materialist thesis. Sparks made the point when he quoted this passage from 'The Supply of Demand', first published by Hall in 1960. Hall wrote:

Even if working-class prosperity is a mixed affair ... it is *there*: the fact has bitten deep into the experience of working people ... There has been an absolute rise in living standards for the majority of workers, fuller wage-packets, more overtime. A gradual filling out of the home with some of the domestic consumer goods which transform it from a place of absolute drudgery. For some, the important move out of the constrictive environment of the working-class slum into the more open and convenient housing estate or even the new industrial town. The scourge of TB and diseases of undernourishment no longer haunting whole regions: the Health Service to turn to if the children are ill. Above all, the sense of security – a little space at least to turn around in.[3]

Here the argument seems to be a modest version of the then influential 'affluent worker' thesis, put forward by Goldthorpe and others. The suggestion seems to be that material changes in the conditions of life of the English working class in the post-war period had changed their political outlook. If the Left was to survive and be victorious, it had to understand this new working-class lifestyle and adapt to it politically and ideologically. The reason why ideological flexibility is needed, therefore, has to do with the effect of changes in material reality and is not simply due to the inherent requirements of theory as such. This search for ideological flexibility and freedom but *within Marxism,* I see as the well-spring of his work. Although, therefore, Hall frequently and commonly uses words such as 'discourse' and 'discursive formation', he has a far more materialist notion of such concepts than Foucault or than many of his readers may realize.

It would be hard to quarrel with this effort to de-Stalinize Marxism though some will question whether this is either possible or useful. Hall clearly thinks that it is essential. Throughout his entire work, this search for a 'Marxism without guarantees' is the fundamental thread which unites it all. This search for democracy and flexibility within Marxism is necessary for anyone who considers themselves progressive in the world today. This is because the body of ideas in Marxism has been and continues to be formative for all critiques of capitalism of any progressive stripe, even when the corpus of Marxism is firmly rejected. To ignore this quest therefore greatly weakens contemporary efforts at progressive social, economic and political reform of whatever variety. Indeed, a classic example of this weakness is risk society theory which has increased the gap between a new brand of marketized social democracy and those who see the need for more radical critiques of capitalism. Thus, the necessity to dialogue with Marxism remains as urgent as ever. At issue is not such a dialogue *per se* but whether the particular manner in which Hall introduces flexibility into Marxism is a viable and promising one, yielding the results which many want. Does Hall's critique work? My argument is that it does not. I argue that, notwithstanding numerous qualifications, Hall ends up by draining politics of economics and by reducing all politics to cultural politics.

On the basis of the above, it follows then that any understanding of Hall's thought must proceed from a recognition of its grounding in materialism. This is particularly obvious in his essay on the problem of ideology published in 1983. Here Hall takes up the questions which we are discussing and resolves them along lines very similar to which are offered here. Very similar but, as we shall see, not the same.

The question that Hall posed in this essay is that of the relationship between consciousness and the economy and the sense in which false consciousness can be said to exist. It is important to appreciate why such an issue should have attained importance at all – the context in which the essay was written. The context was the post-1968 one – both the aftermath of the student rebellion in Paris and the Soviet crushing of reform in Czechoslovakia. This was a context in which a privileged dogmatism of the Stalinist variety was confronted with an equally vanguardist Trotskyism. Both groups – locked in mortal ideological struggle – had this much in common: contempt for the consciousness of 'ordinary folks' (Hall's term) and an overweening sense of possessing the 'truth' of radical politics to which all progressive persons should defer. Part of this contempt for ordinary people was a disregard in particular for the life of ordinary black people and the popular cultural forms which they had developed. Hall's project is to retain the profound insights which Marxism offers into capitalism while rejecting this Stalinist and Trotskyite dogma.

All this was conducted with a central political problem in view. This was the problem of 'the consent of the mass of the working class to the system in the advanced capitalist societies of Europe and thus their partial stabilization, against all expectations'.[4] Both Stalinist and Trotskyist Marxism – indeed, Marxism as a whole – found itself impotent and ineffectual face-to-face with this popular consent. This issue of the failure of revolution in the West was seen as raising mainly the issue of the character of class consciousness versus false consciousness, where and how this consciousness of consent arose and what was the role of the political intellectual in relation to the masses, in the development of consciousness beyond the level of the popular. In other words, the failure of revolution was seen as posing a problem in consciousness and in what one could call the politics of consciousness, not a problem in politics and economics more broadly speaking. The issue was therefore posed as one of how this popular mass consciousness of consent was to be understood and, where necessary, critiqued. These were some of the central questions which arose in the context of the time, which Hall felt it necessary to attempt to answer, within the Marxist framework.

Basing himself on Marx, Hall argued that spontaneous forms of consciousness, popular as well as scholarly, arise from the surface of economic life which is what people actually experience. In the case of capitalist society what this 'surface' amounts to, is the market and exchange relations, be these in consumption, production, finance or the labor market. This reaction to the surface of life as it necessarily appears in consciousness therefore has a material base – conditioned by how and where one is positioned in the marketplace. This is the reason why consumerism, hedonism, narcissism, exhibitionism, self-centeredness – reflexivity if you will – the spontaneous forms of consciousness in developed capitalist societies which, as Weber was at pains to point out, have long relieved themselves of their Protestant ethic. All the efforts of neo-conservatives to revive such an ethic collapse in hopeless failure amidst the consumerist plenty of the developed capitalist economy. The refinements of consumerist luxury prove simply too much to resist, first and foremost for the members of the conservative elite itself. As Weber long ago pointed out, all attempts to give an ethical foundation to modern monopoly capitalist civilization in its present state, are simply non-starters, likely to collapse either in hypocritical farce, or worse, to degenerate into a 'blood and soil' atavism of the worst anti-human kind.

This spontaneous consciousness is therefore 'true' in the sense that it does arise from particular material experiences. However, this is only a *partial* and one-sided truth and therefore no truth at all. This is because experience based on the market actually conceals more than it reveals about the deeper and more far-reaching economic and social processes at work. These processes are to be found in the sphere of production. Even in the sphere of production they are by no means immediately obvious. Only a profound analysis of the 'hidden abode' of production – in other words, intense intellectual effort which critiques the shallowness and one-sided nature of 'experience' – can overcome the false consciousness generated by the capitalist system itself.

False consciousness therefore is a reality and it springs from reality. It is a reality in its popular form as much as in its scholarly and expert form. Indeed, it may be more widespread in academia and among elites than it is among the mass of ordinary people. It is not necessarily superficial, even though it derives from experience. Experience is not disconnected from reality but is an expression of it. Therefore, at crucial moments and when viewed from particularly insightful angles, spontaneous expressions of consciousness often arrive at profound representations of reality. This is particularly true in the field of popular art but, alas, only for a few artistes. Their work attains a lasting status because they capture a particularly telling moment when events force truth to peep out from reality – a moment which we all recognize, if only instinctively.

Therefore, where the falsity of spontaneity derives from is not intellectual error or a failure in reasoning. To argue this way is to pose the problem entirely within the framework of empiricism or of traditional French rationalism. Falsity derives from the very operations of political-economic reality itself. It is a real experience which obscures the fullness of reality and, therefore, it is only real experience which can change it. It is because spontaneous forms of consciousness are anchored in real experiences and social relationships – for example, the real experience of market exchanges – why they arise in the first place and are so tenacious. They are not figments of the imagination – mere 'errors' of reasoning or failures of empirical 'data analysis'. Part of the cunning of reality is just this: it produces both the reality as well as the processes which obscure reality. A complete grasp of reality would therefore go beyond the spontaneous and would explain, not only what the underlying reality consists of but also, even more important, how economic processes themselves operated to generate a *camera obscura*.

Thus far, Hall's account of false consciousness is materialist, some may even say orthodox. Although he does not there acknowledge it – indeed, under the influence of Althusser, Hall explicitly makes a number of anti-Hegelian asides – this line of thinking is clearly Hegelian. Ideas such as the distinction between a 'surface' which is the 'form' of reason and which, while an expression of Reason's 'substance' may obscure its 'essence' are unmistakably Hegelian in nature. In the *Philosophy of Right*, Hegel wrote:

> The great thing is to apprehend in the show of the temporal and the transient the substance which is immanent and the eternal which is present. For since rationality (which is synonymous with the Idea) enters upon external existence simultaneously with its actualization, it emerges with an infinite wealth of forms, shapes, and appearances.[5]

In fact, without resorting to the considerable Hegelian heritage in Marx, it is impossible to arrive at a notion of ideology which is non-mechanistic. Indeed, the basic Hegelian distinction between Understanding (*Verstehen*) which remains at the level of 'show' (*Schein*), and Reason (*Vernunft*), more or less corresponds to the distinction in Marx between false consciousness which is spontaneous and a consciousness which penetrates to the very core of reality and grasps both this core as well as how this core necessarily presents itself to consciousness in particular, distorted, and one-sided experiences. The notion that the 'truths' of consciousness are always relative and partial, that experience generates only a partial truth not to be taken at face value, that, however, this partial truth is a necessary part of reality which reality itself generates and which people actually experience – this is the Hegelian critique of French rationalism and mechanical materialism, which, as Marx long ago pointed out, Feuerbach famously failed to grasp.[6]

Hegelian rationalism was 'Absolute' and far more thoroughgoing and profound than French rationalism. He showed that the process whereby Reason supersedes Understanding is not a subjectively intellectual one produced by superior feats of reason performed by the Cartesian subject. From the Hegelian viewpoint, this is to break the necessary interconnection between subject and object and to elevate the former arbitrarily over the latter. On the contrary, truth emerges from an arduous process of struggle *within* Reason and is a necessary part of the process of the unfolding of Reason itself in a broad social (not personal) sense. In the Preface to *The Phenomenology of Mind*, Hegel wrote: 'The beginning of the new spirit is the outcome of a widespread revolution in manifold forms of spiritual culture; it is the reward which comes after a chequered and devious course of development, after much struggle and effort.'[7]

As Lukács pointed out, there is a striking contrast between early and late Hegel on this issue of the power of consciousness.[8] First, it is vital to note that this is a profoundly historical notion of consciousness. Consciousness does not 'exist,' it *emerges* – it has a history. Second, the history of consciousness is a *phenomenology*. It evolves over historical time as the result of a struggle within consciousness itself, between new and archaic mentalities and outlooks. Third, in Hegel's earlier writings, Understanding (at the social level but expressed in the insights of individual thinkers) is able, as it were, to leap ahead of itself and anticipate solutions to problems yet to fully unfold in Reason. Consciousness is able to sense in 'symptoms here and there ... the undefined foreboding of something unknown – all these betoken that there is something else approaching'.[9] In a letter to his friend Neithammer in 1808, quoted both in Lukács' book *The Young Hegel* and by Avineri, Hegel is more explicit: 'Daily do I get more and more convinced that theoretical work achieves more in the world than practical. Once the realm of ideas is revolutionized, actuality does not hold out'.[10] This was in sharp contrast to the dispiriting view published 13 years later – a view which is far better known. At this later date, Hegel retained the idea that a particular form of Understanding is simply a stage in the fuller evolution of a social Reason itself. Now, however, Hegel asserts that this form can only follow, never anticipate the full emergence of reality. He wrote:

> One word more about giving instruction as to what the world ought to be. Philosophy in any case always comes on the scene too late to give it. As the thought of the world, it appears only when actuality is already there cut and dried after its process of formation has been completed. The teaching of the concept, which is also history's inescapable lesson, is that it is only when actuality is mature that the ideal first appears over against the real and that the ideal apprehends the real world in its substance and builds it up for itself into the shape of an intellectual realm. When philosophy paints its grey in grey, then has the shape of life grown old. By philosophy's grey in grey it cannot be rejuvenated but only understood. The owl of Minerva spreads its wings only with the falling of the dusk.[11]

Such a daunting stoicism introduced a mechanical element into the otherwise more flexible and dialectical body of Hegelian thought. If one sticks with the earlier Hegel, then the ability of consciousness to achieve foresight is preserved, but this is not an easily won and spontaneous foresight. It does not arise arbitrarily but out of the emerging situation itself. It was this conception which gave rise to Marx's well-known formulation to the effect that society only sets itself problems which it can solve, since the emergence of the problem is a sign that the solution is at hand – problem and solution are organically connected and necessarily emerge together as part of a single process. Yet this is not to be understood mechanically and as a fixed relationship: solution may precede problem – consciousness anticipating reality – or arise entangled with it in complex and contradictory ways which pose intense ideological and political challenges.

Hall comes close to this dialectical conception in his well-known essay, 'The problem of ideology: Marxism without guarantees'. The key point made by Hall here is the Hegelian one, 'materialized' by Marx. This is the idea that failures and limitations of popular and individual consciousness do not arise from failures in logic and the process of reasoning. They spring from reality itself. Reality has its own logic and process out of which a grasp of this reality itself emerges. Therefore, it is not truth alone which springs from reality while false consciousness is an intellectual error. On the contrary, both true and false consciousness are organically rooted in the process of the emergence of reality. Therefore, the specific form which both true and false consciousness takes depends on the extent to which the determinations and contradictions in reality have emerged and, so to speak, specified themselves. Both true and false consciousness have a certain necessity, historically speaking. In other words, it is not consciousness which obscures reality. It is reality which obscures itself. Reality presents and conceals truth at one and the same time. On the basis of this approach, consciousness remains anchored in actual political-economic processes – an 'ideology' – and does not float off as a disembodied 'discursive formation'. Nor, given this Hegelian approach outlined above, can there be any simple reflection of the economy in consciousness, least of all a one-to-one correspondence between social class and ideological outlook. The contradictions and determinations of consciousness do not emerge automatically but are the result of the most intense struggle and effort. Mechanistic notions of consciousness, which was a basic staple of Stalinism, are to be abhorred.

Why, then, do I find Hall's conception inadequate and misleading? In the first place, Hall's conception of the failures of consciousness as due to its partial nature is insufficiently historical. The failure as presented by him is a failure of the incompleteness of the perspective which consciousness has on reality – its 'take' on reality and consequent lack of penetration, as it were. Hall does not sufficiently historicize this process, does not sufficiently present this lack of grasp as itself a necessary stage in the emergence of a truthful consciousness – a process governed by its own logic and necessity. Since truth is always relative, in many cases false consciousness is a consciousness which was *once* true. Put in Hegelian terms, there is no *phenomenology* of false consciousness in Hall. Because there is no phenomenology, the effort and struggle for true consciousness to emerge – the arduousness of the process by which truth emerges in a struggle with previous 'truths' and supersedes them – are not appreciated or brought to the fore. Paradoxically, the result of this is to underestimate the role of intellectual effort in the discovery and exposure of the truths of reality.

But there is a more important issue. As soon as Hall recognizes that both truthful and false consciousness arise from actual material experience, he excessively elevates the agency of consciousness. He confines the agency of the economy only to 'the first instance'. Hall wrote:

> It would be preferable, from this perspective, to think of the 'materialism' of Marxist theory in terms of 'determination by the economic in the *first* instance', since Marxism is surely correct, against all idealisms, to insist that no social practice or set of relations floats free of the determining effects of the concrete relations in which they are located.[12]

In other words, material reality is only a 'setting of limits' for consciousness, only a 'defining the space of operations' and not the determining force as such.[13] What this boils down to is the assertion, rejected above, that while true consciousness derives from reality, false consciousness does not. The latter derives from idiom, metonymy and psychology – in this sense, is generated non-rationalistically. Consciousness now becomes 'culture'.

The problem here is not with the assertion of the relative autonomy of consciousness. This much is present in both Hegel and Marx. The problem arises when Hall goes beyond autonomy and then implies that consciousness, although arising initially from material reality, subsequently is not only autonomous but determining. Moreover, Hall's logic of consciousness is a non-rationalistic 'psycho-logic'. The problem therefore is not the relative autonomy of consciousness but its *authority* and *concept*. In other words, as a form of agency, in Hall, cultural agency (language, social and national psychology) trumps both economic-political agency as well as conscious reason. *Cultural* politics becomes the most important form of politics. Let us look at a characteristic passage.

In a discussion of the problem of ideology and 'the ways in which ideas of different kinds grip the minds of masses', he wrote:

> It has especially to do with the concepts and the languages of practical thought which stabilize a particular form of power and domination; or which reconcile and accommodate the mass of the people to their subordinate place in the social formation. It has also to do with the processes by which new forms of consciousness, new conceptions of the world, arise, which move the masses of the people into historical actions against the prevailing system.[14]

Here the conception is not simply one of the autonomy of ideology. Ideology here is conceived of as being able to 'grip the minds of masses' – largely, as it were, by the force of its ideological and emotive power – and, through 'the concepts and languages of practical thought' either stabilize or destabilize political power. In other words, it is not ideology combined with the bitter experiences of material reality which moves people, willy-nilly, often *in spite of* their ideological outlook, to act or not to act in a particular way and, indeed, to reflect on and perhaps slowly change their consciousness. It is 'meaning', by virtue of its mastery of popular idiom and concepts, which is able to convince millions – by virtue, if you will, of its social-psychological penetration, cultural astuteness and dramatic power. Hence the vital political importance of understanding popular 'style' in Hall's thought.[15] Grasp of this style and adaptation to it, not superficially but deeply, are the essential components in making political ideas popular, not the actual ability of these ideas to speak to and really solve the economic and political questions which face millions of people in the world today. Here one encounters the failure characteristic of this line of thinking – a profound underestimation of human rationality. False consciousness, conceived of by Marxism as rooted in the *camera obscura* of reality and in that sense rational, is here presented as hidden deep within the recesses of metaphor and 'multi-accentuated' meaning. Cultural and 'psycho-logics' are the key. In turn, this necessarily leads to a deep disregard of economic issues and the enduring rationalistic connections between the economic, the political and the ideological.

These ideas are elaborated when Hall discusses Laclau's notions of how the inner dynamics of thought enables thought to grip the masses and thus to shape political action – presented as a profoundly non-rationalistic process. Hall wrote: 'But its [consciousness] cogency depends on the 'logics' which connect one proposition to another in a chain of connected meanings: where the social connections and historical meaning are condensed and reverberate off one another.'[16] In other words, the reason why an ideological outlook 'grips the masses' is not because it arises from and is consonant with real economic and political experiences. The development and understanding of popular consciousness are not a rationalistic process in that sense. To understand popular consciousness one needs not logic but 'logics'. What changes or sustains popular ideas is not the real ability to resolve economic and political issues, not, so to speak – the political and economic efficacy of ideology. The relationship is the other way around. It is the 'inner logics' which are decisive. Political, economic or even ideological efficacy – in the rationalistic sense – are neither here nor there. What wins the masses over to a particular outlook is the rhetorical power of ideology rather than its practical vindication in everyday experience. It is inadequate mastery over popular 'common sense' which is the problem.

Hall always argued that the effectiveness of Thatcherism derived from its mastery of a certain kind of populist conservative rhetoric. Of course, given the intractable political and economic contradictions and gross inequalities of our time, no one can deny that social, cultural and racist demagogy of every conceivable kind necessarily plays a central role in helping dominant social groups to maintain power and legitimacy. But such an observation begs the question as to what lies behind the effectiveness of this demagogy. Is it the mastery of idiom – the dialect in which demagogy presents its case? Or are the causes deeper? Hall has never paid much attention in his analyses to the economics of the triumph of Thatcherism or to the glaring failures of the Left and Social Democracy

*33*

to resolve the economic and social problems of our time, especially after the decline of Keynesianism and the Bretton Woods system in the 1970s and the failure of the market reforms in Eastern Europe during the same period. The thought that Thatcherism was in reality superior to the approaches of the Left and social democracy, primarily in its grasp of the crisis facing the global capitalist economy, and, barring this decisive fact, Thatcherite neo-Victorian and neo-colonial rhetoric would have been in vain – such thoughts simply do not arise anywhere in his analysis. As Sparks pointed out, 'the material basis of Thatcher's political success is never investigated' by Hall.[17] This lack of concern for economics continues to this day and is a serious source of theoretical as well as political weakness. What it leads to is a politics long on denunciation and outrage, but short on the presentation of convincing alternatives to the present global capitalist order.[18]

Thus, this line of thinking leads to the conclusion that it is psychological, cultural and semiotic shrewdness which matters most in politics. On this basis, it may not be out of place for an exponent of cultural studies to conclude that Marxism failed not because of its failures in theoretical and applied economics which is simply the obverse side of its failure in politics. The problem was the inadequacy of Marxist 'spin'. The failure of Marxism was a cultural failure – a failure to adapt itself sufficiently shrewdly to specific national idioms – essentially a failure of cultural propaganda. Marxism needs to go back to the drawing board and to repackage itself more idiomatically and metonymically, root itself more effectively in popular culture and organize mass cultural manifestations. As Hall wrote, 'It is only through the way in which we represent and imagine ourselves that we come to know how we are constituted and who we are.'[19] This is psychological and semiotic reductionism and in the end, is irreconcilable with materialism as well as with rationalism.

This argument leads to the view that the process of the development of culture is at its core a self-subsistent psychological and linguistic process. It is mainly a mental process at the mass and individual level governed by its own inner logics and not mainly determined by the economic or political real-life effectiveness of these thoughts. To Hall, while 'meaning' – not 'thought'! – initially arises rationalistically from material experience, having once arisen, thereafter it is free. Indeed, from this point of view, it becomes very difficult to maintain any distinction between the economic, the ideological and the political. Such is the primacy given to culture that economic and political agency – rationalistic agencies of any kind – are themselves treated as expressions of cultural outlooks. The idea of other forms of experience and activity, of 'experience outside of representation' becomes inconceivable.[20] The very term 'representation' is a term loaded with emotion and metaphor – not simply a synonym for 'conception'. Hall wrote, in appreciation of the work of Althusser:

> It opened the gate to a more linguistic or 'discursive' conception of ideology. It put on the agenda the whole neglected issue of how ideology becomes internalized, how we come to speak 'spontaneously', within the limits of thought which exist outside us and which can more accurately be said to think us.[21]

If one accepts this formulation, then it means that one must subordinate the economic to the political and, in turn, the political to the cultural will. In a sense too, it can lead one to go further and deny the distinction between cultural outlooks and action. It is not that Hall takes the absurd view that economic and political realities or actions do not exist, only culture. It is not even that he argues that the economic and the political – all actions – are experienced in and through culture. Hall is always careful to recognize 'the powerful role which the economic foundations of a dominant social order or the dominant economic relations of a society play in shaping and structuring the whole edifice of social life'.[22]

He clearly and repeatedly affirms this 'powerful role'. But the problem is that the economic is not so 'powerful' as to be persistent in its effects. That role is not awarded to consciousness either, which, after all, remains a highly rationalistic concept. It is awarded to culture. Culture envelops consciousness and is more powerful than both politics and economics. Once having arisen, culture – language, music, dance, poetry, literature, folklore, national and social psychology, 'style' – is given the capacity to so shape this economic and this political – all actions – that the latter have little decisive force of their own. Economics and politics, indeed, all human actions – become not merely 'influenced' by culture. They become *determined* by culture. 'Action' too, in such an all-enveloping cultural perspective, becomes, in the final analysis, if not a form of culture, simply an 'expression' of it. Or, if you will, culture becomes a form of action.

This is a very deep denial indeed, or an inability to concede an independent existence to the economic and to a lesser extent to the political – to rationalistic action of any kind. It represents a profound subsumption of them all under the category of culture. It must lead to a privileging of the cultural over all other forms of politics and of politics in general over economics. Although there is an aspect of this which is deeply quietist and contemplative, it is not an apolitical view. In fact, it provides the theoretical rationale for a particular type of politics. Hall is very political, but this is primarily a *cultural* politics.[23] A politics of the powerful gesture: mass mobilizations, marches, street theatre, powerful speeches, well-crafted essays. This approach to the problems of modern capitalist society has shown time and again its inadequacy: it can oppose and denounce, but cannot propose.

This takes us to Hall's treatment of Gramsci. For Hall is aware of the problems posed by his confinement of the economic to only being determining in 'the first instance'. After all, he asks, if the first, why not 'the first, middle and last'?[24] Why not continuously? Sensitive to this issue, he remarked elsewhere that 'Of course, "consent" is *not* maintained through the mechanisms of ideology alone'.[25] Apart from the fact that this is an aside, at issue is not whether ideology acts 'alone'. The issue is whether it is the *main* force. Hall's formulations foster the view that it is.

Gramsci is important to Hall because of his concept of hegemony and the tendency in Gramsci to assign an elevated role to the 'organic' intellectual – a notion which has its roots in early nineteenth-century German anti-capitalist Romantic thought. Hall regards the concept of hegemony as the key to unraveling the riddle of the consent of the contemporary working class to advanced capitalist society. Following Grasmci, this is characterized as due to the process of 'hegemonic domination'.[26] What is at stake here is the basis of consent. The issue is whether the consent of the disadvantaged in contemporary capitalist society is maintained *primarily* by cultural mechanisms or primarily by a rationalistic political economy and ideology. Hall interprets Gramsci as arguing that this is primarily a cultural process in the non-rationalistic sense – the power of religion and the mass media are held to be decisive.

But this may be an unduly culturalist interpretation which downplays Gramsci's rationalistic materialism, especially the vital importance which Gramsci attaches to the economic and social interventions of the state as a means of maintaining the hegemony of the ruling groups and of stabilizing their rule.[27] This was particularly important for Gramsci in his analysis of the effectiveness of the corporatist policies of Mussolini.[28] Of course, brazen demagogy was and is necessarily endemic to fascism. But, in Gramsci's view, what made Italian fascist ideology effective and able to 'grip the masses' was not its 'metonymy'. The point is that fascist ideas were embodied in concrete economic and social projects which incorporated and made material concessions to broad masses of people. Fascism was shrewd and in its own way, highly rationalistic at the level of means-rationality. In other words, it was the combination of ideology with effective practice which was decisive. Needless to say, a decisive part of this 'effective practice' was the ability to take a sober view of the economy and, on this basis, to implement economic policies which had the capacity to address the central problems of the day.

A similar misreading may have occurred in drawing on Gramsci's critique of economism. One of the most important but often unacknowledged features of Gramsci's thought lies in the political context in which it arose. This was not simply a matter of the specifics of Italy and the rise of Mussolini. Of course, these were vital aspects of his context but to confine oneself to these is to be too narrow and, in fact, makes it difficult to really appraise Gramsci's thought accurately within the general body of the socialist thought of the period.

The point to remember is that Gramsci, like all Marxists of that time, was primarily influenced by the Russian Revolution of 1917. His writings, however, are from the period of so-called 'War Communism' (1917–21) and after. In particular, Gramsci worked for the Comintern in Moscow and Vienna from 1922 till 1924 and his thought was greatly influenced by the struggles both of Bolsheviks against Mensheviks and within Bolshevik ranks themselves.[29] To understand his thought in context therefore requires a brief delineation of this context.

Gramsci's critique of 'economism' more or less adopts the famous critique made by Lenin in *What Is to be Done?* This is a critique which argued that the economic determinism of the Second International – primarily Kautsky and Bernstein – relied on the economic evolution of capitalist society to achieve socialism, without the direct intervention of a revolutionary party to overthrow the capitalist state. The point being made was that such an approach of economic determinism was passive and at its core defeatist. It failed to provide for an independent role for ideological and political activity and simply relied on the automatic unfolding of economic events.

Gramsci repeats this Leninist critique. Here is Sassoon quoting Gramsci on the dangers of 'economism':

> An appropriate political initiative is always necessary to liberate the economic thrust from the dead weight of traditional policies – i.e. to change the political direction of certain forces which have been absorbed if a *new homogenous politico-economic historical bloc, without internal contradictions, is to be successfully formed.*[30]

Gramsci's concept, writes Sassoon, is that 'while material structural conditions are given, as a product of the past, an earlier stage of the class struggle, and while in decisive moments the elements of physical force or "military" preparedness is vital, the subjective political dimension is the most crucial'.[31] Whatever one may think of such ideas – especially the idea that 'the subjective political dimension is the most critical' – it is clear that this entire discussion relates solely to the issue of the struggle for power. Indeed, whatever the differences Kautsky may have had with Bolshevism, there can be little doubt that the 'economistic' Kautsky assumed that after power was won, central planning would prevail with the entire economy being treated as 'a single gigantic industrial concern'.[32]

However, it is worth noting that this critique of 'economism' does not exhaust Gramsci's views on the importance of the economy. One must not forget that his theorizing also took place during the period of the first experiment with market socialism – the New Economic Policy (NEP), initiated by Lenin in 1921 and championed thereafter by Bukharin, Rykov and Tomsky. This was before the Stalinist heavy industry drive and forced collectivization of agriculture starting in 1929.

Bukharin, following Lenin, was an exponent of what today would be called market socialism, or, if you will, 'socialism with Chinese characteristics'.[33] A gradual and prolonged transition to socialism was implicitly envisaged by Bukharin, with the Soviet economy having substantial areas of it held in private hands and subject to market forces. And this situation of a 'mixed economy' actually prevailed in Russia during this period. Private capital and trading flourished. So-called 'nepmen' infuriated socialist morality with their new-found and often dubious wealth. This is where the whole notion of 'articulation of modes of production' first arose, originally in the ideas of Lenin. These policies, soon to be dramatically reversed by Stalin, were vehemently opposed by Trotsky and Zinoviev – the so-called Left Opposition.

This debate raged in Russia and the international communist movement especially between 1924 – the year of Lenin's death and 1926–27 when the Left Opposition was finally defeated. This was precisely the years of Gramsci's most active political life up until he was arrested by the fascists in 1929. There can be little doubt that he was aware of this fundamental debate which reverberated throughout the Comintern. Indeed, he commented directly on these issues. Hall refers to the fact that Gramsci had critiqued Bukharin's *Theory of Historical Materialism* published in 1921 for 'vulgar materialism' and 'economism'.[34] One could be forgiven for assuming that Gramsci's position in this critical debate – which Hall does not discuss – would have been against that of Bukharin. However, what is striking is the fact that at this point in his writings Gramsci comes out decisively in support of the position of Bukharin and the majority of the Bolsheviks. Far from an accelerated advance to socialism in the interests of the proletariat he wrote the following:

Yet the proletariat cannot become the dominant class if it does not overcome this contradiction through the sacrifice of its corporate interests. It cannot maintain its hegemony and its dictatorship if, even when it has become dominant, it does not sacrifice these immediate interests for the general and permanent interests of the class.[35]

The point that Gramsci is making here is that the maintenance of the alliance between the proletariat and the peasantry in the context of the Russian Revolution required a profound grasp of the economic situation. The sacrifice of the immediate interests of the proletariat for the peas-ant's interests in the market – in buying and selling and in capitalism – was a strategic requirement. According to Gramsci, this approach to the economy was a fundamental condition for the maintenance of the hege-mony of the proletariat. Apart from shedding light on Gramsci's post-revolution attitude to economic policies, this represents a profoundly materialist not culturalist understanding of the necessary foundations for hegemony. But Gramsci was even more explicit, writing in 1926 before Stalinist extremism took hold:

Today, at nine years distance from October 1917, it is no longer *the fact of the seizure of power* by the Bolsheviks which can revolutionize the Western masses, because this has already been allowed for and has produced its effects. What is active today, ideologically and politically, is the conviction (if it exists) that the proletariat, once power has been taken, *can construct socialism*[36]

This observation speaks directly to the issues which we have been dis-cussing and to the vital importance which practical economic achieve-ments have for the ideas of socialism to 'grip the masses'. Indeed, there can be little doubt that both the economic and political failures of 'real socialism' have exerted a decisive effect on the passive consent of work-ing people to the continued dominance of the capitalist system.

One final word on Hall's ideas having to do with the issue of hybrid-ity and 'black essentialism'.[37] As mentioned earlier, the concept of hybrid-ity, as currently put forward, is an inadequate attempt to capture a far more thorough-going process unfolding as a result of the international scope of the division of labour. In his short paper on 'What is this "black" in black popular culture?', Hall is concerned to combat essentialist notions of blackness in black popular culture. He wrote that 'the essentializing moment is weak because it naturalizes and de-historicizes difference, mistaking what is historical for what is natural, biological, and genetic'.[38] Following his usual line of argument, Hall argues that identification with

*39*

blackness by itself is not enough, quoting Isaac Julien that 'being black isn't really good enough for me: I want to know what your *cultural politics are'.[39]

However, the alternative which Hall proposes to black essentialism is problematic. His argument is that 'black popular culture' – clearly meaning by this term only black popular culture in the West and not in Africa – is a hybrid, not a pure entity. Black culture in the diaspora, because it is diasporic is a 'recombination, hybridization and "cut-and-mix"'.[40] This is so because it was 'over-determined from at least two directions ... Selective appropriation, incorporation, and rearticulation of European ideologies, cultures and institutions, alongside an African heritage'.[41] In other words what we are offered as an alternative to black essentialism is the rather old-fashioned view of black syncretism. What are the problems with such a view?

First, there is the obvious difficulty inherent in using the term 'black' to include people from South Asia as well as people with an African heritage. Often the problematic of this usage is presented as deriving from its firm rejection by overwhelming majority South Asian populations in Britain. This may well be so but there is a larger point. The effect of this usage is curiously to detach blackness in Britain from blackness in Africa and to constitute it simply as a 'construction' peculiar to the British context. This detachment from Africa is extremely problematic. What about the thousands of people in Britain who are of direct African heritage and origin, from Nigeria, Ghana, Kenya and elsewhere – their rootedness in Africa not mediated through the Caribbean? In most discussions of blackness and race in Britain, ironically, much is made of the Afro-Caribbean as well as of the South Asian population. The people in Britain who are directly from Africa herself somehow find themselves erased.

Further, borrowing is hardly a unique feature of black culture – one would be hard-pressed to find a single example of any culture which was not and does not continue to be 'hybrid' in that sense, the claims of cultural nationalists notwithstanding. The fact that a culture has many different sources borrowing from far and wide – for example, Muslim elements in Spanish culture or Swedish elements in Russian culture – hardly means that such a culture has not combined these elements into a new distinctive synthesis – that there is no such thing as Spanish, Russian or Swedish culture. The point that black culture in the West is 'impure' is an irrelevant one, since the same applies to black culture in Africa, indeed, in all cultures. The question is whether black culture in the West has gelled into a new synthesis or simply consists of the 'European' *alongside* the 'African' – a *pastiche*. What constitutes the essence of this historically created synthesis, if such a synthesis is thought to exist at all? What are the historical forces which have shaped it and continue to shape it today? The fact that black popular culture in the West is a *historical* product hardly means that it is contentless, that it is simply oppositional, that it has no constructive distinctive essence of its own, born from its specific aspirations and struggles. As Hegel argued long ago, essence is inherently historical and unfolds as the result of a struggle of the spirit. Reliance on a semiotic view of cultural differences carries the inherent danger of draining each culture of its distinctive, historically determined specificity and reducing it to one in a series of oppositions which have only internal referents. Cultures then become one in a system of arbitrary oppositions. In other words, such an approach leads to the view of cultural difference as inherently without substance in the objective socio-historical sense.

Moreover, Hall, although he affirms the complexity of the subject, emphasizes one particular version of the historicity of black culture – a truncated one which is familiarly held by many anthropologists as well as by the upper middle class which controls the state and cultural life in the Caribbean.[42] This is the idea of African-Caribbean culture as a 'creole' culture. The dominant strata of this brown-black upper middle class is 'hybrid' in the sense that it self-consciously presents itself as an amalgam of 'Africa' and 'Europe' – but more the latter than the former. It likes to think of itself as representing 'the best of both worlds' and therefore with an inherent right to rule over the masses of the black population.[43] The black working class and peasantry and increasingly the newer Caribbean black middle class and bourgeoisie out of which Rastafarianism, Reggae and Dancehall spring, however, perceive and present themselves quite differently. They resolutely identify as 'African' or 'true Jamaican' (as distinct from the brown-skinned, white, Chinese, Jewish and Lebanese elite). Similarly vital class and colour distinctions in culture exist in the African-Caribbean population in Britain, within the staunchly Pentecostal peasant culture of the Windrush migrants as well as with respect to the far less visible and tiny secular brown-black middle class. As often is the case in discussions of black culture in the West, there is a strange silence on the issue of class differences among black people and its consequences for internal cultural difference. In other words, one needs to speak of black popular cultures, not culture and delineate their class content and position within a certain broad unity. One must, as Hegel may have put it, give all the determinations of 'black culture' their due.

Alternative and far richer conceptions of black cultural historicity exist, other than this simple two-segment static model in which, in any event, the segments are implicitly essentialist. It is apparent, for example, that the *inter-African* process of cultural unification among persons of African descent in the West – the process by means of which, for example, Asante and Ibo amalgamated, and tribalism was overcome which began in Africa itself – was and is far more important historically than the African-European relationship. Indeed, the latter is inconceivable and was inseparable from the former. Many years ago, I put forward the thesis that this truly historic process of *becoming* 'African' in the West – in some ways an incomplete process in Africa herself – is the fundamental theme of the history of black people in the West.[44] It is one riven with tensions, violent conflicts, class, color and other contradictions but it has proceeded nonetheless. This does not deny the rather obvious fact of powerful European influences. It simply does not assume that this African-European relationship provides the entire axis on which black culture in the West turns and that this relationship, important as it obviously is, sets the framework for analysis of this historical experience.

This weakness springs from the tendency to discuss black culture in the West, popular and otherwise, solely with reference to the West and without any reference or connection to black culture in Africa. A similar error would hardly have been made if the subject had been that of Scottish culture in Canada. Hall's conception of the 'hybridity' of black culture in the West – regarded by some black intellectuals in the West as 'obviously' the most important part of black culture in general – suffers from a lack of a deep historical perspective which integrates this cultural tradition and experience with its really existing African past.

# THREE Gilroy

## Neither Black nor Atlantic

Whereas in the writings of Stuart Hall one still feels the presence of economics at least implicitly and in the background, this is not the case for the work of Paul Gilroy. One must distinguish in his case between the earlier work (*Ain't No Black in the Union Jack* and *The Empire Strikes Back*) which are written from a structural Marxist and world systems perspective, which is closer to the approach of Stuart Hall, and his later work beginning with *The Black Atlantic*. In contrast to the explicitly social and historicist framework utilized in the earlier work, in the latter work, an analysis is developed which is largely literary and individualistic with little or no appreciation for the specificities of the historical context of any of these literary figures. More importantly, there is little grasp of how this context arises out of a peculiar period in the economic and political development of capitalism which gives the period and the literary figures their peculiar sensibilities and orientation. I shall focus in this chapter on some critical aspects of the well-known book *The Black Atlantic* although the analysis here applies, *mutatis mutandis*, to the central themes of his work as a whole, including his most recent book *Against Race*.[1]

*Black Atlantic*, published in the early 1990s, was written at the height of a particular crisis in the African American community and, equally important, in the aftermath of the long economic and social malaise in Britain during the Callaghan–Heath and early Thatcher period. In addition to the stagflation which gripped the British economy, there was the persistent battles with the militant trade unions and the often violent struggles between the police and some sections of the black community, especially the riots of July 1981. It was also written in the wake of the collapse of socialism in the Soviet Union and the worldwide crisis in all schools of Marxism which ensued. The greater influence of Foucauldian nihilism in *Black Atlantic* is probably due to these factors which are now *passé*. Now, in 2005, we are clearly in a different moment in world history. The present moment is defined by a new 'New Imperialism' – the resurgence of inter-imperialist conflicts between differing geo-political power blocs and renewed efforts to re-divide the world along lines beneficial to one bloc or the other and the inevitably intense nationalist resistance to this entire process.[2] This open re-assertion of power politics in the global reality makes the abstract culturalism of *Black Atlantic* and of *Against Race* appear particularly odd.

In contrast, *The Empire Strikes Back*, especially in its opening essay which discusses some of the economic and political bases of British racism in the 1970s crisis retains much of its relevance today.[3] This period, from 1960 to 1970, was also the period of the rise of elements of a multicultural middle-class intelligentsia in Britain.[4] This intelligentsia, of South Asian and Afro-Caribbean origin, despite the immense racial obstacles faced, developed on a significant scale in the years prior to the Thatcher government and its neo-liberal project in Britain. Although relatively tiny, because it is concentrated in London, this stratum of academics, artists, media persons and young professionals (which has continued to grow even more rapidly under New Labour) constitutes an influential force in contemporary British cultural life. Gilroy, of course, is from this stratum and gives voice to a specific perspective within what is a broad range of views. In this he differs in emphasis from Stuart Hall whose social, political and intellectual formation had an altogether different foundation and ran along a different course. In Gilroy's case, the reservations Hall retained against wholesale departures from Marxism are over time abandoned and it is the Foucauldian side of his work with its focus on disembodied 'discourses' which blossoms.

This tendency was always present in the structural Marxism of his early work with its typically exaggerated emphasis on the role of ideology (read 'discourse'), as for example in his chapter 'Police and Thieves' in *The Empire Strikes Back*.[5] There, the issues of the narrow plebeian nationalism of E.P. Thompson and the racism of the British police are presented primarily as ideological phenomena which presumably require a mainly ideological (read 'cultural') politics to be overcome.[6] In another essay in the same book, Gilroy, from the opening paragraph states that his focus will be on 'the cultural politics of "black" [*sic*] people in this country' and that this requires an approach which 'involved giving due weight to cultural factors, understood neither as purely autonomous nor as epiphenomena of economic determinations'.[7] Further, in this same work

Gilroy clearly conceives of race as an ideological-cultural phenomenon – a 'cultural construction' not constituted by *contemporary* material forces. Racism exists as an ideology without any apparent contemporary material base. Racism is more a 'culture' than an ideology. This culture is modified by historical circumstances but the phenomenon which it references is not constituted by *contemporary* economic and political forces and interests. *Past* bases of racism (slavery, colonialism) were material. *Presently*, however, racism is cultural: 'We must locate racist and anti-racist ideology as well as the struggle for black liberation in a perspective on culture as a terrain of class conflicts.'[8] Gilroy wrote:

> We are fully aware that the ideological status of the concept 'race' qualifies its analytic use. It is precisely this meaninglessness which persistently refers us to the construction, mobilization and pertinence of different forms of racist ideology and structuration in *specific historical circumstances*. We must examine the role of these ideologies in the complex articulation of classes in a social formation, and strive to discover the conditions of existence which permit the construction of 'black' people in politics, ideology and economic life. Thus there can be no general theory of 'race' or 'race relations situations', only the historical resonance of racist ideologies and a specific ideological struggle by means of which real structural phenomena are misrecognized and distorted by the prisms of 'race'.[9]

Racism thus arises subjectively, is the result of an 'error' on a grand historical-cultural scale. Clearly this is a purely constructivist theory of racism. For it implies that there is no objective basis either for a sense of race or for racism. From the point of view of the oppressed black population, it denies that there are significant distinctive characteristics among black people other than what has been imposed on them from outside by racists. Therefore, there is no need to attempt to study how such a sense may have developed, what such distinctive characteristics may be and how they were originated by the creative efforts of black people themselves, often but not always in opposition to an externally imposed racism. There is no need to analyze how these characteristics may have developed and changed over time and what were the economic, political and ideological forces which shaped the black population and were in turn shaped by them. At the same time, from the point of view of racists and racism, the implication is that such an outlook arises simply out of 'prejudice'. In this sense, blackness (and whiteness for that matter) is substance-less – empty signs with no 'there' there, to recall the semiotic formula. White people are people who happen to be white; black people, people who happen to be black. This argument is applied not only to race but also to

45

nations. From this viewpoint, there are no British people, only people who happen to be British. Likewise for the French, Germans or Nigerians, is the implication. These national terms too are merely cultural constructs, products of the collective imaginations of literary and other figures and then transmitted to the wider population.[10]

At the base of Gilroy's thinking, as in Foucault's, are traditional abstract eighteenth-century French Enlightenment concepts of an undifferentiated humanity. Divisions of race, culture, nation and class obviously exist but these do not have the same ontological status as the category 'humanity'. The latter is real but the former are cultural constructs – 'discourses' – distorting the real. One is back to the debate between Kant and Herder (with Gilroy in the Kantian camp) and to the abstract humanism of Feuerbach.[11] This abstract universalism reveals itself especially in his most recent book *Against Race* with its notions of 'planetary humanism' and 'strategic universalism'.[12] Cultural and national difference is thus construed semiotically, as a product of arbitrary, historically imposed, oppositions which, at a deeper level, are substance-less and logic-less. Gilroy's subject is the racism of white people and later, the essentialism of black people. His subject cannot be the historically changing class and national characteristics and development of both the black and white populations due to the changing local, national and global political economy. However, the fact that race is a historical category can by no means make it substance-less. As we shall see below, however, even this semiotic view Gilroy finds too nationalistic, still too divisive of humanity into sub-groups, for his taste.

Thus, this is a theory which, unlike the work of Hall, departs from cultural constructivism and not from materialism. For example, standard Marxist analyses from the time of Engels, which attribute British racism to the material rewards derived from Britain's long-standing colonial history, its monopoly of the world market and export of capital are not even mentioned, much less critiqued. Gilroy emphasizes almost exclusively the role of the earlier colonial period and of slavery in the development of anti-black racism in Britain. This historical experience has obviously been critical. This, however, is a tale *about the past*, not about the present. There is no grasp of the material basis of *contemporary* racism. Gilroy does not grasp the fact that contemporary racism is based in the very real, material, economic and political oppression of entire peoples and groups of peoples by real existing imperialism.[13] He shows little understanding of the development of capitalism – the rise of monopoly capital and its export in the form of finance capital which subordinates national economies worldwide, despite their formal constitutional independence. This perspective which persistently references only slavery and colonialism as distinct from contemporary imperialism as the basis for contemporary racism is one of the major weaknesses of Gilroy's work. As the work of MacMaster and others have pointed out, the transformation in the substance and basis of both anti-Black racism and anti-Semitism in the last quarter of the nineteenth century and into the twentieth century is absolutely crucial for the understanding of these two scourges.[14]

Indeed, Gilroy does not use the concept of imperialism as a critical analytical tool. Instead he relies on the concept 'modernity' which elides different stages of capitalist development, thereby aggregating precisely what needs to be disaggregated. He fails to see that the issue since the end of the ninteenth century is not capitalism in general or 'modernity' in general. It is a matter of a very specific stage of capitalism – monopoly capitalism dominated by the export of finance capital and wars of imperialist conquest – and the growth of a very specific resistance to it in the form of the socialist movements in Europe and the anti-colonial wars then beginning in China, Ireland, India, Egypt and elsewhere at the start of the twentieth century. As is well known, this imperialism, *sensu strictu*, and the anti-imperialism it engendered, mark a qualitative development from the earlier colonialism and the Free Trade period which preceded it. This is the whole point of the work of Hobson, Hilferding, Kautsky, Bukharin, Luxemburg, Lenin and, for that matter, Max Weber with its emphasis on 'bureaucracy', rationality and the 'iron cage'. But this fundamental point eludes Gilroy. He therefore does not grasp that it is this new imperialism and all its requirements and consequences which lie at the root of contemporary racism and necessarily shape the character of the resistance to it, making this resistance also a global one.

The obvious connection between the post-World War II and especially post-Suez loss of these very tangible material and long-enjoyed privileges of Empire and the resurgence of British racism, especially in the police force, is not raised nor discussed by Gilroy. Racism is presented simply as an ideological – a social-psychological and cultural – phenomenon. It is a process wherein certain 'structural phenomena' are 'misrecognized'. Therefore, in *The Empire Strikes Back* we are confronted with the strange phenomenon of a book on the consequences of Empire which has no theory of imperialism. If one roots British racism largely in past economic phenomena such as colonialism and slavery or in police 'attitudes' or the inadequacy of the British educational curriculum (history, literature) or in the narrow nationalism of English cultural studies, then one, in effect, cuts this nationalism and racism loose from its *contemporary* material roots – unmoors it as it were. In that case, racism can have no contemporary, actively ongoing, material root. It once *had* such a root but has one no more. One's explanation of racism then must be that it is due to a sort of historical-cultural inertia on a massive scale. It is primarily a social-psychological hangover from the colonial and slave past, not a resurrection of and reinforcement of that past on the basis of real material interests in the present period. Yet I would maintain that it is impossible to understand the vitality of racism in the twentieth and twenty-first centuries as due to some kind of unspecified ideological momentum from the past. As was the case with the collapse of liberalism and the resurgence of racism in the late nineteenth century, the contemporary imperialist root of modern racism must be the point of departure. From the viewpoint of a materialist theory of imperialism, the deep North–South economic divide and the renewed struggle among the great powers for global geo-political advantage are the root features of contemporary world racism. The huge global political and economic inequalities and the jostling for strategic global advantage inevitably generate a strong sense of racial and 'civilizational' superiority in the developed North. Immigration and the economic pressures engendered by globalization further aggravate these basic tendencies. It is precisely this subordination of whole peoples globally and not just at the local and national levels which is the *differentia specifica* of racism in the imperialist era. Black people are thought of as inferior *everywhere* in the world by very many among all non-black peoples.

As already noted, there is much reference to the influence of colonialism and slavery in Gilroy's work. But the absence of any grasp of the role of finance capital and imperialism as the foundational process of present-day racism remains the enduring failure of his work to this day. His resorting to Vološinov or to Hall's metaphorical statement that 'Race is the modality in which class relations are experienced', apart from begging all the important questions, collapses race into class.[15] One cannot understand the force and durability of racism by seeking explanations of it at purely the local or national level, regional, or even the 'Atlantic' level. The forces which drive racism are global in their very nature. Gilroy's shifting the unit of analysis from single nations – Britain, the United States – to a so-called 'Atlantic' region merely substitutes a less narrow 'Atlanticist' regionalism for a narrower nationalism. Indeed, Gilroy does not take note of the fact that the very creation of communities of Black Atlantic sailors settled in the port cities of Europe is largely a result of the replacement of sailing with steamships and the expansion of shipping after the 1860s. Significant numbers of Black, Indian and Arab sailors were employed as cheap labor on European shipping lines and many of them settled in cities such as Liverpool, Cardiff and Hamburg.[16] Even in this very direct sense then, the Black Atlantic had a material base which is completely erased in Gilroy's account.

So, the elements of his distinctively culturalist approach were already present in Gilroy's earlier work. What seems to have happened in his later work is that, with the crisis in Marxism and the collapse of socialism, the materialist side of his work subsided and the Foucauldian side came more to the fore. It should also be noted that these changes occur also as the subject of his work changes: the earlier material is focused on anti-black racism in Britain and preoccupies itself with the reforms which would be necessary to lead to the incorporation of black persons in British society, culture and historical traditions. His later work continues this same, deeply incorporationist, theme, but in the form of a critique of what he sees as separatist and essentialist tendencies in African-American cultural politics which threaten the larger project of the incorporation of black people as a whole into a transformed (multicultural) British culture.

Of more significance, however, was the situation in the United States when Gilroy published *Black Atlantic* in 1993. This was a period when there had been a profound dissolution of the political economy of urban black America by the processes of de-industrialization, neo-liberalism and globalization. The deep restructuring of American capitalism, which began after the United States abandoned the Bretton Woods system of fixed exchange rates in 1973, culminated in the establishment of the Washington Consensus and the North American Free Trade Association (NAFTA) in 1994.[17]

These measures were both the result of the intense global competition with Japan which decimated the American manufacturing sector as well as the turn to neo-liberalism which attacked the social support systems on which the white and black poor had come to depend in the United States. The collapse of traditional sectors of black employment in the automobile and ancillary industries consequent on devastating Japanese competition, combined with the dramatic reduction in social support, created an unprecedented crisis in the black urban communities of the northern United States. From the vantage point of today, with a renewed round of loss of manufacturing and high-level service jobs but this time affecting primarily white workers and middle-class professionals, it is apparent that the initial process of de-industrialization was simply a first wave. In the case of the first wave, much of the legal rights and social and economic progress won in the civil rights struggles was rolled back: the black working class was decimated at the very same time as a larger upwardly mobile professional black middle class emerged. As is well known, many of this latter group themselves fled the inner cities leaving millions of persons of color abandoned and facing intensified impoverishment. In the absence of a politically effective mass movement, significant numbers of black males resorted to drug running and criminality on an unprecedented scale in a desperate attempt to maintain some sort of economic viability. This was met with an aggressive mandatory sentencing policy for black offenders and the rapid construction of prisons. The so-called 'prison-industrial complex' emerged.

As numerous scholars, but especially William J. Moses, have pointed out, Afrocentricity – Gilroy's *bête noire* in *Black Atlantic* – is an old and deep tradition in the African-American community, long pre-dating the 1980s. It is a deep folk tradition which always re-surfaces during periods of intensified oppression such as in the 1850s and in subsequent periods of segregation and racism.[18] It was against the background of precisely such a renewed phase of immiseration in the 1980s that essentialist ideologies of blackness gained a much stronger hold in the black community. These ideologies had as their main purpose the rejection of this de-industrialization assault on the black community and the unprecedented mass impoverishment which ensued. Afrocentricity was basically an ideology of self-defense. One form which this ideological defense took was the growth of a cultural nationalism championing the integrity and worth of the black community often in an essentialist and extreme form. Gilroy's *Black Atlantic* is a critique of this essentialism. But one reads it in vain to find any reference to the real events shaping the entire politics, culture and debates of the period. What Moses repeatedly decries as 'presentism' prevails throughout.[19]

Critiques of this form of cultural studies have largely focused on its literary nature – its assumption that one can read off the culture of a period by focusing on its literary or popular culture in the main. This objection is obviously valid but does not sufficiently raise the question of how literary studies are to be adequately conducted. Such a critique simply points out the literary illusions behind this approach, whether the culture being depicted is elite or popular. In other words, it takes up the well-known critiques of this form of cultural studies as a simple inversion of Leavisite elite criticism – a form of cultural populism. In this form of cultural studies where material forces have disappeared, broad intellectual, aesthetic and social movements such as black cultural nationalism or, for that matter, music are treated naïvely – simply as the ideas and writings of this or that black intellectual, artiste or activist.

Inherent in this method is the complete failure to treat social movements as anything other than thoughts which spring directly from the brow of more or less brilliant minds. Why these particular minds at these particular times and in these particular places, why these ideas and not others seem to resonate with the thinking of thousands of other black people – this is not even perceived as an issue, much less discussed. The tale is a drama of how ideas of one heroic individual confronted the ideas of another in space and across time. Thus we have here not only an abstraction from the economy, the political situation and history. We also have an abstraction from society as well. It is a drama of one intellect against or in alliance with another. Presumably, since this is how the process unfolded during the times of Delany, Crummel, DuBois and Richard Wright in the nineteenth and twentieth centuries, this is also how it is unfolding today. The 'cultural constructions' of contemporary black and white intellectuals take precedence over the harsh material realities of the struggles of millions of black and white people, such being the power of culture and ideology. We are in the presence of a deep-seated culturalism here.

This is particularly striking in his discussion of the early Pan Africanists – Martin Delany and Alexander Crummel – but it is equally striking in his discussion of the work of W.E.B. DuBois and especially of the work of Richard Wright. In *Black Atlantic* Gilroy preoccupies himself with the issue of the essentialism of this new wave of black cultural nationalists in the United States in the 1980s. His approach to critiquing this group is to argue that, far from being an isolated and inherently pure essence, black culture in the West has always been 'hybrid' and creole and has always transcended purely national boundaries – in this sense is 'Atlantic', neither American nor British. He further argues that this culture is an inherent part of 'modernity', by which he seems to mean that the culture developed within the framework of capitalism from the sixteenth to the twentieth centuries. Black cultures, he states in the title of the first chapter of the book are 'a Counter Culture of Modernity'.[20]

By this phrase, obviously influenced by writers such as Bauman and the Adorno–Horkheimer branch of the Frankfurt School, Gilroy draws closer to Central European anti-modernism and anti-Enlightenmentism. Black cultures are argued to have been *against* modernity because they were *of* modernity. His point is that the Black Atlantic – itself a very problematic concept – has always been an integral but unrecognized part of modernity while all the time being critical of the failure of modernity to eliminate racism and to realize its promises of equality and fraternity. A major part of Gilroy's mission is to rectify this 'misrecognition' and to put black back into the Union Jack. The literary culture created by the black population in Europe, the Caribbean and the Americas must find its rightful recognition from the white intelligentsia and become part of the established corpus of European literature.

Gilroy begins *Black Atlantic* with an account of the writings of Martin R. Delany, the early African-American physician and black nationalist, writer and explorer of Africa who lived from 1812–1885. Delany is useful to Gilroy because he was claimed by Afrocentrists as a progenitor. Gilroy aims to show that in fact Delany, while adhering to a variety of essentialist ideas, did not conceive of his desired black nation along mainly Afrocentric lines because he once favored Nicaragua as a possible location for the establishment of an independent black nation. Gilroy wrote: 'Delany's primary concern was not with Africa as such but rather with the forms of citizenship and belonging that arose from the (re)generation of modern nationality in the form of an autonomous, black nation state.'[21] Delany too had 'outgrown the boundaries of North America' – traveling to Canada, Africa and Britain – the Black Atlantic. In other words Delany was not narrowly Afrocentric nor purely American.[22] This seems thin grounds on which to dissociate Delany from the tradition of Pan Africanism which finds one expression in Afrocentrism. For it is clear from other studies of Delany as well as from Gilroy's own quotations of his work, that Delany championed notions of the unique cultural characteristics of people of African descent throughout thousands of years of history – notions which Gilroy would characterize as essentialist – as well as being willing to locate his desired nation–state outside of Africa if necessary. Moses calls attention to the 'Egyptocentric' feature of Delany's thought[23] and quotes the following characteristic Afrocentric paragraph from Delany's *Principia of Ethnology*:

> And the enquiry naturally presents itself: How do the Africans of the present day compare in morals and social polity with those of ancient times? We answer, that those south of the 'Sahara,' uncontaminated by influence of the coast, especially the Yarubas [Yorubas], are equal in susceptibility and moral integrity to the ancient Africans. Those people have all the finer elements of the highest civilization.[24]

In other words, Delany held *both* views which are by no means as contradictory as Gilroy suggests. Such an approach, far from being less, was in fact, *more* essentialist and Afrocentric. The willingness to locate a nation for people of African descent anywhere implied that 'Africanity' was so inherently enduring that a nation–state for people of African descent did not need to be located in Africa in order to unfold its inner Afrocentric essence.

Gilroy presents many details of Delany's personal life but he fails to locate Delany in a particular historical period with distinctive socio-cultural, political and economic characteristics. Yet as Moses points out convincingly, it is impossible to understand Delany and the Pan Africanists of this period without understanding that they lived in the shadow of the Fugitive Slave Act of 1850, and the Dred Scott decision of 1857 leading up to the Emancipation Proclamation of 1862 in the United States. This was the period which Moses characterizes as 'Classical Black Nationalism' – from 1850–1862.[25] The central point to understand when reading these writers is the fact that they lived and wrote during the pre-Civil War period when the bourgeois North seemed to be evading a clash with the slaveholding South.

This was a period of political maneuvering when it seemed that the struggles to abolish slavery would be defeated and the political and economic interests of the semi-capitalist slave-holding plantocracy of the South would prevail, because of the pusillanimity of the Northern bourgeoisie. It was the pessimism induced by this period, as Moses points out at length, that explains the revived interest in Liberia among black nationalists of the period and their attraction to the idea of the establishment of a black nation in Africa or anywhere, in spite of the fact that such projects had always been associated with the denial of the rights of free persons of color and the deportation projects of the pro-slavery American Colonization Society. Gilroy does observe, in relation to the later shift in Delany's position away from emigrationism to what Gilroy dubs 'patriotism' – that 'the civil war was the catalyst'.[26] But a firm grasp of the precise specifics of the historical context is not presented as central to the analysis of Delany's life and work. On the contrary, 'presentism' prevails.

For example, in a long quotation, Delany is excoriated for his mid-nineteenth-century Victorian patriarchal beliefs about the family.[27] This, of course, is an easy ahistorical point to score from the standpoint of late twentieth-century feminism. In fact, it is certainly possible to read Delany's ideas in favor of the education of women in the nineteenth century in precisely opposite terms – as in keeping with the most advanced views of his time. This kind of 'presentism' also leads to speculations in a psychoanalytical vein about Delany's ideas, all of which are unsupported by any further evidence. The following is a typical passage:

Campbell saw Africa as his motherland while Delany, even when he referred to Africa with the female pronoun, persisted in calling the continent the fatherland. I want to suggest that this obstinacy expresses something profound and characteristic about Delany's sense of the relationship between nationality, citizenship, masculinity. He was probably the first black thinker to make the argument that the integrity of the race is primarily the integrity of its male household and secondarily the integrity of the families over which they preside. The model he proposed aligned the power of the male head of household in the private sphere with the noble status of the soldier-citizen which complemented it in the public realm. Delany's appeal today is that of the supreme patriarch.[28]

No evidence is offered to support the assertion that late twentieth-century interest in Delany is due to his alleged patriarchalism. Nor is any evidence offered for the pronouncement that 'Delany can now be recognized as the progenitor of black Atlantic patriarchy.'[29] This psychoanalytic approach leads to a narrowing of the significance of Delany and, *a fortiori*, of the struggles of black people in that period for a better life. It is certainly not how Delany is treated in the work of other scholars.[30] More importantly, such an approach obscures just what is distinctive in Delany's writings – his typically (bourgeois) mid-nineteenth-century emphasis on the importance of the establishment of a strong black nation–state. This same outlook also shows itself in his commitment to economic development for black people in America and also to the development of Africa. This was undoubtedly progressive for its time. One only has to consider the positive development of African-American life during the period of Black Reconstruction and the disastrous deracination which followed its destruction, as well as the current economic crisis in African-America and in Africa, to appreciate the prescience of Delany's ideas.

Gilroy also presents an analysis of Delany's novel *Blake; or, the Huts of America*, first published in 1859 and contrasts it with the far better known and influential political and ethnographic work of Delany such as *Principia of Ethnology: The Origin of the Races* or of *The Condition, Elevation, Emigration, and Destiny of the Colored People of the United States* (1852). Moses' analysis of these works make it clear that Delany was very much a black nationalist of his particular era and presents Delany as precisely the type of black nationalist that Gilroy says he was not.[31] But *Blake* is important for Gilroy's argument because he uses it to argue that 'the version of black solidarity *Blake* advances is explicitly anti-ethnic and opposes narrow African American exceptionalism in the name of a truly pan-African diaspora sensibility'.[32] But this again is another case of Gilroy reading his own notions into Delany. For, taking into account his work as a whole including *Blake* and, especially the *Principia*, it is clear that Delany derives his sense of Africanity and his rationale for a black nation–state broadly in the familiar romantic nationalist *Volksgeist* terms, characteristic of nineteenth-century German, Polish or Italian nationalism. In this respect, as in all these cases, including the Zionist case, national consciousness is not at all thought to have arisen from and to express a diasporic experience of the transnational, as Gilroy argues.[33] On the contrary, the national essence is thought to have survived *in spite of* the diaspora, in spite of the dispersal of the putative bearers of this essence across many alien national lands. Therefore, Delany's is no disembodied 'Atlanticist radicalism', to use Gilroy's term.[34] He was a nationalist and essentialist of the familiar nineteenth-century kind as Gilroy eventually concedes.[35]

Gilroy's project is to undermine all nationalism, especially black nationalism and to replace it with an undifferentiated internationalist humanism. He asked rhetorically 'whether nationalist perspectives are an adequate means to understand the forms of resistance and accommodation intrinsic to modern black political culture'.[36] It is precisely this abstract universalism which leads him even to be critical of what he calls the 'pluralistic position which affirms blackness as an open signifier' – a possible allusion to some of the positions of Stuart Hall.[37] This criticism arises because Gilroy says that he found this latter position to be 'insufficiently alive to the lingering power of specifically racialised forms of power and subordination'.[38] Although somewhat obscure, the criticism seems to be that the pluralist position of Hall in its acceptance of a 'strategic essentialism' makes too many concessions to nationalism. It operates at what Gilroy calls 'the politics of fulfillment' but does not rise to the level of what he calls 'the politics of transfiguration' which represents his ideal.[39]

In passages of unparalleled romanticism, Gilroy attempts to elucidate the difference between these two politics. The first – the politics of fulfillment – while admirable, limits itself to a rationalistic critique of racism and essentialism. It is the call for 'bourgeois civil society to live up to the promises of its own rhetoric. It creates a medium in which demands for goals like non-racialised justice and rational organization of the productive processes can be expressed.'[40] This ('semiotic' and 'pluralist') politics, however progressive, champions only the rights of a particular nationality and not of an abstractly 'singular' humanity as a whole. This is why the concept of 'diaspora' is so important for Gilroy as he argues that it is precisely this diasporic absence of rootedness in any single nation–state which imparts to the black struggle a unique cosmopolitanism. It is this diasporic quality which is thought to allow black struggles to rise above parochialism to an undifferentiated, universal, 'human' level – to rise above the 'binary opposition' of essentialism and pluralism.[41] The significance of the concept of diaspora for Gilroy is revealed in the following, typically lyrical, passage: 'This diasporic multiplicity is a chaotic, living, disorganic formation. If it can be called a tradition at all, it is a tradition in ceaseless motion – a changing same that strives towards a state of self-realization that continually retreats beyond its grasp.'[42] This view of black culture comes close to denying it any specificity or any continuity with Africa whatsoever. Gilroy presents the purported absence of strong national specifics as precisely the quality which is the most positive feature of the black experience. This must give us pause. For it is these very 'chaotic' and 'disorganic' features of black life which generations of black leaders have regarded as the bane of black existence and a contributory factor to black subordination. Yet these are here presented by Gilroy as the highest virtue. The question therefore arises: which section of the black population experiences their life in this wholly 'chaotic' and 'disorganic' manner? For whom does Gilroy speak?

But to dwell on these, purely negative implications of Gilroy's conception of diaspora would be to miss a larger point. This point is that the positive substance in Gilroy's emphasis on diaspora is really a call to eschew parochialism and ethnocentrism in the struggle for black emancipation and development in an era of imperialism. It is Gilroy's way of insisting that the black struggle must see itself as a part of a larger, international struggle, and ally itself with, not cut itself off from, internationalism. In a sense, the concept of diaspora is an abstract recognition of the fact that, in an age of imperialism, all progressive struggles – both national and class ones – must proceed on the basis of international alliances or face certain defeat, for capital is clearly global.[43] According to Gilroy, the interests of black people, as well as of humanity as a whole, require this broader viewpoint which must govern how even the most justly held nationalist struggle is conducted. This is the positive content in his diasporic concept. The problem is that Gilroy moves between a position which calls for the black nationalist struggle to be waged within a framework of international alliances[44] and another, more frequently expressed position which calls for the black struggle to be dissolved into an abstract internationalism in which a national agenda does not figure. These are two entirely different political positions with radically different consequences. Gilroy sensed the necessarily international character of every national and class struggle in an era of imperialism and tried to capture this in his concept of diaspora. But he did not grasp the reasons why internationalism was strategically essential in our time. As a result, his internationalism was formulated in an abstractly universalistic manner which is highly problematic.

It is this broader, abstractly universalistic viewpoint which the concept of a politics of transfiguration is said to address. Gilroy wrote:

> This [the politics of transfiguration] emphasizes the emergence of qualitatively new desires, social relations, and modes of association within the racial community of interpretation and resistance *and* [*sic*] between the group and its erstwhile oppressors. It points specifically to the formation of a community of needs and solidarity which is magically made audible in the music [of black people] itself and palpable in the social relations of is cultural utility and reproduction.[45]

This notion of 'erstwhile oppressors' begs all the questions. What is 'erstwhile' about contemporary racism or the current immiseration of Africa – an entire continent? What is 'erstwhile' about the regimes imposed on the developing world by the International Monetary Fund, the World Trade Organization and the entire apparatus of globalization? This is an extraordinary formulation on the part of Gilroy which brings out dramatically the difference between his viewpoint and that of Stuart Hall referred to earlier. By declaring oppression 'erstwhile', Gilroy arrives at a politics of solidarity between the oppressed and oppressor groups without qualification. And this consigning of the material basis of racism to slavery and to the colonial past – the assumption that racism has no *contemporary* material basis – plays a major role here in the formulation of such a political approach. This politics of transfiguration is conceived of as superior and elevated in comparison to the less lofty nationalistic struggles of particular groups of people. Since oppression is now erstwhile, 'transfiguration' – an appropriately mystical term – supersedes the need for a politics of national struggle. But the need for national (and class) struggles to rise above the purely local and national is not a metaphysical quality deriving from a 'politics of transfiguration'. It arises from the global nature of the system of finance capital and of imperialism. Far from requiring the dissolution of a national struggle into an international one, imperialism requires that the national (and class struggle) be internationalist in their strategy. Both the national and class struggle have to be conducted in a strategic framework in which they make common cause with other, similar, national struggles as well as with the class and other struggles of those strata of the 'erstwhile oppressors' *to the extent that these strata oppose the oppressive activities of their own group over other peoples.* But none of this means that nationalist struggles have lost any of their vital importance.

It is vital to appreciate that 'transfiguration' is not presented in this manner by Gilroy – as a politics of solidarity between differing class and national groups. In fact, 'transfiguration' in any meaningful sense poses the biggest challenge for progressive members of the oppressing group who are often called upon to oppose the policies of the government of their nation. Gilroy does not, however, pose the issue in this manner.

In his argument, the onus seems to fall on the oppressed. Nor is the idea one of the international unification of particular streams of national struggle into one single Bandung-like flood. Such conceptions would be too 'pluralist' in Gilroy's terms and nowhere are presented. Instead, what is presented is the need to dissolve all national struggles into a direct struggle for rights for all, without reference to the struggle for the particular needs of any particular nation.

Gilroy does not grasp that the universal goals of a united humanity are contained *within* the struggles of particular nations for national development, not *in opposition to* them. He does not seem to grasp that the entire point of national struggles is precisely to place all nations on an equal footing as a part of humanity – so that one can speak honestly about a really equal humanity which is not just another empty ideal in the head of some demagogic politician. Gilroy does not grasp that the humanity of which he speaks has to be created in reality, not simply asserted in books. Without this struggle for national emancipation and development the unification of humanity as is, in the present circumstances of gross global inequalities between and within nations, can only lead to the disarming of the oppressed and the domination of the weak by the strong. Pursuit of the national, racial, class and gender struggles is the only route to the unification of humanity on a really equal basis. This is the route to humanism, not a departure from it. Since oppression is far from being erstwhile and, in practice, all struggles necessarily have their national peculiarities, the 'politics of transfiguration', as Gilroy presents it, would not only lead to the abandonment of struggles for the rights of nations; it would lead to the abandonment of the struggle to create a real and not just imaginary humanity as well.

Gilroy presents little empirical evidence of the existence of this 'politics of transfiguration', said by him to be expressed in the black musical tradition 'on a lower frequency where it is played, danced, and acted, as well as sung and sung about'.[46] He is of course aware that such claims are reminiscent of those made by essentialists, in fact, seem indistinguishable from them. He offers the following rhetorical clarification:

> This subculture often appears to be the intuitive expression of some racial essence but it is in fact an elementary historical acquisition produced from the viscera of an alternative body of cultural and political expression that considers the world critically from the point of view of its emancipatory transformation.[47]

This seems to be suggesting that it is the unique historical experience of plantation slavery rather than the inherent qualities of black culture which have led to these transfigurative impulses lodging themselves in the 'viscera' of black musical popular culture. If this is the argument – it is by no means clear – then it is simply a repetition of the tendency, already noted, for Gilroy to locate the material sources of contemporary oppression in past historical processes. Moreover, as pointed out above, this kind of opposition between culture and history is a false one which de-historicizes culture. In any event, such an argument would not explain why, as Gilroy claims, black *Atlantic* culture (or any other culture, for that matter) should take a transfigurative rather than any other form, such as the form which he describes as 'fulfillment'. Unless one accords some special virtue to 'Atlanticism', why not black culture in Africa itself? It would seem that given the depredations which followed the Conference of Berlin in 1884–85 and the unprecedented immiseration proceeding in Africa today, the continent itself would be the appropriate place in which to locate the center of black struggles. Gilroy continues the annoying practice of presenting black intellectuals and people in the West as in the vanguard of the struggles of peoples of African descent. Once again, the intellectuals and peoples of Africa herself bring up the rear.

Gilroy, as mentioned before, has no concept of a new stage of capitalism emerging at the end of the nineteenth century with the consolidation of the power of finance capital. He conceives of current history simply as a 'post-slavery experience'.[48] He does not grasp that imperialism marked a new era in human history which has resumed with unparalleled intensity with the collapse of socialism. Instead he wrote vaguely and abstractly of the political history of black struggle being divisible into 'threefold processes', of which the third is a 'pursuit of an autonomous space in the system of formal political relationships that distinguishes occidental modernity' – in plain language – the anti-colonial struggle for politically independent states in Africa and the Caribbean.[49] This notion of an abstract 'modernity' as already pointed out, completely obscures the distinctiveness of the stage of monopoly capitalism and imperialism.

Gilroy living in the twenty-first century, does not grasp what DuBois grasped in the early twentieth century, that the black nationalist and Pan African struggle necessarily entered a new, anti-imperialist stage. Even though, for obvious reasons, he does not formulate the change in these terms, Moses implicitly recognizes this when he distinguishes the period 1895–1925 as a unique period designated the *Black Nationalist Revival*.[50] This was the period of Marcus Garvey and the early DuBois. In DuBois' case the anti-imperialism becomes as explicit over time as that of George Padmore or C.L.R. James. In the case of Garvey, whatever his own predilections, the realities of imperialist division and re-division of Africa compelled him to move in an anti-imperialist direction. Garveyite anti-imperialism was expressed in the well-known slogan 'Africa for the Africans, at Home and Abroad' which all the Great Powers regarded as subversive and which brought him and his followers into direct confrontation with imperialist forces, at home and abroad.

Given only the vague grasp of the significance of imperialism, it is difficult for Gilroy to give a coherent account of the work of either DuBois or Richard Wright. For it is obvious that both are products of a different era from that of Delany. Theirs is not the mid-Victorian period of bourgeois liberalism, optimism and Free Trade during which the Civil War was fought and emancipation from slavery won. Nor is it the period of Black Reconstruction which followed. DuBois and Wright are products of the collapse of Reconstruction, the rise of the robber barons, the deracination of the rural black population in the South and the mass migration to Northern cities. This is one and the same process which leads to the Italian migrations to America, to the McKinley Tariff, to the Homestead Strike, to the 'big stick' policy of Theodore Roosevelt, to the Spanish-American War, the entry of the United States into World War I and the emergence of America as an imperial Great Power at Versailles in 1919. DuBois analyses this process sociologically and politically, Wright depicts it in his novels.

Wright is the chronicler of the saga of the deracinated black peasant from Mississippi who flees Jim Crow in the South only to encounter the all-powerful racism of the North. Wright understands well the experience of deracination and presents fierce and powerful characterizations of the inner rage which it produces in its black victims. But Wright does not understand the emergence of a different kind of black person out of this capitalist cauldron. This is a person driven not by *ressentiment* – by bitterness and rage springing from the experience of seeing the entire social and personal basis of their life destroyed while being powerless to do anything much about it. This newer consciousness was to be found in the black person who is rooted in Northern industrial society and who is located at the heart of the very process of capitalist production – in some of its most important industrial enterprises. Such a black person is driven not by rage at what has been lost but by hope for what can be. The personal and social psychology is different and is generally not to be found in Wright's works.

It is in this sense that Wright's artistic power can be said to have declined when he went to live in Paris. Wright's dilemma derived not simply from being an American in Paris but was more specific, as Arna Bontemps long ago pointed out.[51] Bontemps made the telling point that Wright's alienation derived from being rooted in the poverty and racial oppression of Mississippi – 'the *bottom* South' as Bontemps specifies it, and the tragedies and atrocities which capitalist deracination threw up in that rural and small town locale. Therefore, had he remained in the North in the United States, Wright would not necessarily have resolved his alienation. For new social processes were now unfolding, shifting the center of gravity of the drama of black struggle to a new locale different from the one he so deeply knew, felt so keenly, and depicted so vividly in his work. The failure to understand Richard Wright is yet another instance of a lack of social and historical specificity in Gilroy's work which renders it highly problematic.

# FOUR Globalization and Risks

The failure to theorize monopoly capital and imperialism (in relation to race) which characterizes Gilroy's work is also a critical weakness of the work of other important scholars, such as Giddens, Lash and Urry and Castells. In the work of these scholars, notions of 'risk', technology and globalization play a critical role but they do not connect globalization to any of the theories of imperialism (Hobson, Hilferding, Kautsky, Luxemburg, Bukharin, Lenin, Harvey). Although they point to the severe inequalities of the global economy (see Giddens, *Runaway World*), they do not characterize globalization as a return to a further and more intense phase of imperialism, especially consequent on the collapse of the Soviet Union in 1989. I shall discuss the work of Giddens first.

The strength of the sociological theory of Giddens derives from his recognition that the liberalization and deregulation of capital and currency markets, combined with the large-scale deployment of information technology, have ushered in a new phase of capitalism. Although not characterized as such, this is, indeed, a restoration of an era of Free Trade but under infinitely more monopolistic and globally competitive conditions. It is precisely this gigantic concentration of monopoly capital and its unification with immense pools of finance capital – all privately held and driven by market forces – that account for the ferocity of global competition. Giddens understands that these changes in the global economy deeply affect even the most intimate areas of everyday life everywhere in the world. There is therefore a certain inescapable uniformity in the consequences which globalization has for the entire world. The key point for him is that these are forces which not only affect developing countries, as the older analyses tended to argue. Globalization also contains very serious 'risks' for developed societies as well. In other words, there is a sense of foreboding in Giddens's work as to what this new era actually holds for the world. This is a very British sensitivity to the dangers of globalization, born, I would argue, out of the historically disastrous effects which a previous era of globalization had for British economy and society.

It is incontestable that the restoration of Free Trade in capital and currency under the conditions of late twentieth- and twenty-first-century monopoly capitalism imposes a nearly uniform fiscal and monetary policy on all nations (except the United States) who do not wish to see their currencies devalued and who do not wish to experience massive capital flight and economic collapse. That this was so for the most developed as well as least developed of economies was one of the brutal lessons of the 1992 Swedish financial crisis as well as of the later Asian crisis. This fundamental fact of global capitalist life also sharply constrains the left-wing regime of Ignacio 'Lula' da Silva in Brazil. However, this vulnerability of the developed economies is not new. In many ways, it is the story of the decline of the British economy during the last part of the nineteenth century which the restoration of Imperial Preference in 1932 was designed, unsuccessfully, to halt. All British social scientists are only too familiar with the ultimately disastrous effects of this previous era of globalization – the loss of Britain's monopoly position on the world market – and all the attendant social and political consequences which reverberate to this day.

This loss of a manufacturing monopoly as a result of the export of capital and the rise of manufacturing competition elsewhere in the world are today being repeated in the United States. As was the case in Britain at the end of the nineteenth century, a similar anxiety is beginning to grip American policy-makers. Giddens understands this history and these processes only too well. He affirms the inevitability of the new Free Trade era but with some hesitancy, especially as to its social and personal and even, ultimately, some of its economic consequences. Free Trade in conditions of monopoly capitalist competition on a global scale, while offering new opportunities for British capital, without doubt also carries enormous economic and political 'risk'. This emphasis on 'risk' – increasingly the main theme in Giddens's writings – creates the impression that the level or 'risk' for developing societies is no more than that faced by developed societies – that there is a level playing field of 'risk', as it were. 'Risk' becomes an abstract metaphysical quality inhering in and pervading 'late modernity'.

But it can hardly be said that developed and developing countries are on the same footing in global capital or currency markets or in the global merchandise or service markets. Giddens mentions but does not dwell on this point – that the consequences of the restoration of Free Trade for developing countries (for example, in Africa) is qualitatively of an altogether different order. The 'risk' here is not recession or a temporary reduction in living standards: one is dealing with the subordination and immiseration of billions of people on a global scale.

Giddens's work is a synthesis of the ideas of Max Weber and Emile Durkheim, with a marked leaning in the functionalist, Durkheimian direction. The Weberian influences are expressed in his emphasis on the concept of 'risk' with its deeply rationalistic overtones. It is also expressed in the emphasis given to the single actor's point of view in the well-known manner of Weber's sociological methodology. This focus on risk and the need for calculation to assess and minimize risk gives his most recent writings a pessimistic, modernist cast which is also reminiscent of Weber's lamentations on the 'iron cage' of modernity. This modernist pessimism about the humanly 'manufactured' dangers of globalization and modernity suffuses his Reith lectures published as *Runaway World*.[1] Giddens balances uneasily between cautious optimism and this heightened sense of pessimism. This pessimism springs from this heightened sense of the fragility of the contemporary global social and political order and the need to shore this up with 'tradition' of some kind. It is as if Giddens sees clearly all the national and global contradictions generated by the global capitalist system – the injustices and virulent hostilities which it generates. At the same time he remains wedded to this system, warts and all. Growing anxiety over the potential for social and political chaos in contemporary global and national society therefore more and more becomes the main concern of his work. Hence his preoccupation with the issue of 'structure' or what used to be called 'the problem of order'.

Others have observed that Giddens's notion of structure in his 'structuration' theory is very much derived from Durkheim. 'Structure' is conceived of as a social-psychological code of norms and values free of deep class contradictions and not based on an economic-political structure in the materialist sense. This is yet another example of the unmooring of social analysis from political economy which is one of the themes of this work. Unsurprisingly, Giddens's solution to the perceived problem of order is also the Durkheimian (and very French) one. What is needed is the invention of 'tradition' but on a rationalistic basis: in plain language a kind of modern civic religion, but of a British not French variety. Giddens wrote this about the importance of tradition: 'In my view, it is entirely rational to recognize that traditions are needed in society. We shouldn't accept the Enlightenment idea that the world should rid itself of tradition altogether. Traditions are needed, and will always persist, because they give continuity and form to life.'[2]

And in a more Durkheimian vein, on the vital importance of preserving a space for 'the sacred' in modern society, he wrote further:

'Yet fundamentalism isn't just the antithesis of globalizing modernity, but poses questions to it. The most basic one is this: can we live in a world where nothing is sacred? I have to say, in conclusion, that I don't think we can. Cosmopolitans, of whom I count myself one, have to make plain that tolerance and dialogue can themselves be guided by values of a universal kind.'[3]

Although Giddens does not elaborate, unlike Durkheim, such 'sacred' traditions would not be inculcated by the education system or some form of *dirigiste* syndicalist corporate state. Neo-liberalism rules out *dirigisme* and the militantly left British trade union leadership are unlikely partners for the Giddens's venture into 'organic solidarity'. Instead what is proposed as means to the same end are various forms of legislation, social reforms and the incorporation of single-issue civic activism such as the environmental movement. In practice, this area is a bastion of the civic-minded middle and upper middle class which is hardly where the problem of alienation from monopoly capitalist society lies. These groups are already influential in society, already 'organic'. The problems of alienation, or to use the Durkheimian term – *anomie* – lie elsewhere.

They are several additional problems with Giddens's approach. In the first place, what is the root source of this lack of 'continuity' and of 'form' to modern life referred to in the quotation above? Is this a metaphysical human deficiency of all times and all eras – characteristic of the human condition in general – or is this 'discontinuity' and 'formlessness' the result of a specific organization of society in a particular period of history? If it is the former, then clearly Giddens is right. One has to make the best of a bad situation, introducing what reforms one can but ultimately one must resign oneself to this existential reality. If, on the other hand, it is the latter, then the preservation of non-rationalistic traditions would serve only to obscure, temporarily, the real nature of the problem.

Moreover, a rationalistic 'invention' of modern civic ritual is an inherently contradictory venture which may have been viable in the nineteenth or even early twentieth century. Then literacy levels were low, the mass media were underdeveloped and, most important of all, the mass of the people had not fully entered the political arena. People deferred to 'their betters' – especially in the British aristocracy and monarchy. Millions of people were still struggling to form their independent political judgments and organizations and were still very vulnerable to the blandishments of opportunistic politicians. Today, however, much (but not all) of that initial political naïvety has largely passed. The harsh blows of experience have taught people in the mass to be deeply skeptical of the grandiose promises made by politicians and to look behind the glitter of monarchies. It will take more than the promotion of middle-class civic activism to address this very hard-headed, political and social popular realism. As recent experience with the Blair regime and the British monarchy has shown, efforts such as Giddens's are far more likely to be dismissed as 'spin' than to be accepted as 'sacred' in the manner proposed. After all, millions of people around the world have had decades of real, everyday, practical experience with 'real existing socialism' as well as with contemporary monopoly capitalism and globalization. The profound skepticism towards the self-serving claims of disinterestedness made by public figures of every stripe are hardly likely to be dispelled by rationalistic or non-rationalistic rituals or constitutional devolutions of any kind. People judge the state of the British National Health Service not by statistics emerging from Downing Street or by criticisms coming from the militant left. They judge it empirically by their practical experience. Likewise, the issue of nationalization or privatization of the British rail system is not judged by the public on an ideological basis. It is judged on the basis of comparing their past experience of the British nationalized system, the present effectiveness of the state-owned French system, and their dismal experience of privatized rail in Britain. It is 'really existing state socialism and monopoly capitalism' which have been put in the dock, not ideological concepts. Giddens himself notes: 'The communications revolution has produced more active, reflexive citizens than existed before.'[4] But it is more than just communications and more than just 'reflexivity'. Indeed, this very concept of 'reflexivity' is an intellectualizing of a process which has far deeper foundations in actual practical political, economic and social experience. Neither intellectual reflection nor the effect of the growth of mass communications adequately captures what has occurred, although these obviously play a role. It has been the tumultuous practical political and economic experiences of the twentieth and now of the twenty-first century which have made hundreds of millions of people worldwide into hard-headed skeptical empiricists!

At the same time, the notion of a new civic religion for the age of globalization – on the face of it, a bizarre idea – is unlikely to satisfy conservative (not to mention fundamentalist) adherents of tradition within Western society, not only in the United States but also in Britain. They are likely to see it as a hopelessly outdated rationalistic maneuver – just what one would expect from a secular humanist cosmopolitan intellectual. From this point of view, the very notion of a 'rationalistic sacred' represents the kind of liberal oxymoron which neo-conservatives abhor and which, in the view of conservatives, is the embodiment of that very approach which has landed bourgeois society in its contemporary crisis. Moreover, the problem is deeper. This liberal approach, advocated by Giddens, fails to appreciate that the problems of capitalist society at this stage of its development are too acute to be overcome by rationalistic traditionalism of the well-established British or French type. From the point of view of conservatism, liberalism is now a very dangerous part of the disease, not part of the cure.

How will the 'sacred' remain sacred, given the powerful doses of rationality which have already been injected into public life, they rightly ask? How will one justify privilege, even 'meritocratic' privilege, in the face of mass rationality and cynicism? One can have an effective bourgeois monarchy, but not when the full glare of twenty-first-century tabloid rationality is turned on it, as both the British and the Dutch cases prove. Manipulations of patriotism combined with lofty proclamations of universal human rights do not survive for long in the real world of the plunder of natural resources, the greedy scramble for lucrative international contracts and the ruthless grasp for global geo-political advantage. The zone of the 'sacred' must be cordoned off from public rationality if it is to operate effectively.

It is hard to see how such a cordoning off can be accomplished today within the framework of democracy, given the power realities of the contemporary global political economy. This strategy was already tried in the nineteenth and twentieth centuries but has now exhausted itself. Indeed, it was precisely the ritualistic and self-serving manipulations of notions such as equality, democracy and human rights which have generated the widespread disenchantment with democratic politics which Giddens laments.[5] Thus, from the point of view of the ruling elites, the problem of mass rationality becomes daily more acute. Elaborate and expensive mass media manipulations are now accepted as an integral part of the political management of the population within democratic regimes. Yet these exercises serve only to generate further cynicism and alienation in the citizenry. Increasingly the only solution seems to be the curtailment of liberal democratic rights.

Giddens is aware that 'old forms of pomp and circumstance' will not work in the conditions of today.[6] As an alternative, he proposes a series of reforms to 'deepen' democracy such as devolution of power, constitutional reform, people's juries and civic associations.[7] This, as is well known, is more or less the approach of New Labour in Britain under the leadership of Tony Blair. These proposals for a stronger civic democracy reinforce the impression that Giddens, like New Labour, has embarked on an updated version of the Durkhemian search for 'organic solidarity'. It would be extremist to argue that such reforms could have no positive effect whatsoever in stabilizing contemporary society. But the question would be, for how long? How meaningful would any such solidarity be under the conditions of real existing monopoly capitalism in unrestricted competition on the world market?

Will increased devolution of constitutional processes to the local level, while leaving monopoly capital intact, not have the effect of revealing the real political powerlessness of the local except over relatively secondary issues? Will devolution not expose how concentrated and centralized real power necessarily is in a society based on monopoly capitalism, much as was the case with state socialism?[8] Will this not lead to an intensification of cynicism and alienation and a further destabilization of society? Is it not, in the end, an artful evasion of the difficult task of facing up to the real issues of power and privilege which bedevil modern society? For decades, the standard undergraduate criticism of functionalism and of Durkheim's thought has been that he attempts, unsuccessfully, to evade the issues of real power and real conflicts in society and tries to paper them over with a civic religion. The neo-functionalist orientation of Giddens is open to a similar criticism.

Although not exclusively constitutional-political – for example, in ideas such as the 'baby bond' and expanded universal early childhood education – the approach is predominantly so. The reason for this is clear: the essence of New Labour's 'Third Way' is the rejection of traditional social democratic approaches which attempt to curtail some of the rights of monopoly capital in the economic and not just in the social sphere. The rule under New Labour is that privatization must dominate and markets must always prevail in the economy. Social reforms are to be sought, but strictly within this framework. They must not encroach on the rights of private monopoly capital in the economy. This means that any attempt at old-style Keynesian social democratic redistributive demand management ('tax and spend') is out of the question.[9] Although obviously influenced deeply by the Eastern European economic and political reform struggles from 1968, it is fundamentally different from the 'Third Way' approach of 'plan and market' developed by the Czech economist Ota Sik.[10] In fact, it agrees with and has been deeply influenced by the conclusions arrived at later by the Eastern European economists Kornai and Brus that the 'plan and market' compromise model simply does not work in practice.[11] It is either the full market or nothing.

Giddens argues that the new global economy has eroded (or is erod-ing) the old solidarities of class and community in both developing and developed societies. He no doubt has in mind the break-up of the old European industrial working-class communities on which the social democratic parties had traditionally been based. Such communities are gone for good. New social strata have emerged, both at the levels of the working and middle classes. Therefore, 'social solidarity can effectively be renewed only if it acknowledges autonomy and democratization – as well as the intrinsic influence of social reflexivity'.[12] However, for Giddens, this fragmentation is precisely what generates anxiety and a sense of 'risk'. These new sources of instability have to be addressed on a modern basis. One cannot simply succumb to the Thatcherite recipe of a free market in the economy constrained by Victorian values in social life which, in any event, does not work. This is 'the old pomp and cir-cumstance of the past' and is completely outdated and ineffectual in the world of today – an example of non-rationalistic, as distinct from ratio-nalistic tradition. This Thatcherite 'first way' is too archaic and leads to social fragmentation, alienation and ultimately social and political insta-bility.[13] More meaningful concessions to democracy and to the aspira-tions of these new social strata are needed. The Eastern European socialist 'third way' of 'plan and market' is ruled out by its failure in real life. But there is a British 'Third Way'. Although economic policy is basi-cally a given and the State must leave the economy alone, it can and must actively intervene in society.

But the interesting question is *how* and *where*? The answer is that, in the new phase, State intervention is needed in the national, regional and global lifeworlds, especially at the level of community.[14] This is, the argu-ment goes, because it is above all in the sphere of civil society – in the family and the community – that liberalization and information technol-ogy have wrought the deepest changes. There is no going back to the days (which never existed) of the stable nuclear family and full employment. What is needed is 'positive welfare' to encourage a new code of 'respon-sibility'; investment in education, in order to enhance productivity and a new alliance between the State and community organizations or the development of an entirely new sector of 'civil labour'.[15]

This approach differs from the approach which sought the extension of quasi-markets in the health service and the educational system.[16] That Thatcherite programme is not the programme of New Labour. Public pro-vision of social services is acceptable but not public provision in any of the main sectors of the economy. This must have a predictable result: if monopoly economic power remains intact, indeed, is strengthened, as has happened under the Blair regime, then monopoly political and social power must be strengthened as well. The devolution of power and the other civic measures proposed by Giddens cannot be a substitute for measures to address the democratization of the enormous concentrations of economic power of global monopoly capitalism. Surely these will turn out to be yet another cruel illusion and undermine even further public confidence in the political process?

These theories raise the fundamental question of whether lifeworlds at the local or community levels can be significantly altered without encroaching on the rights of monopoly capital at the center, either by resorting to the large-scale redistributions of the old welfare state or by interventions in the relations of production. Can the new social strata which have arisen in the latest phase of capitalism, by dint of their new-found sense of responsibility and with opportunities provided by the State, forge their own destiny against the immensely powerful structures of finance capital at the local, national and global levels? At best, this is a dubious proposition. It brings us face to face with the reality that for democratic constitutional reforms, devolution, social provision or civic activism at the local or regional levels to be meaningful, then reforms at the economic and political center will be essential. The really critical issue is the continued concentration of political and economic power at the national and global center and how to democratize that point of concentration. Regional devolution of power over secondary matters and single-issue activism do not address this reality.

There is a general tendency in risk society theory to make broad generalizations about globalization which do not take into account the continued, indeed enhanced role, of developed national economies in the world market and the role of force.[17] Risk society theory also does not take account of the fact that capital since the late nineteenth century has been finance capital and that this inherently seeks a monopoly over world markets and the division and re-division of the world as new centers of capital arise and old ones decay. It is an inherently unstable system based upon the dominance of the weak by the strong.

The instability derives from the fact that monopoly capital, although hugely concentrating capital to an unprecedented extent, *does not abolish the capitalist market*. It still operates on the basis of private ownership of the means of production and of the consequent capitalist market relations. In the very nature of the system, now some groups of monopolists advance while others retreat and vice versa. Some parts of the world, experience unprecedentedly rapid rates of economic development while others, especially in the old manufacturing countries such as Britain and the United States, decline. Uneven development derives from the persistence of market relations and the private property which undergirds it.

The balance of economic and thus of political forces between different centers of capital regularly changes, as the market rewards now this center of capital and now another. The political need to regularly re-divide the world to realign it with the changing balance of forces arises as a constant element in international relations. During periods of relative stability (when the balance is more or less fixed) international law can prevail within the boundaries of power politics. During periods of change in the balance of forces such as now, international law necessarily is disregarded as force is used to establish a new balance. Hence the inescapable instability of national and international relations under monopoly capitalism and imperialism. To attempt to grasp this extremely unstable situation by the term 'risk society' is to remain at the level of symptoms without getting to the root causes of the 'risk'. It expresses a determination not to address these root causes but to remain at the level of anticipating, containing and restraining the symptoms.

In what is perhaps the most comprehensive account of shifts in the contemporary global economy, Dicken calls our attention to the conditions of volatility – the 'risks' – which prevail in the world economy today:

> Rates of growth during the 1980s were extremely variable, ranging from the negative growth rates of 1982 through to two years (1984 and 1988) when growth of world merchandise trade reached the levels of the 1960s once again. Overall, growth—albeit uneven growth—reappeared. But then, in the early 1990s, recession occurred again. In 1994 and 1995, strong growth reappeared, especially in exports. A similarly volatile pattern characterized the last years of the century.[18]

He goes on to point out that transnational corporations (TNCs) now operate on an enormous global scale, accounting for two-thirds of world exports of goods and services, much of which is intra-firm trade which does not even enter market relations – a most interesting form of the abolition of commodity relations under highly developed capitalism.[19] In the United States, the model for this relative abolition of commodity production within capitalism is the massive retail chain Wal-Mart. In many ways, especially in their electronic data management systems which have an international reach across the borders of nation–states, they are, ironically, models of socialism in a purely economic sense. While the United States leads in the erosion of market relations in distribution and retailing, the iron link between banking and industrial capital has clearly gone furthest in Japan. The Japanese *keiretsu* system has far surpassed anything J.P. Morgan could have

Table 4.1 Distribution of banking assets of the top 25 banks by country, 2000

| Country | Assets ($millions) | % |
|---|---|---|
| Japan | 3,780,037 | 25.8 |
| Germany | 2,418,502 | 16.5 |
| United States | 2,259,744 | 15.5 |
| United Kingdom | 1,593,912 | 10.8 |
| France | 1,568,411 | 10.7 |
| Switzerland | 1,267,941 | 8.7 |
| The Netherlands | 884,837 | 6.0 |
| China | 865,713 | 6.0 |
| Total | 14,639,097 | 100.00 |

Source: Adapted from Dicken (2003).

dreamed of. Dicken gives the example of the well-known Japanese electronics firm, Toshiba. He writes:

Toshiba is itself a parent company controlling hierarchically substantial numbers of satellite companies including parts suppliers, in a vertically integrated Toshiba group. At the same time, Toshiba is also a member of the horizontally integrated Mitsui industrial group. In fact the webs of inter-relationships are extremely complex ... The organizational scale of the leading keiretsu is immense. For example, the eight leading horizontal keiretsu ... consist of around 900 separate companies but in effect, they control, in total, some 12,000 companies. In the early 1990s, the 163 leading companies in the six major keiretsu effectively controlled more than 40 per cent of all Japanese non-financial enterprises and some 32 per cent of total assets.[20]

To which it should be added that the recent years of stagnation have resulted in an even greater concentration of Japanese finance capital, with huge banking consolidation which left the Mizuho Financial Group (a result of the merger of the Mitsubishi Bank and the Bank of Tokyo) as the largest financial group in the world. In 2000, six of the top 25 banks in the world were Japanese with about 25.8% of the banking assets in this top group. Only Germany came close with four banks in the top 25 representing about 16.5% of banking assets.[21] Such is the immense scale that social production has achieved under monopoly capitalism, dwarfing anything imagined in the writings of Hobson, Hilferding or Lenin. Table 4.1, adapted from Dicken, shows the relative distribution of banking assets in the top 25 world banking groups by country in 2000. Apart from the absence of the South Korean, Taiwan and Russian banking groups, it gives a fairly accurate picture of world geo-finance.

The basic issue, therefore, which is not addressed in risk society theory is what to do about this concentration of power at the global and national center. The issue is the provision of really existing everyday material and social equality and power to ordinary people, both at the national and the global levels, without which meaningful changes at the community levels – as advocated by risk society theory – cannot be meaningful. In the absence of measures which address this concentration of real power at the center, it is difficult to see how any attempt to construct a modern 'organic solidarity' will be effective. Recent evidence indicates that this failure to address basic production relations is already having a predictable effect. Under the Blair regime, Third Way policies have led to a significant expansion of inequalities, to the persistence of major social problems and to a significant undermining of the Blair project itself.[22] It is unlikely that the $65 billion social expenditure program of the Chancellor of the Exchequer announced in 2000 affected the trend towards growing income inequality.[23]

Giddens senses that his approach may not be viable. This is the significance of the priority which he gives to the concept of 'risk'.[24] But this notion minimizes, even trivializes, the enormity of the challenge which hundreds of millions of people around the world face today at the global, national and local levels. For these millions, it is far from being the case that life in the main is positive but there are some clouds on the horizon – some 'risks'. For these millions, the crises of impoverishment, unemployment, hunger and disease are not at all secondary features of life which can be avoided by careful calculation – by 'reflexivity'. On the contrary, poverty and hardship are the very core of their life experience. Oppression and exploitation inhere intractably in the basic structures and processes of global society and cannot be so easily disposed of by concepts such as 'risk'.

Giddens argues that in the main the opposition to globalization derives from the fact that it necessarily undermines non-rationalistic traditions and ancient ways of life sanctioned by age-old customs and religions. This is the explanation which he presents for the growth of fundamentalism – either Islamic or Christian. Fundamentalism is presented as a reaction against modernity. There is obviously an element of truth to this argument but it by no means emphasizes the main truth. The truth of Giddens's argument lies in the fact that both Christian and Islamic fundamentalism in fact face a common enemy: the national and globally dominant finance capital. Still, politically, these are two radically different phenomena. Christian fundamentalism in the United States arises in a highly developed capitalist society among groups – often sections of the white working class – who have been discarded by the ruthless march of American monopoly capital – especially the export of millions of jobs overseas. Islamic fundamentalism arises in societies which have a low level of capitalist development and which also are subordinated by global finance capital. In the first case, Christian fundamentalism is part of a sharp turn to the right and provides a popular base for the militias, for anti-black and anti-Semitic racism as well as for extreme neo-conservatism. In the second case, Islamic fundamentalism is part of a virulently extremist plebeian third world nationalism. The social and political significance of these two fundamentalisms is quite different.

What is more, by one-sidedly conceptualizing fundamentalism as primarily one of a social psychological reaction against the erosion of tradition, the problem is assimilated to that of yet another emotional reaction, in the long list of non-rational reactions to modernity, as in the second half of the nineteenth century in Western Europe. But by this approach the basic reality of the world dominance of monopoly and finance capital is obscured. The problem is not 'modernity' in general but the very specific form of 'modernity' produced by monopoly capital. It is the reality of grossly intensified global, regional and national inequalities of economic and political power and of military might. The white worker in upstate New York who finds himself thrown into unemployment by the decline of manufacturing notices that this is occurring while spectacular profits are being made by a few not so far away on Wall Street. He may well be attracted to Christian fundamentalism and join a right-wing militia as was the case of the Oklahoma bomber, Timothy McVeigh. What is driving such a person to fury is by no means a simple rage at the inexorable march of modernity eroding the not-so-rustic New York wilderness. What infuriates such a person is the injustice of it all and his complete powerlessness before the bankers and the state which facilitates them. This is the root of the fundamentalist response and not simply a generalized anti-modernity as such. The point is that the 'erosion of tradition' is not proceeding under conditions of relative equality, democratic discussion and consent. It is increasingly obvious to millions of people that this is far from being the case. The reason why the response to globalization and the erosion of tradition take a virulently fundamentalist form in some and is likely to grow more so, is because globalization is proceeding under such manifestly unjust and unequal conditions with such glaringly harsh consequences for the vast majority of humankind, including tens of millions in the United States itself.

The erosion of tradition is a real issue in its own right, although there is also much evidence of a willingness of hundreds of millions to embrace new ways of life when given the opportunity to do so. However, it is impossible to arrive at a viable approach to the issue of the erosion of tradition or even to discuss it rationally while globalization takes the grossly unequal form which it presently does. The source of the problem of fundamentalism, therefore, is not the erosion of tradition by itself, but the manner in which the erosion is proceeding – throwing hundreds of million into the direst poverty and threatening millions more, including increasingly, millions in the United States and the United Kingdom. The problem is not globalization *per se*. It is globalization led and exploited by finance capital.

# FIVE Capitalism Organized and Disorganized

Third Way or Global Civil Society theory is an attempt to formulate theoretical and political positions which address the tensions arising from the impact of globalization on contemporary society without addressing the roots of these tensions. Theories of 'disorganized capitalism', of 'economies of signs and space' and of 'network society' are closely connected to risk society theory but go further. These theories have the advantage that at least implicitly they accept the reality of the emergence of monopoly and finance capitalism since the beginning of the twentieth century as the dominant national and global political and economic reality. Although these theories do not discuss monopoly capitalism at length, nevertheless the very concept of a capitalism which is now 'disorganized' presupposes the prior domination of the 'organized', monopoly capital variety. The main point of these theories now becomes the argument that this monopoly capitalism – glossed as 'organized capitalism' – is only one version of modernity and, moreover, one that is being superseded by the reassertion of neo-liberalism, recent technological developments and the 'flows' of globalized capitalism. It is because network society theory and theories of 'disorganized capitalism' share the common assumption that, *pace* Dicken, an economic (and implicitly, political and social) path is unfolding which supersedes monopoly capitalism that they justify being treated together.

The most important and unacknowledged version of these theories is that associated with the work of Lash and Urry, reviving the idea of Hilferding and others about 'organized' versus 'disorganized capitalism' and proposing notions of the emergence of new 'economies of signs and space'.[1] In many quarters – especially in the United States – this body of theory, under the rubric 'network society theory', is associated with the work of Manuel Castells. But in fact, Lash and Urry – publishing in

1994 – were the first to work out a general sociological theory of the effect of new manufacturing methods and information technology on society as a whole. Castells developed similar ideas at about the same time but his full exposition in his three volumes came two years later. It is evident that Castells was aware of the arguments of Lash and Urry since he makes the same reference to one of their main works towards the end of the first volume of his trilogy as well as in the second volume.[2] Later I shall discuss the work of Castells – the idea of a 'network society' – and the important way in which it differs from the theory of Lash and Urry.[3]

The two books by Lash and Urry – *The End of Organized Capitalism* (1987) and *Economies of Signs and Space* (1994) – have to be taken together as one is clearly a sequel to the other. Published in 1987 and 1994, the works by Lash and Urry present the crisis of the contemporary world as resulting from the 'disorganization' of modern capitalism. They argue that one can distinguish between a capitalism which is 'organized' and one which is 'disorganized' – with the first case representing a monopoly capitalism combined with the post-war social democratic state and the second, resembling more a technologically updated reprise of the liberal English small and medium-sized enterprise economy of the middle of the nineteenth century. This latter 'new economy' – a term not used by Lash and Urry – is held to be the state of affairs evolving at the end of the twentieth century.

To understand the work of Lash and Urry one has to appreciate its context. It arose at the height of the 'disorganizing' Thatcherite neo-liberal moment – after the decisive defeat of the 1984 miners strike – and the collapse of the Soviet Union in the late 1980s. Above all, it is an expression of the collapse of the Keynesian social democratic compromise between labor and capital which arose out of the defeat of fascism in World War II and which more or less persisted into the 1970s. It also embodies the end of the post-war boom which the Keynesian compromise had produced and the intensification of the assault by capital on the positions won by labor as their rate of profit diminished. Both 'disorganizings' loom large in the books, with hope found in a third 'disorganizer' – Japanese flexible specialization production systems, information technology and global flows of capital.

The second work in particular – *Economies of Signs and Space* – reflects what one could call the dot.com moment. It is suffused with illusions about the emergence of a 'new economy' which ran rampant during the frenzied bubble economy of the 1990s. The weakness of both books lies in their failure to grasp that this global triumph of neo-liberalism, while undoubtedly 'Undoing Culture' as Featherstone memorably put it,[4] and undermining many old verities of the post-war social democratic welfare nation–state, at the same time was part of a new 'organizing' moment of monopoly and finance capital on an unprecedented global scale. It was therefore far from being the case that the hegemony of monopoly and finance capital was being 'disorganized' by small-scale production of the old liberal or 'new economy' sort. As Lash and Urry's discussion of finance capital itself indicated, what was really occurring (as far as the British economy was concerned) was the subordination of British capital in the City of London by American and Japanese finance capital.[5] What was occurring was the displacement of an earlier, less 'organized' form of what Cain and Hopkins famously characterized as 'gentlemanly capitalism' by an even more highly 'organized' form of finance and monopoly capital.[6] It was not a matter of 'disorganization' but of the re-structuring and re-organization of capitalism on a grander, global scale. This point is easier to see now, when the economic consequences of the entire process have played themselves out more fully and the geo-political consequences as well. No great effort has to be mounted today to convince that this entire process has culminated in a new round of naked imperialist aggression. But when Lash and Urry wrote, the dot.com surge seemed unstoppable and it was by no means obvious that this would be the course which events would take.

Hence their work (both books taken together) stresses throughout the chaotic and dissolving consequences of the radical free market policies of Thatcher and even of the 'new economy'. In the first work in particular, Lash and Urry document in detail the dismantling of the post-war welfare state then unfolding with full force in Britain and spreading to the rest of the European continent.[7] Their work is therefore characterized by the same profound pessimism which suffuses the work of Giddens and which has already been noted. This is less so in the second work – *Economies of Signs and Space* – than in the first. This difference between the two works is important because this second work is conceived of as having found a solution to the problems posed in the earlier work but whose solution eluded Lash and Urry at that time. Here is a characteristic passage:

> The abstraction, meaninglessness, challenges to tradition and history issued by modernism have been driven to the extreme in postmodernism. On these counts neo-conservative analysts and many Marxists are in accord. In any event not just are the analyses surprisingly convergent, but so too are the pessimistic prognoses.
>
> Now much of this pessimism is appropriate. But it is part of the aim of this book to argue that there is a way out. It is to claim the sort of

'economies of signs and space' that have become pervasive in the wake of organized capitalism do not just lead to increasing meaninglessness, homogenization, abstraction, anomie and the destruction of the subject. Another set of radically divergent processes is simultaneously taking place. These processes may open up possibilities for the recasting of meaning in work and in leisure, for the reconstitution of community and the particular, for the reconstruction of a transmorgrified subjectivity, and for hetero-geneization and complexity of space and of everyday life.[8]

This statement has to be seen as a critique of the postmodern nihilism – Baudrillard in particular – prevalent at that time. Lash and Urry deny that we are lost wandering in a vale of meaninglessness or, that all that was solid has melted. They see possibilities for 'the reconstitution of community' arising out of 'economies of signs and space' which ironically arise in the wake of the 'disorganization' of capitalism by the Thatcherite neo-liberal onslaught and the accompanying technical changes in pro-duction and information systems. These new flexible production systems of the modern economy – portrayed as based on 'flows' and 'processes' rather than on 'structures' – are presented as pointing a 'way out' which may rescue the age-old 'subject' and 'self' of the liberal bourgeois imagi-nation from inner chaos and collapse.

In this sense, although they pose the issues differently, their work is driven by a more profoundly Weberian problematic than is the case in the work of Giddens. As was the case with Weber, the issue for them is how to rescue this subject, this individual, imprisoned now not by an iron cage but by postmodern chaos and 'disorganization' on a global as well as a deeply personal scale – a chaos created by the latest mutation of the cap-italist system itself. As is well known, Weber, although profoundly seized by the bureaucratic transformation of capitalism, clung firmly to rational-ism, refusing to give ground to the contemporary trends of modernism and nihilism which had already developed strongly in his time, for example, in the life and work of Stefan Georg and his circle. Yet Weber's work found no satisfactory solution to this fundamental problem – the collapse of liberalism and the irrevocable bureaucratization of modern capitalism – leaving one in a state of profoundly pessimistic resignation.

Here in the work of Lash and Urry, as in postmodernism, it is not the threat to the subject posed by bureaucracy and monopoly capitalism which is the focus. The decay has become more penetrating, the threat more menacing than was the case with turn-of-the-century modernism. To con-ceive of this crisis as a 'risk' to society is blissfully absurd since what is gone forever is precisely the coherent personality capable of rationalistic calculation in the classic bourgeois manner – those personalities whose self-interested interactions sustained the traditional Hobbes–Locke–Adam Smith civil society order. In the case of postmodernism, late twentieth-century subjectivity is no longer intact and can no longer be healed by art or psychoanalysis, least of all by a politics of rationalistic calculations of the Weberian or Giddens sort. In Lash and Urry the focus is on this corrosion of the very soul. It is the inner psychological disorientation produced by late twentieth-century capitalism which preoccupies these scholars. This aspect of Lash and Urry's analysis leads one to recall Lukács's commentary on the work of Thomas Mann and the famous 'Schopenhauerian attitude' of Thomas Buddenbrooks or Gustave von Aschenbach – inner psychological collapse masked by outward fastidiousness – the so-called 'ethic of composure' – a parody of the once healthy Protestant ethic, now decaying from within.[9] Except that in postmodernism and, implicitly in the work of Lash and Urry (though not of Giddens), the process of fatal psychological decay has gone much further than anything Tonio Kröger or Hans Castorp could have dreamt of. Hence also the great emphasis on 'meaning' and on 'the aesthetic' in the work of Lash and Urry since it is this loss of inner coherence of the self which seizes them most.[10]

In keeping with this focus on the inner life and their sense of the acuteness of the crisis, Lash and Urry argue – apparently differently from Weber and Lukács – that it is the very collapse of 'organization' in late twentieth-century capitalism that shatters possibilities for individual rationality. One writes 'apparently' because this seems the very opposite of the Weberian thesis that the weakening of bureaucratic organization, while no longer feasible for technical reasons, were it to occur, would open up fresh spaces for individual freedom. But this is only a surface difference because the crisis of the liberal bourgeois subject has gone much further since the days of Weber: the crisis now is from within. The proliferation of human-created 'risk' on a massive and all-enveloping scale is not seen here as an *external* threat, as it generally is in the work of Giddens and Beck. The point for Lash and Urry is that this threat is deeper, it has penetrated to the core of the modern personality. It is this worm within which is the source of modernist and postmodernist *angst* and explains its potency. At the same time, the technical innovations of flexible specialization which follow and supersede this disorganization in their later work are celebrated as offering a new opportunity for the reconstitution of the self.

But although the threat to subjectivity is different from that perceived by Weber – more inward, more subjective and therefore more acute and intense – the goal of Lash and Urry is, broadly speaking, the same. The aim is to recover some ground for liberal social and cultural life, for 'reflexivity' and individual rationality, however small, in a world which has become profoundly hostile to liberal values of any kind. *Economies of Signs and Space* is Lash and Urry's *Protestant Ethic* with 'reflexivity' now supposed to carve out the space in which the threatened liberal subject can nervously survive.

The fact that Lash and Urry, like Weber, raise the issue of monopoly capital in this abstract form of the levels of 'organization' (or 'bureaucracy') of 'society' and not of capitalism *per se* makes it difficult for them to come to grips with the phenomenon with which they are dealing. Lash and Urry's emendation of Weber makes matters worse in one sense. At least in Weber's case it was easy to 'translate' bureaucracy into monopoly capital and thereby to understand more comprehensively the reasons for the rise of bureaucracy, the collapse of the liberal bourgeois competitive economy and with it the liberal democratic political project – the accompanying breakdown of the inner coherence of the bourgeois self and the rise of modernist disenchantment. Indeed, it is not hard to place certain aspects of Weber's ideas within the general context of the body of literature at the end of the nineteenth or early twentieth century, which includes writers such as Hobson, Hilferding, Rosa Luxemburg, Kautsky, Bukharin, Lenin, and, from another angle, Freud, although, as was to be expected, Weber himself resolutely resisted any such contextualization.[11] In particular, as Mommsen points out, Weber was opposed to Marxist theories of the concentration of capital from which the entire theory of monopoly and finance capital as well as of imperialism springs. If anything, Weber was more open to the views of 'evolutionary socialism' put forward by Bernstein, according to which the growth of monopoly ('organized') capital – cartels and the like – opened the possibility for a more harmonious capitalism which would be self-regulating – a capitalism evolving towards socialism.[12] This is ironic for, as has often been pointed out, Hilferding's notions of 'organized capitalism' sowed similarly fatal evolutionary illusions among Social Democrats in Weimar Germany.[13]

Notwithstanding this attitude on the part of Weber, the fact remains that he was dealing with the same problems posed for liberalism by the supersession of liberal competitive capitalism by monopoly capitalism, but dealing with them from a liberal-conservative viewpoint. *Pace* Weber's well-known sardonic remarks ridiculing socialist critiques of the anarchy of production under capitalism and his argument that socialism only aggravated the problems of bureaucracy which had developed under monopoly capitalism and that, therefore, socialism was bound to lead to the final loss of all personal freedom – all these viewpoints notwithstanding, Weber's problematic places him squarely within this body of literature.[14]

But Lash and Urry, while pursuing their project to rescue the liberal subject's autonomy ('reflexivity'), place themselves in a worse position than Weber for arriving at a solution. In this connection it is important to note that Lash and Urry struggle to maintain a critical stance against communitarianism, in spite of the fact that they are obviously attracted to aspects of it, for example, in the work of Charles Taylor.[15] Unlike some of Giddens's work,[16] they are by no means taken in by Heidegger whom they correctly interpret as an ultra-conservative ideologist hostile in the very fiber of his being to the liberal values which they hold dear. But this leads them, in the end, back into deeper pessimism since they in fact have little faith that communitarianism, especially in the Heideggerian or, for that matter, Alasdair MacIntyre versions, can accommodate liberal values of any kind, much less lead in a progressive direction. In a vitally important passage which many may have missed, they wrote:

> This rooted and Heideggerian phenomenon of 'the we', which is worlded rather than global, seems to open up political spaces for the new communities, including the 'new social movements'. In its departure from the subject–object assumptions of the abstract 'I', it opens up space as well for ecological thought. But the Heideggerian anti-discursive world of shared meanings, background practices and building, dwelling and thinking is at the same time and proximally the world of racism and ethnic hate. It is not, *pace* Adorno and Bauman, only the 'technology' of bureaucratic reason which was responsible for the Third Reich, but also these very rooted worlds of shared meanings, habits and shibboleths.[17].

Lash and Urry thus rightly reject the thinking of those in the anti-globalization movement, such as Gray, who draw their anti-global inspiration from a deeply held position of conservative Tory localism.[18] So, in the end, although Lash and Urry intermittently pursue it, they themselves turn out to be skeptical of their own technological communitarianism. It proves to be of dubious value as a solution to the problem of rescuing liberal values. Lash and Urry sense that the only solution to the preservation, indeed extension of liberal values, and for an overcoming of the incoherence of the self is the idea laid down from 1848 in *The Communist Manifesto* wherein 'the free development of each is the condition for the free development of all'. But because they conceive of the current process of contemporary capitalism as deeply 'disorganizing', they fail to grasp the fact that globalized monopoly capital, while laying the foundation for a new individuality, at the same time makes its realization impossible. It exploits this enormous social and individual potential for the private interests of a tiny minority of individuals. In their highly abstract formulations of 'reflexivity', they sense that, as usual and paradoxically, it is the very development of capitalism itself – this time on a global and truly vast social scale – which is laying the foundation for a new social order in which individual freedom thrives on a very broad social basis. But they do not see that the bars of our contemporary global iron cage are even 'harder than Krupp steel'.

Lash and Urry are prevented from seeing this by the abstraction of the concept of 'organized' capitalism which fails to deeply capture the peculiar combination of monopoly and competition which is the hallmark of monopoly capitalism. Such theories overlook the fact that capitalism is at one and the same time both 'organized' and 'disorganized'. It is organized in that, since the nineteenth century and especially today, it has achieved unprecedented levels of concentration of capital, of a far deeper international division of labor – an immense level of socialization of production. On the other hand, it is 'disorganized' by the persistence of private ownership of the means of production and by the world market. The acuteness of this contradiction – at a pitch never seen in human history before – is at the root of the problems of our age.

In this connection and as an aside, it is worth noting that too much attention has been riveted on the issue of free versus regulated trade. Monopoly and finance capital proceeds and dominates in both, prefers now one, now another, as the conditions of market competition change. In the United States – since the 1980s the bastion of neo-liberalism and the Washington Consensus – the tradition of economic policy historically has been a protectionist one. One only has to go back to the McKinley Tariff in the nineteenth century for this to become clear. Today, opposition is growing to Free Trade in the bourgeoisie itself – for example, in the group around the financier George Soros – as these lines are being written. Much is being made of the necessity to have 'fair' and not simply 'free' trade and of the need to regulate the global financial markets because of the fear of 'contagion' – the dangerous experiences of the Mexican Crisis of 1994–95 and of the Asian Financial Crisis of 1998. When one develops a balance of trade deficit of over $500 billion dollars ($120 billion with China alone in 2003) and one's currency begins the inevitable slide, neo-liberal free trade dogmas suddenly lose their attractiveness!

Because Lash and Urry characterize the state of affairs abstractly in a manner which misses the critical features of the modern economy, they are unable to understand how this globalization is also a process of the extension of the social division of labor on a global scale which opens the door to a solution to the problem which grips them. When to this is added their notion that capitalism today is undergoing a fundamental disorganization, then it becomes practically impossible for them to grasp the substance of contemporary social, economic and political processes and to formulate a credible way out.

The hope expressed by Lash and Urry is that the new 'information-rich production systems' introduced especially in the United States following the disorganizing neo-liberal reforms will also have an individualizing and liberating effect. This aspect of the argument in *Economies of Signs and Space* is explicitly different from that presented in *End of Organized Capitalism*. In their earlier work, Lash and Urry explicitly characterized the changes wrought by flexible production systems – only then reaching their full potential – as 'an integral part of the  disorganization of contemporary capitalist societies.'[19] But in *Economies of Signs and Space* Lash and Urry reject their earlier formulation as too one-sided – 'because of an overly structuralist conception of social process'.[20] What this point refers to is the conception of flexible production and the global economy as based on 'flows' rather than on structure – a weakness in their argument to which I shall return. In *Economies of Signs and Space* also there is an emphasis not only on the emergence of flexible production systems but on the role of the new information industries, and this emphasis was not present in their first work and points forward to the work of Castells'.[21] They now take the opportunity to argue that these production systems require a better educated and more autonomous worker with independent access to information on a variety of subjects. Thus, a new kind of citizenry will arise who will be able to circumvent and challenge the knowledge power of bureaucratic experts. As a result of this greater individuation of those now caught up in the extension of market relations and the spread of technology, citizens will now exercise greater individual judgment – greater 'reflexivity'. Thus the unintended consequence of marketization and the spread of technology, flexible production systems and new global flows of capital – 'disorganized capitalism' – will be that a more informed, critical and demanding citizenry will arise and this can only mean greater democracy and accountability. They wrote:

> This growing reflexivity is in the first instance part and parcel of a radical enhancement in late modernity of individuation. That is there is an ongoing process of de-traditionalization in which social agents are increasingly 'set free' from the heteronomous control or monitoring of social structures in order to be *self*-monitoring or self-reflexive. This accelerating individualization process is a process in which agency is set free from structure, a process in which, further, it is structural change itself in modernization that so to speak forces agency to take on powers that heretofore lay in social structures themselves.[22]

Thus, 'agency is set free from structure' and their problematic of rescuing the liberal subject is apparently resolved.

But only apparently. For this is hardly a convincing account of the conditions of the subject in modern global capitalist society – neither of the bourgeois nor of the proletarian subject. Such conclusions are colossally premature. They are based on an elementary misconception about the character of the latest phase of capitalist development which bears little relationship to the real-life experiences of billions of people in either the developed or developing world. Lash and Urry disregard the obvious fact that the technical changes in productions systems are occurring within the framework of the enormous growth in the power of global corporations and of international finance. This power dwarfs the governments of powerful nation–states, much less the detached 'reflexive' individuals of whatever social class in the corporation-dominated capitalist marketplace. Let us set aside the question of the agency of a member of the working class in the developed countries or of a member of the urban poor in the Third World in the contemporary conditions of global corporate capitalism. It is obvious that the power of 'knowledge', 'meaning', or of 'aesthetic' agency here celebrated by Lash and Urry is a feeble thing indeed when confronted with the immense resources of transnational corporations, the trillions of dollars traded daily on international currency markets, or the military might and *Realpolitik* of an international state system dominated by a 'hyperpower'.

Their highly unrealistic analysis bears little relationship to the real powerlessness which hundreds of millions of working-class and poor people tangibly feel everyday worldwide. More interesting, however, is that this profound sense of powerlessness and lack of agency is not confined to the proletariat or to small farmers. On the contrary, large numbers of middle and upper middle-class persons in the developed world have this same sense of their inability to influence the central social and political decisions which have a powerful effect on their lives. The greater sociality contained in contemporary capitalist production forces (rightly identified by Lash and Urry as having a liberating human potential) cannot realize itself as long as it is trapped within the iron cage of corporate capital. No solution to the crisis of the subject and the inner incoherence of life in contemporary bourgeois society can be found as long as the social forces which contain the possibility for solution remain the private property of a few. To be a consistent liberal today requires liberals to become socialists, as Lukes concluded.[23]

It becomes clear that Lash and Urry themselves sense the weakness in their own arguments – they display little confidence in their own solution – that 'reflexivity' by itself will rescue the modern liberal subject. They conclude their introduction to *Economies of Signs and Space* with the following gloomy prognostication which recalls some of their earlier formulations in *End of Organized Capitalism*:

> Disorganized capitalism disorganizes everything. Nothing is fixed, given, and certain, while everything rests upon much greater knowledge and information, on institutionalized reflexivity. People are increasingly knowledgeable about just how little they do know. Such increasingly uncontrolled economies of signs and space are inconceivable without extraordinarily complex and ever-developing forms of information, knowledge and aesthetic judgments. The unintended consequences of reflexivity – that is, the effect of reflexive agency on increasingly contingent structure – often lead to yet further disorganization.[24]

In other words, the crisis persists, perhaps on an even more daunting and thoroughgoing basis – indeed, aggravated by the rise of 'disorganized' capitalism.

Lash and Urry rightly sense that, indeed, the overall direction of world economic and social development is laying the only possible foundation for the re-constitution of the coherence of the liberal subject through the growth of a new international division of labor. They sense, in other words, the salient paradox of our age – that individuality today can only have the scope and depth which it has because it is based on an immense sociality. They sense the limitations in the traditional liberal concept of individuality as based on the autonomy of the subject from social ties (conceived of as 'constraints') in the sense of the 'negative' liberty of Isaiah Berlin, as Lukes points out.[25] But they do not see how they can go beyond this concept and retain their liberal values. They thus fail to grasp that, in contrast to the liberal bourgeois conceptions of individuality – associated with one brand of nineteenth-century liberalism – modern individuality is unique precisely because of the extensive social relations on which it is founded and on which it depends.

This adherence to a notion of individuality which derives from one particular historical experience of liberal bourgeois economy and society and which has certainly not been tenable since the beginning of the twentieth century, if not earlier, is at the heart of their difficulty. Indeed, Lukes points out that this view represents only one particular part of the liberal tradition – mainly that derived from the British experience. There is an equally important tradition associated with Rousseau which is preoccupied with the issue of the connection between individuality and sociality – with the social basis of individuality. This line of reasoning is embodied in Marx's outlook – not only in his earliest writings but right through to the *Grundrisse*. Durkheim's critique of the 'utilitarian egoism' of Spencer also has its roots here, as does the anarchism of Kropotkin.[26] It is not confined to Continental Liberalism because Lukes demonstrates that this line of thinking also influenced the Left liberalism of Oscar Wilde and Hobhouse.[27]

If subjectivity is formulated in atomistic terms – as synonymous with a self-generated and self-sufficient personal autonomy which is absolute in the Kantian fashion[28] – then, as Weber discovered, it becomes impossible to find a solution to alienation in modern society. This is because it is obvious that every single social and economic trend is ineluctably developing away from autonomy in the absolutist sense towards some kind of 'iron cage'. What is clearly needed, as has been repeatedly argued, is for a different concept of individuality to be worked out which is consonant with the actual conditions of modern life. This can only be an approach based on the fact that the distinctive feature of modern individuality – its newly found scope and depth – lies in its social derivation and connectivity. Connectedness and the economic, social, cultural and political dependence of billions of individuals on each other provide the preconditions and bases of modern individuality.

This is fundamentally different from the conception of individuality whose ideal is the independent consumer acting independently in the market and living the private bourgeois life. No such independence exists nor can it exist today or in the future. The point therefore is not to seek to recover an autonomy for an individual cut off from the social as the basis for a newly minted 'reflexive' subjectivity. The point is not to 'oppose man as a social being' to 'the self-sufficient individual'.[29] For a very long time there has been no such thing as a 'self-sufficient individual'. Sociological theories of the socialization of the individual 'self' – such as that put forward by George Herbert Mead – are one recognition of this reality.[30] Nor should our thinking be governed by the equally erroneous idea that the purpose of re-asserting the 'social being' of humans is to subordinate individualism. The entire point of the re-assertion of sociality is not to overcome, but to realize, individuality. The entire point is not to use sociality to crush individuality but to establish sociality as the basis for the free individuality of all. The point is to 'supersede' (in the Hegelian sense) the achievements of liberalism – individual freedom, individual rights, individual ethics, rationality – by retaining them, overcoming their limitations, expanding and supplementing them. As Lukes demonstrates in his complex and subtle analysis of individualism, Dumont missed the point completely when he set up a simple opposition between individualism and 'holism'. When the issues are thought through in the light of contemporary developments, these are far from being 'two mutually irreconcilable ideologies' – a kind of structuralist either–or.[31]

The point is to find a way for individuals to gain control over this new global-social which offers possibilities for a new individuality, on a scale and of a scope unthinkable to some theorists of liberalism such as, for example, Locke. Then the autonomy of the individual will not be confined to his or her private life. In combination with the autonomy of other individuals, it will be extended to the public sphere. It is not the mutual enmeshing in a global social network of social and economic relationships *per se* which threatens individuality. It is the absence of democratic control over this immense system *at its center* and the fact that it remains in the hands of a small minority of privileged individuals and corporations. In this sense the social crisis is not just a crisis for collectivities of people. The social crisis is simultaneously the root of the crisis of individual subjectivity as well.

Looked at from this point of view, modern individuality cannot flourish without the individual gaining a control over the determining social forces which she or he obviously does not possess today. Gaining control over these immense global social, economic and political forces on which the individual is inescapably dependent and to which he or she makes his or her contribution is not for the purpose of asserting some new form of totalitarian collectivism. On the contrary, the recovery of control over the social is a *sine qua non* of rehabilitating the self and an indispensable precondition for securing modern individuality and for restoring coherence to the subject, but on a broad social basis. The fundamental question, of course, is how to accomplish this in a democratic manner – both procedurally and in terms of substantive outcomes. We have no choice but to begin this process and the only way to begin is by an honest admission that all Marxist attempts to achieve social emancipation so far – in particular the Stalinist-inspired ones – have not only failed dismally: they have had disastrously inhumane consequences which are the very opposite of the approach which needs to be taken.

The specific notion of subjectivity to which Lash and Urry hold is also connected to their reductionist account of the roots of modernism and postmodernism which Featherstone and others have shown to be untenable.[32] This is the line of analysis which explains the spread of postmodernism directly as a 'reflection' of the development of flexible production systems. In *End of Organized Capitalism* Lash and Urry qualify their analysis by insisting 'that we are not arguing that there is any one-to-one, reductionist state of affairs in which postmodernist culture is somehow a reflection of the phase of disorganized capitalism'.[33] But they persist in what is at its core a reductionist argument nevertheless.

From a purely empirical, historical, point of view it is impossible to link postmodernism to changes in production techniques in this direct and mechanical sense – wherein 'flexible' production systems show themselves, if you will, in 'flexible' imaginations. Such mechanistic notions reflect a profound lack of grasp of the Hegelian nature of Marx's argument. The simple empirical fact is that modernist disenchantment began to develop many decades *before* the emergence of new production techniques while the liberal bourgeois economy was still the order of the day or just beginning to be superseded by monopoly. Modernist *angst* and postmodernist nihilism are a much broader and deeper phenomenon than simply a reflection of a change in production technique or in the scale and character of global capital flows. In the case of modernism what was at stake was precisely the collapse of liberal democratic ideals which began to occur even before the rise of monopoly capitalism. Even before then in Western Europe, with the failure of the 1848 revolutions and the suppression of the Paris Commune, it became apparent that bourgeois society not only could not make good substantively on its promises of freedom, but that the bourgeoisie would fight to defeat the very ideals which it once championed. The rise of global corporate capitalism and imperialism brought this crisis to a boil as Weber's own work and life demonstrate most vividly. The carnage of World War I was the culmination of this very broad cultural crisis – expressing itself in all areas of intellectual, political and aesthetic life.

Likewise for postmodernism. We are here confronted with a cultural expression not of a production technique but of something much deeper. This is the deeply intractable contradictions of the broad way of life created by a system of monopoly capital and the complete failure of all attempts to resolve the social and psychological contradictions and crises which it generates – including crises for the well-heeled bourgeois personality far removed from the production process. The social and personal contradictions generated (crime, social bitterness, personal emptiness) are such that especially for the well-provided for, life has to be lived in a state of relative social seclusion which, however, offers no real respite – simply making bad worse. For the rest of us, it is the despair generated by the repeated failure of the remedies for capitalism – each of which seemed to hold such promise and then turned out to be at least as bad as the disease, if not worse – which is one major sources of the postmodern turn. Such an acute, sense of despair had developed even while 'real existing socialism' seemed to have some viability in the world. The collapse of bureaucratic socialism in the Soviet Union in 1989 was perhaps the final straw. Now not even modernist *angst* was sufficient to express the depths of felt despair. Even modernism – especially modernism – was said to be a ridiculously optimistic metanarrative. A much more complete decay of subjectivity had occurred and therefore a more totalizing rejection of rationality was required. Even Nietzsche was insufficient – one had to cast one's eyes further back, with the assistance of the compleat anti-rationalist – Martin Heidegger.[34]

Thus, in the case of postmodernism, one is faced with a much more deeply felt, thorough-going and rooted crisis of despair than reductionist analyses of 'reflection' are willing to concede or able to grasp. As previously pointed out, the emphasis on 'meaning' in Lash and Urry's work is an expression of this fact. Nor is this crisis within the reach of such blithely rationalistic concepts such as 'reflexivity' or 'risk'. This crisis cannot be 'managed' by some skilful modern adaptation of the ideas of Hobbes, Locke, Rousseau, Adam Smith, Durkheim, Weber, Marx, Freud or of one or other high priest of the tried and trusty civil society tradition, national or global. Althusser is dead. Foucault, with his quaintly inverted French rationalism, seems hopelessly old-fashioned. Nothing seems meaningful anymore, not even the emptiness of parody, since even parody assumes a coherent subject. All one can do is nurse one's fatally wounded subjectivity. The point therefore is that those who reject the reductionist and mechanical materialist explanations of modernism and postmodernism have no confidence whatsoever in such rationalistic nostrums. To them this is an impasse which can only be suffered, never resolved. In this sense, for all their idealism, scholars such as Featherstone, in the end, have a deeper grasp of the intractability of the pitiless crisis which monopoly capitalism has created both for the individual and for global society as a whole.

This leads us to consider what I would characterize as Lash and Urry's rootedness in the notion of the nation. This, to be sure, is not a matter of nationalism or even of the 'Englishness' of Christopher Hill, or, of a writer such as E. P. Thompson for that matter, or of the 'Welshness' of Raymond Williams. On the contrary, Lash and Urry's work is explicitly comparative and seeks to go beyond the *inter*national to a truly *supra*national global. Yet their work takes as its unit of analysis the modern developed nation–state – be it Britain, Germany, Sweden, Japan, France or the United States. One can go further – their perspective remains deeply national (not nationalistic) in so far as an important source of their sense of the 'disorganizing' effect of contemporary global capitalism is its erosion of the power of the nation–state and its ability to independently regulate its economic, political and cultural affairs. As was the case with the subjectivity of the individual, global 'disorganized' capitalism is perceived to have also placed the 'reflexivity' of the nation in receivership. Although therefore a forerunner of what would now be regarded as a truly global approach, Lash and Urry did not themselves propose such an approach. They remain mired in what Beck has designated 'methodological nationalism', even as they pointed out that this national framework for social science analysis has collapsed.[35]

In *End of Organized Capitalism* no less than four of the fourteen points which they argue lead to the 'disorganization' of capitalism have to do with the erosion of national level processes and control. These include: 'the decline in the importance and effectiveness of national-level collective bargaining'; the 'increasing independence of large monopolies from direct control and regulation by individual nation–states'; then there is 'the spread of capitalism into most Third World countries which has involved increased competition ... and the export of the jobs of part of the First World proletariat'; finally, there is 'the considerable expansion in the number of nation–states implicated in capitalist production'. One could even add their final point about the spread of popular cultural forms across national boundaries independent of national cultural processes and policies.[36] Lash and Urry do not mention the growth of international migration in their first book, but this worldwide phenomenon would fit well with their overall analysis.

This sense of the complete collapse of the old national entities – economically, culturally and politically is even more developed in *Economies of Signs and Space*. Here Lash and Urry emphasize seven critical points which point to the fact that the old developed European nation–state is no longer a 'national community of fate'.[37] The first factor is the immense scale of transnational financial flows. The second is the severe structural inequalities of the process at the global level which is a consequence of the domination of the process by the developed capitalist countries of Western Europe, North America and Japan. The third factor is the inability of national governments to effectively manage domestic economic affairs in the light of the scale of international financial flows in a deregulated world free market. The fourth is the tendency which this has created for the integration of states into regional blocs. Fifth is the necessity which has thus resulted for there to be new forms of global governance. Sixth is the fragmenting effect which this has had on the traditional international order defined by the nation–state. Finally, Lash and Urry conclude that all this is leading to the creation of an entirely new form of international order in which the sovereignty of nation–states is no longer the accepted principle organizing global relations between peoples.[38]

One cannot comment in detail here on these extremely controversial propositions which, in some respects, could be interpreted as legitimizing the intervention of stronger states – those who control the UN Security Council (but not, of course, the General Assembly!) – in the internal affairs of weaker states. The issue is not that such processes are not occurring or that they are of little significance. On the contrary, one would have to be blind indeed not to see that very powerful global forces have been unleashed in the world today across wide areas of social, economic, cultural and political life which put all nation–states – developing and developed at 'risk'. One only has to consider the current enormous growth of protectionist sentiment in the United States – grossly under-estimated in Europe and around the world. There is a very strong souring on globalization in key sections of the American political elite due to the effect of globalization in undermining their hegemony over American society. Severe political setbacks threaten the social position of key allies of this elite (especially in the Southern and Midwestern United States) as 1.5 million manufacturing jobs have been lost from the national economy since 2000 and as their current account and budget deficit soars to unprecedentedly high levels. Because the political hostility to globalization is most intense at the State rather than the Federal level, the intensity of the hostility to globalization among broad social strata in the United States is not perceived. Yet at least eight states (Indiana, Michigan, Washington, South Carolina, Delaware, Nevada, Minnesota, Missouri) have either passed or are considering the passage of 'Job Protection Acts' and many more are likely to follow. The aim of these acts is to make it illegal for jobs funded by state funds to be outsourced overseas. The issue of the loss of jobs to China, India and Mexico is likely to be one of the most important issues in the Presidential elections of 2004.

As I write these lines, the estimated budget deficit for the financial year is $521 billion or about 4.5 percent of the gross domestic product of the United States. It now turns out that, as was the case with Britain at the end of the nineteenth century, the assumptions that the benefits of globalization would simply 'flow' to the United States were unfounded. One can expect that American equivalents of Joseph Chamberlain – Free Trade and Pro-Imperialism politicians who suddenly reverse themselves and become vociferous protectionists – will emerge at any moment. This entirely new and unexpected but perfectly predictable tendency is, indeed, what the turn from neo-liberalism to neo-conservatism portends. It has become so marked that Giddens and his colleagues have found it necessary to invent a new term to capture it. 'Regressive globalizers' is the new term coined for these newly-founded anti-globalizers from the political

Right.[39] But this term fails to appreciate that the hostility to globalization in the United States has a very broad social base. There is a growing perception that, as Harold Meyerson put it in a column in *The Washington Post*, 'in the age of globalization, the interests of many U.S.-based corporations grow increasingly divergent from those of the American people'.[40]

The social and economic consequences of corporate globalization are only too painfully real, as even the most powerful economy in the world is now realizing. Nor is this process confined to the economic sphere as scholars such as Apparadurai and Hannerz have repeatedly pointed out.[41] One does not have to agree with their particular conception of the specifics of the process ('hybridity', 'ethnoscapes') to see that their general argument that broad global cultural forces are abroad on a scale and comprehensiveness hitherto unknown is incontestable. For example, pointing out that this internationalization of culture is an unequal and uneven process which is driven by power and reproduces exploitation and elitism is true but does not undermine their core argument. How else could global cultural processes unfold under corporate capitalism?

Likewise, to point out in contestation of Hannerz's notions of the 'creole' or 'hybrid' nature of important segments of contemporary world culture, that all cultures have always been hybrid and that Hannerz's arguments only make sense if one assumes a closet essentialism – this too misses the central point. Only cultural nationalists and the anti-immigrant racist Right argue from an essentialist position of the 'purity' of local cultures. It cannot be doubted that all cultures, especially Sweden's, has a centuries-old history of hybridity and intermixture. What Hannerz is pointing to, however, is something different. His point is that this time-honored and very human process of cultural mixing is now not simply taking place between a single culture or number of cultures and others. The process is not taking place on a bilateral but on a global scale – as is conceptualized in Featherstone's concept of the emergence of 'third cultures' which Lash and Urry cite approvingly.[42] This therefore is an altogether more far-reaching process than the complex interactions across continental distances which have always taken place in world cultural history.

Alongside national cultures, a global culture is struggling to emerge. That this global culture is unequal, commercialized, dominated by pusillanimous media corporations seeking only their selfish interests, is difficult to deny. Indeed, one of the most effective parts of Lash and Urry's argument is their critique of Baudrillard which makes precisely this point.[43] The cunning of the 'reason' of the transnational cultural corporations and the many devious ways in which they are able to commodify and render harmless even tendencies to 'resistance' in popular culture and movements is one of the most telling points that Lash and Urry make. Nevertheless, none of this should lead one to overlook the fact that this global culture has emerged, warts and all, in complex interactions with national and sub-national cultures and this is a positive development of world historical significance. This is the crucial point.

The interesting question therefore is not the existence of this extremely important global phenomenon but one's attitude to it. Lash and Urry treat new cultural trends as prime instances of the deeply 'disorganizing' effects of contemporary capitalism.[44] Despite the calm language, they seem seized by the innumerable instances of brazen manipulations of popular culture and the multiple misuse of modern technology by the transnational and corporate media. The substitution of 'image' for 'product'; the promotion of shallow spectacle instead of meaningful art; the deliberate merging of fantasy and reality via the proliferation of a world of images and media – all these and more are instanced by Lash and Urry as examples of the nefarious cultural maneuvers of contemporary 'cultural' corporate capitalism – global *panem et circenses*.

Their concern in *End of Organized Capitalism* is that all of this has intensified changes in economic, social and political life – especially in the area of industrial relations and collective bargaining – which have completely undermined the power of the organized industrial working class in the developed capitalist countries, Britain in particular. Lash and Urry are deeply concerned with this historic loss which they rightly regard as irreversible. The old factory proletariat concentrated in council housing in large cities which was the foundation of the British trade union movement, the British Labour Party and the social democratic British state is no more. But this approach is very one-sided. The fundamental weakness in Lash and Urry's attitude to the collapse of 'organized capitalism' lies in its uncritical attitude to the long-term sustainability of the post-war Keynesian social democratic compromise. This unsustainability was not anticipated by social democrats or the Left as a whole during that period and is still not clearly grasped by Lash and Urry in their work. Yet the Keynesian compromise, with its high level of social concessions from capital to labor, although leading to an unprecedented post-war boom, also led to an over-capacity crisis and an eventual decline in the rate of profit for capital.[45] This crisis showed itself in the prolonged 'stagflation' of the 1970s. Such a crisis had to be resolved, either by a rolling back of the historic concessions to labor or a further encroachment on the rights of capital. Given the balance of forces in the world at that time, capital almost inevitably won out.

The stability (complacency?) and level of organization of the old industrial working class in Britain also derived from the privileges enjoyed by British capital in the world market, some of the profits from which benefited sections of the leadership of this very same working class. Moreover, the record of this working class in the sphere of consistent opposition to British colonialism and imperialism is an inconsistent and inglorious one. Likewise its attitude to anti-black racism and immigration. Some sections of this European industrial proletariat were internationalist in outlook and activity. But others were not renowned for selfless acts of international solidarity or for their revolutionary spirit. On the contrary, what often struck outsiders was their nationalism and, at times, chauvinism. Lash and Urry's portrait of the 'organized' and then 'disorganized' European proletariat starts from a somewhat idealized baseline. It is insufficiently critical of the 'organized' proletariat, especially its political and intellectual leadership. To some extent, it could be argued that a ruthlessly cosmopolitan corporate capital has taught this 'organized' working class of Europe a cruel lesson and made them pay a high price for not seeing beyond the immediacy of the post-war compromise. They, or at any rate their leaders, may have been the authors of their own misfortune.

But there is a more important point. This has to do with the way in which the new world developments in culture and economy are perceived simply as bringing 'disorganization'. This can only be an appropriate term if one takes the nation–state as an inescapable ontological and practical reality in the manner of 'methodological nationalism'. It is indeed the case that, from the point of the view of those who have been habituated to take the old nation–state structures for granted, the new globalization processes are profoundly 'disorganizing'. But to see only this negative aspect is to miss the point that they are also profoundly 'organizing' but on an infinitely larger global scale. Especially in *Economies of Signs and Space* Lash and Urry recognize this point. There they argue that, as a result of information technology, 'disorganization' creates new opportunities for progressive political movements.[46] They affirm that the new changes are irreversible and that there is no going back either to the old culture, the old social solidarities, the old economy or to the politics of the old working-class trade union and labor movements – *a fortiori* to the old welfare state. But they reject the idea that these changes mean the end of all progressive politics.

Here, their argument takes a truly fascinating turn which, I would argue, is also a result of the embeddedness of the idea of the nation–state in their thinking as well as their notion of finance capital as consisting simply of 'flows'. Lash and Urry argue that the future of radical politics lies in alliances with the new social movements which are arising alongside and partly as a consequence of the new cultural, economic and political forces. They have in mind in particular the environmental movement. Lash and Urry obviously entertain the hope that such an alliance can provide a social and political basis for the reconstitution of the social democratic agenda in the new global conditions which have emerged.

Striking here is the fact that these are social movements which have arisen overwhelmingly in the developed capitalist countries, especially in Western Europe. One also cannot help noting that these new social movements in Europe, in particular the environmental movement, are dominated by members of the professional middle and upper middle class. Indeed, in his emphasis on new notions of citizenship and of democracy, it could be argued that this is the Global Civil Society agenda in which the radical working-class movement is swallowed up by the interests and aspirations of the liberal urban upper middle classes which dominate the contemporary British Labour Party.

One would have thought that the very analysis of Lash and Urry would have led them further afield both socially and politically – to a politics beyond the boundaries of the nation–state. Both in *End of Organized Capitalism* and *Economies of Signs and Space* they point to the global reach of contemporary economic relations and the spread of capitalist manufacturing in particular to parts of the developing world – especially to Asia. At the same time, they repeatedly make the point that this new wave of capitalism spreading rapidly in parts of the developing world is accompanied by a closer integration of the developed capitalist economies – the European Union being the most obvious by no means only example. Yet Lash and Urry do not see these processes as providing the basis for the construction of a new progressive politics. Although there have been many examples of the importance of transnational solidarity – either in transportation strikes in Europe or in the inter-locking parts of the European motor car industry or in the international farmer movements[47] – the issue of a transnational strategy for a global progressive movement is not raised, much less discussed. The importance of such an alliance is even greater if one considers the issue of the export of jobs and capital from developed to developing countries and the 'race to the bottom' between developing and, for that matter, developed capitalist countries, in their competition to attract capital. Again, Lash and Urry's work does not conceive of the development of such an alliance between various social movements in developed and developing countries as a priority. In short, Lash and Urry under-estimate the potential for progressive transnational social movements arising in the developed countries and forming alliances with similar movements in the developed world, although that is precisely the tendency in the global justice movement This weakness is made even worse by an uncritical borrowing of extremely dubious characterization of areas inhabited by impoverished (black) people in the US 'wild zones'. This term simply shows how far most European scholars are from an understanding of the continuing strength of progressive movements among African Americans – indeed, of American politics as a whole – as well as in the developing world.

Yet it has become exceedingly obvious to most people – including people in the developed countries – that the present global order has been established by global monopoly and finance capital to meet their interests and no one else's. If this is the case, it would seem obvious that the only viable answer is an equal – indeed stronger – transnational organization across the boundaries of the nation–state of the forces which are opposed to the dominance of monopoly capital – including working-class, Green, gender and national and social movements in the Third World. In so far as one remains wholly within the boundaries of the nation–state therefore, it would seem that the chances of reconstituting a progressive politics are practically non-existent.

This would not mean that such a transnational politics would abandon or ignore nation–state boundaries for this would be both premature and suicidal. Corporate capitalism, while it fosters internationalism, is a global force which is still firmly rooted in the inter-relations between powerful nation–states which protect the interests of its corporate capital against the interests of others. What is more, the historic task of national liberation and national economic development is a very long way indeed from being exhausted for the billions of peoples in the developing nations. Because of the collapse of the Non-Aligned Movement, the depth of their debt crises, the feebleness of their economies and the postcolonial demoralization and decay from which their populations and nationalist political movements suffer, the usually Eurocentric analyses of globalization simply take it for granted that no significant global political actors are to be looked for from this Third World quarter. By one cliché or the other – 'failed states', 'wild zones' and 'black holes' – they are easily disposed of. But the idea that the historic aspirations of billions of human beings have somehow ceased to exist and are no longer a significant national and global political force is a wrong-headed and extremely dangerous one.

This geopolitical reality in which national power is intertwined with and in contradiction to international power, particularly evident today, is not affected by the fact that the system of global corporate capital is far more powerful than any single nation–state – including the most powerful. This is because, global or not, corporate capital is still capital – that is, like all capital it remains based on private ownership of the means of production and therefore is driven by market competition. A critical part of this competition remains the battle to hold on to one's home market while seizing hold of as much of the market of other nations as possible. Indeed, globalization has made this competition between transnational corporations for global market share more intense than ever. Loss of one's home market – due to trade deficits, or current account deficits, currency depreciation or non-economic factors – is a crucial strategic loss in this battle, quite apart from its political consequences. It is therefore absolutely essential for transnational corporations and global finance to be able to mobilize their own nation–state or regional bloc or multilateral agency – the European Union, the Group of Seven meetings of the main developed countries, the International Monetary Fund or the World Trade Organization – on their private behalf. Moreover, in the very nature of monopoly, victory is neither sought nor won by resorting simply to traditional competitive means. Threats, power politics, militarism, geopolitics – all means foul and fair – now become standard operating procedure. The conflict between the European Union and the United States and the finely calibrated political counter-response on steel tariffs vividly demonstrated the close inter-connections between these geo-economic and geopolitical realities. Likewise for recent divisions between the United States and Britain, on the one hand, and France, Germany and Russia, on the other. Adopting an internationalist perspective is therefore not a matter of abandoning national politics. It is a matter of understanding how such politics are pursued. National politics now has to be pursued within a context of the new, much more strongly integrated, international systems if it is to be effective. National politics has to operate within and be a part of a truly global politics.

It is striking that nowhere in the analyses by Lash and Urry or any other theorist of the 'new economy', was the emergence of the anti-globalization movement anticipated. One critical reason why Lash and Urry failed to grasp this central economic and political reality has to do with their conceptualization of international finance capital as a series of 'flows' which move now in this direction, now that, completely disregarding national frontiers.[48] But surely it should be obvious that these 'flows' move in certain channels directed by transnational corporations and in the international currency and capital markets controlled by the large Japanese, American and German investment banks? It is hardly the case that such 'borderless flows' are random and 'disorganized'. How can one miss the elementary fact that these 'flows' are part of the reproduction process of monopoly and finance capital on an immense global scale? If, however, one fails to see that the issue is not 'flows' but monopoly, then, of course, there will seem to be no point to the development of a politics which gives centrality to an anti-monopoly strategy.

# SIX Network Society Theory

The analysis of globalization as a 'space of flows' is developed more fully in the work of Manuel Castells.[1] In an eclectic and wide-ranging analysis, Castells' work contains the most comprehensive assertions on the effect of the then new information technology on the entire character of world society. Published at the height of the dot.com boom, we are here confronted with a kind of dot.sociology in which the technological changes in the production process are presented as ushering in an entirely new historical era with a new social formation – the 'informational' society. While similar to many of the ideas presented in the work of Lash and Urry as discussed above, the work of Castells actually proceeds from an altogether different inspiration and therefore has to be treated separately.

Lash and Urry's work, like that of Giddens, is a relatively sober Anglo-Saxon exercise in rational analysis – evaluating social 'risk' and the crisis of the bourgeois individual – while eschewing communitarianism and its accompanying identity politics. But Castells' entire point of departure is precisely a lament for the loss of community – Catalonia, Chiapas, the local or national community, 'place', 'culture', 'nation' – and a search for its restoration by means of modern communications technology and the 'network enterprise'. Unlike both Giddens and Lash and Urry, Castells is a champion of identity politics. The issues covered are similar, but Castells' analysis both departs from and arrives at a wholly different place. In this sense, Castells' work is much closer in spirit and inspiration to the mysticism of Heidegger which Lash and Urry rightly rejected.

Here is a classic example of Castells' romantic 'identitarianism' and colorful language which recur frequently throughout the text in the three volumes. He is discussing what he regards as tendencies to the postmodern in contemporary European architecture – its reliance on 'the space of flows' – using as an example the Barcelona International Airport, designed by Ricardo Bofill. Castells wrote:

> No cover-up of the fear and anxiety that people experience in an airport. No carpeting, no cozy rooms, no indirect lighting. In the middle of the cold beauty of this airport passengers have to face this terrible truth: they are alone in the middle of the space of flows, they may lose their connection, they are suspended in the emptiness of transition. They are literally in the hands of Iberia Airlines. And there is no escape.[2]

This juxtaposition of the banal and the high-flown is typical of Castells. We are here in the presence of an eclectic romantic communitarian ethos, supported by a mass of empirical data, and spiced with a plebeian anarchism which now abhors, now admires, capitalism and globalization.

It is not hard to demonstrate that Castells, although superficially influenced by Weber, has little faith in the rationalistic paradigm and is not a part of the liberal Harrington–Hobbes–Locke civil society tradition to which Weber himself belonged. Indeed, his frequent resort to metaphorical language which annoys many writers, for example Henwood,[3] springs precisely from this profoundly romantic anti-capitalist orientation which drives his entire work. It is this irrevocable attachment to the local which leads Castells to assert what amounts to the primordial priority of 'identity'. For him it is self-evident that 'Identity is people's source of meaning and experience' – without qualification.[4] That class, trade unions, political parties, civic associations, the market, business organizations, corporations, the Protestant religion – rationalistic forms of organization and consciousness of all kinds – have been and continue to be the dominant sources of 'meaning' in bourgeois society for hundreds of years does not move him. It is as if Adam Smith, Hegel and Weber, not to mention Marx, never lived and wrote.

Castells' Continental European anti-rationalism, although obscurely expressed, is unmistakable. This is the meaning of the elaborate discussion at the beginning of *The Power of Identity* in which he attempts to distinguish between 'the process of construction of meaning on the basis of a cultural attribute, or related set of cultural attributes' and 'roles, and role-sets.'[5] 'Culture' in this sense is an original and deep-rooted *Blut und Boden* – 'the construction of identities uses building materials from history, from geography, from biology' – while 'roles' spring from 'the institutions and organizations of society' and 'depend upon negotiations between individuals and these institutions and organizations'.[6] In other words, 'Identity', which springs from 'culture' is *Gemeinschaft*; roles and institutions are *Gesellschaft*. The first is the domain of ineffable, primordial, Catholic sentiment; the second the domain of self-serving calculation – Protestant and bourgeois to the core. The first is *Germania Sacra*, the second, *la perfide Albion*. This is the outlook which led Castells to write the following:

> Identities are stronger sources of meaning than roles, because of the process of self-construction and individuation that they involve. In simple terms, identities organize the meanings while roles organize the functions ... I also propose the idea that, *in the network society*, for reasons that I will develop below, for most social actors, meaning is organized around a primary identity.'[7]

This 'primary identity' is anchored in a sense of 'place'. Castells observes ambiguously that 'Places are not necessarily communities, although they may contribute to community building.'[8] This is true in the sense that he wants to preserve the option of locating the given 'community' at the local, regional or national level as the need arises – but never at the international level. His entire definition and discussion of 'place' rest on 'identitarian' assumptions. According to his definition *'A place is a locale whose form, function and meaning are self-contained within the boundaries of physical contiguity'*[9] – a definition which Henwood finds vague and useless. However, to dismiss this definition is to miss the depth of Castells' communitarianism. The operative word here is 'self-contained'. The notion is of a social group with a certain self-sufficiency and autonomy from the rest of society – living within self-contained boundaries imbued with deep emotion. Thus, in discussing Belleville – a suburb of Paris – Castells attempts to show how, despite many changes over the centuries, Belleville has retained its distinctive identity:

> Its dwellers, without loving each other, and while certainly not being loved by the police, have constructed through history a meaningful, interacting space, with a diversity of uses and a wide range of functional expressions. They actively interact with their daily physical environment. In between home and the world, there is a place called Belleville.[10]

Thus a 'place' is to be distinguished from a mere 'space' in that the former is a 'meaningful interacting space' which 'history' has infused with 'meaning'. A 'space', on the other hand, is simply an arena for calculating, self-seeking activity by the egoistic bourgeois. This terminology reflects a profound cultural conservatism in which 'meaning' arises strictly from the past – from 'history' in that specific sense of the archaic. Meaning never springs from the present and even less can it arise from future history – from a sense of the prospects which the future may hold. The point to note also is the opposition made between 'the home' and 'the world' between which twenty-first-century Belleville is now said to uneasily sit – not as communitarian as when Castells first moved there as an exile from Fascist Spain in 1962 but still clinging to some vestige of 'placeness'. Castells does not, in the manner of Giddens, for example, present 'the home' as thoroughly penetrated by and integrated into the bourgeois 'world' such that the Thatcherite project of affirming 'Victorian values' while pursuing marketization with unprecedented vigor was caught in a fundamental contradiction. Indeed, the entire argument of Giddens around the unviability of 'tradition' in the culturally conservative sense and the need for tradition to be made rationalistic, rests upon the notion that such oppositions as that of 'home' and 'community' to 'the world' are simply a figment of the romantic conservative imagination. Deeply rooted as he is in British history and its early development of capitalism, for Giddens, 'home' and 'community' have long been captured for bourgeois culture and the private life. To think otherwise is simply yet another example of the forlorn attempt (frequently made by sections of the capitalist class itself) to idealize an earlier phase of capitalist society in contrast to the economic, political, social and cultural *Sturm und Drang* of the current phase. It is as if the capitalist class itself takes fright at the volatility and contradictions of the world which they themselves have made and recoils from them. Giddens rightly sees that, from the point of view of an upholder of civil society, this approach is counter-productive because it ends up aggravating the contradictions which are already acute enough. Like it or not, all 'homes' and 'communities' have for centuries been in and of this capitalist world – the more so since the aggressive marketization project of the Thatcherites in the 1980s. Yet it is precisely on this anti-modernist notion that the structure of Castells' thought rests. This is yet further proof – if proof were needed – that Castells does not belong to the rationalistic civil society tradition from which Giddens, Lash and Urry obviously spring. Let us pursue this point further.

Castells, in the elaboration of his thesis on the centrality of identity politics to the world today, distinguishes between three types of identity. According to him there is 'legitimizing identity', 'resistance identity' and 'project identity' – a framework obviously borrowed from Weber's typology of domination.[11] These distinctions are critical to Castells' entire analysis of the present moment in world social development as well as his notion of the direction world development is likely to take as a result of the spread of the 'informational' society. At first sight, 'legitimizing identity' seems to be very similar to the concept of legal domination, especially since Castells says that it 'generates' (?) civil society.[12] One immediately thinks that one is in the presence of the familiar Hobbes–Locke–Smith conception of individualistic market society based on bourgeois concepts of *contract* rather than on feudal notions of *status*, in which law plays a critical role in legitimizing, indeed obscuring, the domination of the bourgeoisie. One thinks not only of Weber but of Hegel whose entire *Philosophy of Right* devoted itself to putting this law on a more solid rationalistic foundation.

But Castells immediately dispels this idea as he goes on to qualify this characterization by explaining in just what sense he is using the concept of 'civil society' and just what is his attitude to the world which the bourgeoisie has made. In the same sentence he goes on to state that civil society 'generated' this 'legitimizing identity' and produced organizations and institutions 'as well as a series of structured and organized social actors, which reproduce, albeit sometimes in a conflictive manner, the identity that rationalizes the source of structural domination'.[13] The crucial point here is in the last phrase – 'the *identity* that rationalizes the source of structural domination' [my italics]. Because Castells' position is an anti-capitalist one grounded in the past, he is loath to concede the progressive democratizing consequences of bourgeois civil society relative to the other historical forms which preceded it. All he sees from his communitarian perspective is that this bourgeois society defeats and subordinates all communities and is to be steadfastly opposed for this reason. This is why he rejects the democratizing and civilizing claims for civil society in the writings of Gramsci and Tocqueville for the more hostile notions of civil society in the works of Foucault, Sennet, Horkheimer and Marcuse. Where others see democracy, enlightenment and the rule of law, Castells says that this group – and this is certainly true in my estimation of Foucault, Horkheimer and Marcuse – sees 'internalized domination and legitimation of an over-imposed, undifferentiated, normalizing identity'.[14] In this connection, it is not without significance that Castells makes Gramsci 'the intellectual father' of the civil society concept, neglecting its roots in the English Revolution and the Scottish Enlightenment more than 250 years before.[15]

Such a viewpoint bears a superficial resemblance to critiques of bourgeois society from within the socialist tradition. This would, however, be a fundamental misunderstanding. It is not only at variance with the socialist tradition, it is also incompatible with the liberal tradition from which socialism itself springs. As Fritsche has pointed out in his brilliant analysis of Heidegger's anti-capitalist romanticism, there is an extremely strong tradition of anti-capitalist communitarian conservatism – especially, but by no means only, in Catholic parts of Europe – which celebrates the purity of the rural community and the notion of the nation as a 'community' in this emotion-laden sense.[16] Fritsche wrote:

> From the perspective of right-wing authors, society was a realm, or a form of synthesis of individuals, in which isolated persons act for the sake of their selfish interests. In this view, the only bond between individuals in society is the common assumption that each individual acts on behalf of his or her selfish interests, while regarding other individuals exclusively as a means in the pursuit of his or her interests. Thus, this bond is not a 'real' bond, since the individuals are connected only in a superficial or – as it has been put – in a mechanical way and are therefore not really united as all ... In contrast to society, community and the different communities – family, the village or small town, the *Volk*, the nation, for some also the state – provide individuals with a stable identity through traditions, customs (*Sitte*), and feelings uniting individuals on the deep level of 'positive' emotions.[17]

The point here is not that Castells is a right-wing author because he manifestly is not. The point is that his approach – as we shall see, similar to the approach of many in the global justice movement – is inspired by cultural assumptions and approaches commonly found in communitarian anti-capitalism. What grips them is the world we have lost or are in danger of losing, not the world which may yet come. This is a critique of capitalism looking back to an allegedly more harmonious, more humane form of human society, which harmony, capitalism – especially global capitalism – has ruthlessly destroyed. This viewpoint does not accept that the advance of capitalism is a dialectical one. It rejects the notion – common to liberalism and socialism alike – that capitalism, at the same time as it subordinates and exploits local communities, constitutes a profound historical advance. This viewpoint does not agree that capitalism, while indeed dissolving human bonds at the communal level, lays the basis for a humanity united by an international social division of labor and a common humanity. By its globalization, capitalism, unintentionally, actually creates the conditions in which 'a real existing humanity' is created in actuality, in a truly global sense. On the contrary, in the anti-capitalist viewpoint, capitalism is perceived and portrayed as an entirely negative development 'normalizing' the local. The political challenge therefore is not to advance to a new form of society for which capitalism has created the foundation. The task is to use the latest technology of capitalism to administer life-support to prolong the life of a communitarian existence already in its death-throes.

Likewise, the claim that the forms of association and consciousness – 'identity' – which capitalism introduces and propagates in the world are fundamentally different from pre-capitalist forms, is rejected. The argument is made that, contrary to its presumptuous rationalistic metanarrative, civil society depends on its own kind of primordialism just as much as communitarianism does. Its claims to generate a 'consciousness' – based in the rational interests of the individual or of groups – are rejected as hypocritical and false. It 'generates' simply an 'identity' rooted in its own – equally non-rational, equally primordial – dogma of individualism and self-seeking. To that extent civil society forms of thought and association are no different from any other 'identity' – in fact, they are worse, since they seek to 'normalize' (crush, pulverize) the only form of 'identity' which is truly genuine – the communitarian one. From this viewpoint, all is 'identity' much as Weber tended to argue that all was 'domination' – which did not, however, prevent him from believing that some forms of domination – liberal rationalism – were superior to others. Indeed, it is striking that one of the few lengthy quotations of Weber which appears in what is, in many ways, a Weberian-inspired work, is the well-known apocalyptic passage from *The Protestant Ethic*. Here, Weber – in full Nietzschean flight – broods over the irresolvable crisis of bureaucratic capitalist civilization.[18] Yet, notwithstanding his deeply felt sense of crisis, Weber remained a determined advocate of his own brand of liberalism and for a public life governed by an authoritarian but rationalistic 'ethics of responsibility' rather than by a 'prophetic' and unaccountable 'ethics of conviction'.[19]

In Castells, the strong emancipatory claims of rationality and democracy – the English, American, French and, especially Russian revolutions – are rejected as simply Enlightenment 'ideology'. The fact that bourgeois ideology – *liberté, égalité, fraternité* – obscures the domination of society by the bourgeoisie is taken as grounds for the dangerous implication that there is no content whatsoever in these democratic and rationalistic claims. From this viewpoint there is not much to choose between capitalism and Soviet-style state socialism since both suffocate the local community, both are guilty of 'the confinement. of power to the state and its ramifications' and of 'an over-imposed, undifferentiated, normalizing identity'.[20] One also senses here what could be called 'communitarian anarchism' – the vision of an ideal world as one composed of a collection of semi-autonomous congealed identities.

The upshot of this particular concept of 'legitimizing *identity*' – not 'legitimizing *consciousness*' – is the downplaying of liberal rationalism of any kind. This leads to the notion that 'identity for resistance' which Castells explicitly identifies with Etzioni's 'communes', 'may be the most important type of identity building in our society'.[21] Hence the effort which is placed on celebrating the Zapatista and feminist movements – although it is highly questionable whether the term 'identity' adequately captures feminist (or any other) consciousness and it is clearly the case that his analysis of the Zapatistas was suffused with romantic illusions. The most interesting aspect of the analysis, however, has to do with his concept of 'project identity'.

Castells uses this innocuous-sounding term to characterize what happens 'when social actors, on the basis of whichever cultural materials are available to them, build a new identity that re-defines their position in society and, by so doing, seek the transformation of overall social structure'.[22] In other words, unlike 'resistance identity', this form of iden- tity ceases to be purely defensive. It does not merely 'resist' but is also able to put forward positive alternatives to the status quo. In a word, 'project identity' is transformative of the fundamental conditions which produces its oppression. It addresses root causes, not simply symptoms. One could say – Castells does not say this – it is revolutionary rather than reformist even though Castells' terminology makes it sound almost like a technical process in which intellectuals may dabble – a 'project'. However, of greater importance is Castells' portrayal of this process. Although 'pro- ject identity' is said to seek 'the transformation of overall social struc- ture', it does so, according to Castells, 'on the basis of whichever cultural materials are available to them'.

In other words, 'project identity' is put together from the group's own inner cultural resources, perhaps long suppressed by an oppressor but kept alive in popular memory. Long underground, it now resurfaces as 'project identity'. It therefore does not represent a fundamental transfor- mation of this consciousness but a kind of ideological resurrection. Nor does it require the group to rise above any parochialism to which it may have been prone. Castells operates with a hierarchy of types of identity modeled to some extent on Weber's treatment of types of domination: 'resistance identity' can rise to the level of 'project identity' and the latter can degenerate into 'legitimizing identity'. But 'project identity' is generated from *within* the group, is, as Castells puts it, the result of an 'expanding' and occurs 'on the basis of an oppressed identity' – a recrudescence.[23] In other words, this is, indeed, an 'identity'. Structural transformation does not require rationalistic forms of consciousness in order to achieve its goals. All that is required is a recovery of the com- munity self – a Heideggerian revelation of 'authentic *Dasein*'.[24]

Castells goes on to explicitly contrast his 'project identity' with Giddens' ideas of the requirements of 'late modernity'. As one would expect, the difference which Castells draws between his concepts and those of Giddens turns precisely on the issues raised above. In the first place, Giddens' line of thought is deeply individualistic in the standard manner of the Anglo-Saxon civil society tradition. Castells had already rejected this individualism in his discussion of the work of Touraine. This work was necessarily problematic for him since Touraine not only is individualistic in his analysis but he also places the individual in opposition to *both* the market *and* the community. Consistent with his communitarianism, Castells points out that while Touraine's 'subject' was the individual, his was the 'collective social actor'.[25] Giddens too is concerned with how the individual uses his or her rationality to negotiate the 'risks' of the modern world. According to Giddens, 'reflexivity' is the key tool which the individual uses to sustain rationality in the challenging circumstances of the globalized world. Castells quotes Giddens' statement that:

> The more tradition loses its hold, and the more daily life is reconstituted in terms of the dialectical interplay of the local and the global, the more individuals are forced to negotiate lifestyle choices among a diversity of options ... Reflexivity organized life-planning ... becomes a central features of the structuring of self-identity.[26]

In other words, for Giddens, as already pointed out, the bourgeois self retains its coherence. It has the weapon of 'reflexivity' in its psychological arsenal and deploys it with skill to effectively win its battles in this globalized world. But for Castells no such coherence is possible for the vast majority of the population under the conditions of global capitalism. With a characteristic rhetorical flourish he insists that 'reflexive life-planning becomes impossible except for the elite inhabiting the timeless space of flows of global networks and ancillary locales'.[27] Giddens' rationalistic optimism will not work. For Castells what is required instead is 'a redefinition of identity [which is] fully autonomous *vis-à-vis* the networking logic of dominant institutions and organizations'.[28] There then follows what one would have to describe as a hymn to communitarianism and identity politics:

> The search for meaning takes place then in the reconstruction of defensive identities around communal principles ... I propose the hypothesis that the constitutions of subjects, at the heart of the process of social change, takes a different route to the one we knew during modernity, and late modernity: namely, *subjects, if and when constructed, are not built any longer on the basis of civil societies, that are in the process of disintegration, but as the prolongation of communal resistance.*[29]

Thus, the process of identity formation today is understood as fundamentally a 'defensive' one. There is no going forward, one can only look back. Civil society is seen by Castells as 'in the process of disintegration' and can provide neither a basis for the reflexive reformism of Giddens nor for the even more rationalistic aspirations of a revolutionary socialism. Therefore the political task is not the supersession of parochial identities by a process of *Aufhebung* which recognizes, incorporates and qualitatively transforms 'resistance' – raising it and humanity to an altogether higher level of (international) social existence. The vision here is different and irreducibly communitarian: 'project identity, if it develops at all, grows from communal resistance'.[30] The vision is even more deeply pessimistic than is the case with the writings of other scholars discussed above.

Castells' notion of a 'space of flows' is part of this communitarianism. Since for him a communal identity is the primary ontological reality, it follows that social and economic relations which operate outside of and beyond communities necessarily operate in an alienating 'space' – a void which never achieves the 'meaning-full' interactions of 'place'. This 'space' is simply a 'space of flows' – a realm of alienation impacting on 'fully autonomous' communities from outside. It is able to subordinate, exploit and even crush communities, without penetrating and profoundly transforming their very nature and inner social characteristics. Thus, interestingly enough, although the thesis is about the triumph and all-pervasiveness of 'network society', there is no 'network *identity*' – not to mention 'network *consciousness*'. Castells specifically rejects the notion that network society is a new (international) culture 'because the multiplicity of subjects in the network and the diversity of networks reject such a unifying "network culture"'.[31] 'Identities' and 'flows' occupy different worlds and have radically different characteristics: 'networks' simply 'link' identities which are the real, ontologically privileged, cultural actors in human history.

This attachment to identity also explains Castells' critique of neo-liberalism, his preference for the East Asian developmental state and what, given his communitarianism, may appear to be a surprising affirmation of a strong role for the state.[32] Neo-liberalism is rejected from the communitarian standpoint as a 'project' inherently antithetical to identity. By foregrounding the free market, it threatens to undermine the very foundations on which identity rest. Castells' attitude to the state is more complex. It depends on the type of state and the role which it plays vis-à-vis identity. He is, as one might expect, highly critical of the Soviet state and sees its bureaucratic rigidity as the main reason for the failure of the

Soviet Union to master information technology. This failure Castells puts forward as the central reason for the collapse of the Soviet Union. However, his attitude to the East Asian developmental state is quite different and it is interesting to note why this is so. According to Castells, the 'project' of the state in East Asia 'took the form of the affirmation of national identity, and national culture, building or rebuilding the nation as a force in the world, in this case by means of economic competitiveness and socioeconomic improvement'.[33] Thus, the developmental state is to be lauded because it was an identity-affirming, identity-strengthening project – in the sense not of local, but of national community, while the neo-liberal minimalist and the totalitarian Soviet states are to be rejected because both, in different ways, sideline and subordinate identity. One does too little to affirm identity – indeed, corrupts identity with rationalistic self-seeking; the other swallows up identity with its all-pervasive political and police mechanisms, imposing 'an exclusionary ideological identity'.[34]

This approach to neo-liberalism and the primacy of identity necessarily means that Castells also cannot accept the view of globalization which sees it as nullifying the power of the nation–state.[35] Indeed, he goes to some lengths to distinguish the nation from the state and, as one would expect, to give primacy to the former over the latter. It is the nation – the community writ large – which is his primary reality and the state is simply an instrument which should be made to properly service this 'project identity'. From this viewpoint – a kind of communitarian nationalism – Castells affirms the persistence of the power of states even where, on other grounds, one may expect his position to be more localist, because states serve the communitarian identity of the nation.

At the same time, he necessarily argues that for this and other reasons, there are powerful 'limits to globalization'.[36] What could these limits be? There are political and economic factors which establish these limits. The political factors have to do with the role which the state plays in shaping the architecture of global economic and other agreements – the very framework in which globalization occurs. In addition, states also intervene very directly to support the interest of particular transnational corporations which originate in the home nation–state. The economic factors include the fact that most transnational corporations maintain their decision-making headquarters, main assets, key technological and financial operations in their home nation. Moreover, Castells points out that both trade and investment penetration continue to be very uneven – with the penetration of especially the Japanese market being very limited. The most interesting factor, however, is the way in which Castells sees the 'identity' (my term) of transnational corporations. They are conceived of as cultural expressions of their particular nation – champions, and the necessary economic underpinning, of national identity. Thus, he wrote that 'German multinationals (such as Volkswagen) have disinvested in West European countries to undertake financially risky investments in East Germany to fulfill the national ideal of German unification.'[37] In Castells' communitarian world, even powerful transnational capitalist corporations are regarded as 'identities'. They no longer make their decisions primarily on the basis of rationalistic calculations of profits – for example, the immense tax and other incentives offered to West German investors in East Germany. Nor does he attempt to explain the quite marked tendency of German automobile and other manufacturing companies to invest overseas in order to avoid the relatively higher labor costs in Germany. Corporations are governed by 'national ideals' not by profit and loss and by the unforgiving quarterly evaluations of the stock market. If those in the very vanguard of capitalist globalization – transnational corporations – are themselves embodiments of identity, then globalization necessarily has strict limits indeed. But how would this utterly naïve outlook explain the ruthlessness with which American corporations have unhesitatingly transferred millions of American jobs overseas? Or the similar actions of British finance capital at the end of the nineteenth century?

This approach to transnational corporations helps to explain an apparent inconsistency in his work. On the one hand, Castells' argument is structured along the lines of technological determinism. The first volume is largely about technology and its effects, and the very first chapter in this volume (after the Prologue) is *The Information Technology Revolution*. Information technology develops and then transforms the business and other operations across the world, creating a 'network society'. On the other hand, Castells denies that his is a technological determinism – 'the new organizational changes I have described are not the mechanical consequence of technological change'.[38] They 'required a change of mentality rather than a change of machinery'.[39] Significant cultural variations continue to persist between nations, and the world is one of permanently differentiated national identities and their associated regional blocs (civilizations?). Castells insists that 'Japanese uniqueness or Spain's difference are not going to fade away in a process of cultural differentiation, marching anew towards universal modernization'.[40] Powerful though the role of technology may be – and a simple examination of the structure of the three volumes will easily reveal that technology is the driving force in his argument – it is not powerful enough to undermine the cultural differences established by 'history' and long-standing primordial identities. These continue to have an irreducible character.

There is a real contradiction in Castells' work between this technological determinism and his 'identitarianism'. This stands out clearly if one goes back to an earlier essay written in 1993 and a later work by Carnoy.[41] In Castells' analysis in *The New Global Economy in the Information Age*, the entire thesis rests upon technological determinism. In the chapters by Carnoy and especially Cohen, but also by Castells himself, there is no mention of the role of culture, community or identity in the new global economy, although this work is clearly an important early version of Castells' later ideas.[42] It is the transformations wrought by Japanese production systems and information technology which are held responsible for the transformation of the global economy and even the collapse of the Soviet Union.[43] Moreover, the analysis of the position of transnational corporations in this work does not in any way put forward the thesis that their power is in any way diminished by these technological changes. On the contrary, in the chapters by Carnoy and Cohen, it is precisely the opposite point which is repeatedly made. The adoption of Japanese production techniques, flatter organizational forms, and the application of information technology have, if anything, made transnational corporations even more powerful, both in the national and world economies, as Harrison established more than ten years ago.[44] Harrison proved that flexible production systems did not simply create 'network enterprises' but 'large firm-centered networked production systems'.[45]

At the opening of his chapter published in 1993, Carnoy, for example, wrote:

> Large multinational enterprises (known as MNEs) continue to grow rapidly and to influence changes in the world economy. They also dominate trade among the industrialized countries and control international capital movements. In the rapid informatization and internalization of production and distribution, much of the innovation (R&D) in information technology takes place in the MNEs or is financed by them, especially as the cost of innovation has risen.[46]

Even Castells himself in his chapter, although he refers to a new 'flexibility and decentralization in production and management', shows his general line of argument is the same as the book as a whole: A technological revolution has transformed large corporations and the world economy which they continue to dominate.[47] It is true that all the authors of this work, Carnoy and Cohen in particular, strongly uphold the thesis that the global 'geo-economy' is one dominated by the most powerful nation–states in which countries the most powerful corporations originate and are based. But the grounds on which this is maintained are not communitarian ones.

It has nothing to do with the unconquerable 'spirit' of the identities at the core of nations and even less to do with imagined primordial identities of transnational corporations. It is a pragmatic and empirical argument, as one would expect from writers such as Carnoy and Cohen who generally work firmly within the Anglo-American civil society tradition. The dominance of powerful nation–states which allows them to pursue meaningful macroeconomic policies at the national level derives from the economic strength of the corporations which originate and remain there. But it is clear that this dominance can be lost. Indeed, the entire point of Cohen's chapter is to warn the United States that it is losing its dominance precisely because it has allowed its corporations to be by-passed by the latest technological changes in the production process.

This contrast between a rationalistic technological and an identitarian culturalist argument stands out even more when one considers Carnoy's later work. In this work Carnoy shows great foresight. Four years before it became a major political issue, he was preoccupied with the severe crisis which globalization and the new production systems was generating in the American labor force and in undermining family and community life, as well as living standards. These concerns have an unmistakably communitarian ring. Carnoy now is alarmed about the vulnerability of the professional strata of the American labor force to competition in the global labor market made possible by information technology. He thus moves strongly away from his old position and is inclined to reject his old thesis on the persisting dominance of the nation–state. He is now inclined to argue that globalization and the transnational corporation are clearly in the driver's seat and in danger of triumphing over the nation–state.[48] In defense of his earlier thesis about the persistence of the power of the nation–state he, rather unconvincingly, resorts to an identitarian argument for the first time. He simply expresses the hope, without any of his traditional empirical support, that 'it is likely that societies with strong national identities and group cohesiveness provide the kind of stability under which financial risk can be accurately assessed, productivity can be raised with new team-based production innovations, and educational institutions work reasonably well'.[49]

Thus, the earlier work of Castells (and of Carnoy) bases itself on technological, not identity, arguments. When, therefore, Castells moves into a phase of his thinking which is suffused with notions of identity, he faces the task of reconciling these ideas with the older, rationalistic, technological positions. The upshot is an unhappy amalgam. Castells tries to reconcile the irreconcilable by arguing that technology is not wholly a rationalistic means–end application of science to production processes.

It is this but much more. Technology is a cultural phenomenon which springs out of and is closely tied to the peculiarities and identities of particular national groups. 'It can be shown', wrote Castells, 'that patterns of business organizations in East Asian societies are produced by the interplay of culture, history, and institutions with the latter being the fundamental factor in the formation of specific business systems.'[50] Castells regards this as an updating of the Weberian thesis and even attempts to locate and characterize a 'spirit of informationalism'.[51] Thus, information technology may have originated in the United States and network forms of business organization may have originated in Japan but they are then 'diffused', nineteenth-century style, from their centers of origin to various locations around the world, 'leading to a multi-cultural frame of reference', to which all countries have to adapt.[52] Castells denies that this argument is based on 'cultural economics' on the ground that for culture to be economically effective, it has to be institutionalized and these institutions are means–ends organizations 'invested with the necessary authority to perform some specific tasks on behalf of society as a whole'.[53] In other words, culture may be the source of technology and organizational forms but when operating in the economic sphere these forms have to pass a pragmatic test: do they serve the material needs of the nation in the competition with other nations or not – do they deliver high rates of GDP growth? Thus, in the economic sphere culture has to give way to such means–ends issues and in this sense Castells rejects the notion that culture is the main determinant of economic institutions. Culture may be the source of particular economic practices but the extent to which these practices sustain themselves and becomes 'institutionalized' depends on the demonstrated means–ends effectiveness of these practices.

This does introduce a certain flexibility into Castells' notion of the relationship between culture and the economy. It is not a straight line relationship and is not simply a matter of 'identity'. Because of this means–ends criterion, economic institutions, which originate in one culture, will 'diffuse' to another as these institutions demonstrate their superior effectiveness even as, at the same time, they necessarily have to adapt to the specific cultural context of the particular 'identity' to which they are diffused. This flexibility, however, does not alter the main point: 'identity' is at the root of all aspects of society, including technology and the economy. Moreover, the objectives which economic institutions ultimately serve have to do not with the interests of individuals or of classes or of 'humanity' – as in the liberal or socialist traditions. The pragmatic means–ends test which all economic institutions (and corporations?) must pass is the test of serving the needs of their given 'identity'. Thus while Castells' approach bears a superficial resemblance to Weber's, it is fundamentally different. He does not demystify 'identities' into various status groups rationally pursuing their self-interests, competing with each other and deploying *Realpolitik* to weaken their opponents and to strengthen their position in the 'nation'. Unlike Weber, Castells does not see that the claims of 'meaning' presented by the particular groups who compose the 'identity', while sincerely held, also embody certain fundamental (status group) situational interests. Castells does not share Weber's sense that identities are strategic creations ultimately to be understood rationalistically. One cannot simply take the primordialist claims of identities seriously as Castells is inclined to do.

Only after one has understood these fundamental orientations of Castells' thought can one begin to understand the particular manner in which he analyzes the global economy and what his concept of 'network society' actually implies. For his concepts of the global economy and of transnational corporations have to subordinate themselves to his 'identitarianism'. It is essential for him to paint a picture of relatively weakened and transformed transnational corporations which link or exclude but do not penetrate national identities – other than, of course, their own national identity of origin. These corporations remain the champions of their own nation's identity. But as for their global operations, these giant business enterprises and immense concentrations of speculative financial capital must be presented as somehow not engulfing the nation–states whose economies they penetrate and often undermine. Castells achieves this in the following manner.

He argues that a new technical basis for economic life has arisen throughout the globe. In an analogy with the notion of industrial society, Castells dubs this 'informational society'. This includes not only Japanese production techniques and *keiretsu* forms of business organization, the Korean *chaebol* and the family-based business of the overseas Chinese, but the regional economies of Emilia-Romagna in Northern Italy as well as the restructured organizations of American corporations in the early 1990s. In one way or another, and taking account of the different cultural contexts, these business organizations have one fundamental thing in common, according to Castells: they are all based on networks. The interesting point though is the character of these networks. His key point is that this inexorable tendency to business networks has become so strong that it has undermined and transformed the traditional 'vertical' organizations and even the power of transnational corporations *at the global level*. This is an astonishing claim but one which it is necessary to make if the ontological primacy of national identities is to be maintained.

Castells qualifies this untenable claim from time to time. For example, he concedes that Harrison is correct when he demonstrates that the significant small business networks are not stand-alone operations but in fact subcontracting captives of transnational corporations. Referring to small and medium business, Castells wrote:

> It is true that small and medium businesses [*sic*] appear to be the forms of organization well-adapted to the flexible production system of the informational economy, and it is also true that their renewed dynamism comes under the control of the corporations that remains at the center of the structure of economic power in the new global economy.[54]

But this concession is immediately qualified in the following sentence by noting 'the crisis of the traditional powerful corporate model'.

He goes on to assert that this traditional corporate model is in 'disintegration' and has moved from a 'vertical' to a 'horizontal' structure. As a result 'a new organizational form has emerged as characteristic of the informational/global economy: the *network enterprise*'.[55] But his fundamental point is this:

> Since most multinational firms participate in a variety of networks depending on products, processes, and countries, the new economy cannot be characterized as being centered any longer on multinational corporations, even if they continue to exercise oligopolistic control over most markets. This is because corporations have transformed themselves into a web of multiple networks embedded in a multiplicity of institutional arrangements'.[56]

But the unreal and idealized representations of both international finance and global information technology in Castells' thought somehow neglects to foreground the obvious fact on which all agree. Transnational corporations have concentrated greater wealth and are more powerful than ever before in national and global economies. The very firms he quotes as examples of crisis and misplaced arrogance – IBM, Philips and Mitsui – are more powerful than ever.[57] Mitsui – one of the original *zaibatsu* – includes giant firms such as Toshiba and NEC. The fact that large transnational corporations restructure and develop networks of inter-relationship can hardly be taken to mean that they are less powerful. This is the very opposite of the true situation. The trillions of dollars of international financial transactions are not flowing freely between all individuals in an undifferentiated 'network'. This capital has owners – a small minority of persons who are the real lords of the universe. The same applies to the concept of an 'informational' society. Internet or not, the significant means of global information technology production in both software and hardware is among the most highly monopolized and contested areas in global capitalist competition, as the anti-monopoly suit against Microsoft by the European Union amply illustrates. In this sense the notion of an undifferentiated 'network society' is also deeply misleading.

The idealized treatment of these issues in Castells' work shows itself vividly when one compares it with the presentation of the very same issues in the work of Dicken, which also refers to transnational financial linkages as a network.[58] In Dicken's analysis, however, a substantial body of data is analyzed to show how concentrated international finance capital is and the extent to which it is essentially the preserve of a handful of big banks in three countries – Japan, the United States and Germany. Likewise, Dicken presents a fascinating account of monopoly practices and ruthless competition in the global semi-conductor industry which has undergone repeated restructuring as a result of the bitter fight between Japanese, American, Taiwanese and now South Korean chip manufacturers. There are now only ten huge global firms which control 50 percent of total world production of semi-conductors. Three US firms – Intels, which has the dominant position in the world market, Texas Instruments and Motorola – control as much as 24 percent of world production.[59] Three Japanese firms – NEC, Toshiba and Hitachi are second with 13 percent of the global market. Three vast European monopolies – led by Infineon, a subsidiary of Siemens, and receiving massive state assistance – have recently staged a comeback and now control 9 percent. Most striking, however, is the growing presence of Samsung – the giant South Korean electronics firm which was totally absent from the world market until 1990. They have now risen to singlehandedly control 4.2 percent of world semi conductor production which makes them the fourth largest producer in the world.[60]

This graphic and realistic account tells us far more about the realities of transnational corporations and the global 'informational' economy and society – who really controls the hardware without which there is no 'flow' of global information and no 'flow' of trillions of dollars of 'hot money' through the London money market. It is quite obvious that, far from becoming a new source of a new organizational form – the 'network enterprise' – global information technology has become yet another source for the accumulation and concentration of capital by global corporate monopolies.

In general, network society theory averts its eyes from the harsh realities of a world based on developed capitalist relations: huge transnational firms – the top 52 of which are among the world's 100 largest 'economies';

a multi-trillion dollar global stock market; an unprecedented concentration of wealth in all countries leading to a situation in which the total income of 582 million poor people in the developing countries is 10 percent of the income of the top 200 billionaires ($1,135 billion) in 1999. The tendency is to dissolve all into 'networks' in which the power of money and military might is dissipated by 'knowledge' and information.

Castells' cultural communitarianism also connects with multiple modernity theory which preceded it, although multiple modernity theory is more rationalistic in its line of argument. If this somewhat fashionable term – multiple modernity – had any substance, it was not merely because it drew attention to stylistic variations on the modernity theme. Why should anyone care – except the Chinese people themselves – whether capitalism or socialism had Chinese characteristics? It was rather that these non-Western modernities (a polite term for monopoly capitalism) were thought to hold out (or to have once held out!) the prospect that a more just modern world was not only possible but also actually unfolding in a materialist sense. In other words, what was of interest was the question of whether these non-Western capitalisms had new and positive social outcomes, whether they seemed to be solving some of the age-old problems of capitalism which had proved so intractable in the Western (especially Anglo-American) forms. In other words, we are back here to the discussion of monopoly capitalism and how it can be overcome. Multiple modernity theory in fact posited a cultural 'solution' to these long-standing socio-economic and political contradictions.

This search for real existing alternatives *within the framework of capitalism* inevitably intensified after the collapse of socialism and with the injustices of global free market monopoly capitalism becoming ever more glaring. This led to the idea that the problem was not monopoly and finance capital *per se*. The problem was the cultural traditions within which the dominant (Anglo-American) forms of monopoly capitalism arose. In this analysis the social and economic failures of Western forms of modernity had to do with the incorrigible individualism of this tradition, especially in its dominant Anglo-American version. Some Asian countries were thought to be convincingly demonstrating that the old connection between individualism and modernity was an ethnocentrism of modernization theory and a peculiarity of Western history.

The apparently necessary connection, famously and grandly set out by Weber in *The Protestant Ethic* was purely adventitious, contextual and limited to the West. Asia was showing that, on the contrary, one could have both community and modernity, no Protestant individualism, low unemployment, limited economic inequality (relative to Anglo-America) and little class conflict. This body of thought was a communitarian emendation of Weber's famous thesis to allow for the possibility of a capitalism with a more communitarian rationality to emerge from the religious ethics of the East. To this extent there is a real connection between multiple modernity and network society theory in so far as both yearn for the preservation of some form of communitarianism.

Indeed, it was claimed that East Asia showed that such communitarian 'economies of signs and space' might be more effectively modern – *more rationalistic*, purely from the point of view of productivity and scientific and technical rationality.[61] Monopoly capitalism was being superseded by this new model of capitalism which, because of its proven competitive superiority, was becoming a worldwide trend. 'Reverse convergence' – the Anglo-American economy converging towards the Japanese model – was becoming the order of the day.[62]

Initially, because of the work of Dore, in particular in the pioneering *British Factory, Japanese Factory*, and in other works on Japanese 'relational contracting', this idea gained currency – that a really radically new production system had emerged in Asia which resolved the age-old social conflicts of capitalism as well as being more productive and efficient.[63] Today this idealizing of the Japanese production system may seem far-fetched, after the collapse of the 'Bubble Economy' in the early 1990s and the prolonged deflationary crisis from which Japan is only now finally emerging. But one must remember the context in which Dore conducted his research. This was, above all, in a context defined by the failure of the nationalization policies of the British Labour governments of the 1960s and the seemingly inexorably stagnation and then decline of British manufacturing and the British economy as a whole. It was in the face of this intractable 'British disease' – the anarchy of shop floor strikes, the incompetence and disaster at British Leyland – that Dore turned his attention to Japan. He was astonished at the contrast in the state of affairs in Japanese production systems even from this early date – well before it became fashionable in Western business circles to make the pilgrimage to Japan.[64]

The sense was that the Japanese or Italian models held out the hope of an apparent supersession of the age-old contradictions of monopoly capitalism. A new era which combined modernity with community was evolving from within the womb of capitalism itself in which the rationalistic potential of capitalism would be realized at the collective level – for the benefit of society as a whole. It is this claim which is the source of the appeal of multiple modernity. I would argue that multiple modernity theory is less communitarian and more rationalistic in comparison to network society theory. This is readily apparent if one carefully compares the work of Castells and that of Dore.[65] Dore's vision is in the British rationalistic tradition. His concern is how this Anglo-Saxon rationality can be supplemented by Japanese rationality – broadened from the individual to the firm and to society – including global society, so-called 'reverse convergence'. Yet the common idea which connects all these outlooks – multiple modernity and network society theory – is the thought that information technology offers society an opportunity to return to a more communal way of life on a modern basis. Even authors who attempt to develop a socialist alternative to monopoly capitalism looked mistakenly to the model of the Japanese 'communitarian firm' presented by Dore, as an institution which provided a model for overcoming worker alienation at the enterprise level.[66]

The key point in multiple modernity theory therefore was to detach capitalism as an economic system from the particular individualistic cultural form which it takes in the West. The implication was that it was from this individualism that the worst problems of poverty, oppression and exploitation arise, not inherently from monopoly capitalism as such. In fact, there may not be any such thing as 'the capitalist system as such' – only various 'modernities' – neither capitalism nor monopoly capitalism but simply 'capitalisms'. It was reasonable, therefore, to hold out the prospect of different, more just forms, of modernity arising in other cultures – in India, Israel, China, the Arab world, Africa, as, it was claimed, had already occurred in parts of East Asia. But these uncritically idealistic assessments of the Toyota production system, the 'three sacred treasures', the Third Italy or Scandinavian socio-technical systems have more or less been exploded.[67]

Nevertheless, all these sociological theories – risk society, 'disorganized' capitalism, network society – have a major advantage over the theories of cultural studies. This has to do with the fact, that all of them to varying degrees attach central importance to an analysis of the economy. In the writings of Giddens, Lash and Urry and Castells, there is not the preoccupation with the issue of 'economism' in such a manner that the entire economic sphere is practically excluded from the analysis. On the contrary, a large part of their sociological conclusions is based on the ideas which they have of how the modern global economy functions. Their weakness is not the neglect of economics but the particular way in which the economy is incorporated into their analysis. In the theories of Giddens and those influenced by him, because of the abstraction of the market from the relations of production, it is the economy as a global marketplace – exchange relations and trade alone – which become central. This comes out most clearly in the work *Global Civil Society* published by a group of scholars at the London School of Economics.[68] In the theories of Lash and Urry and Castells, the focus is on the economy as a system of production. But this system of production is perceived as technologically, not socially determined. In the end, therefore, these sociological theories prove inadequate since they do not incorporate the economy into their analyses as a social system of production. Most important of all, by relying on concepts such as 'modernity', 'risk society', 'economies of signs and space' and 'network society', the central economic and political challenge of our age – the concentration of power at the global and national center due to the dominance of monopoly capital – is minimized.

# SEVEN 'Localization' Explored

In the light of the arguments presented above, I now turn to the critical issue of the alternatives to monopoly and finance capitalism proposed by the anti-globalization movement – or the 'global justice' movement as they have been latterly and significantly re-named. Here I present what I regard as a friendly critique of the thinking of the anti-globalization movement. I make this point initially because most of this chapter occupies itself with pointing to what I regard as the dangerous fallacies in this thinking which render these ideas unfeasible in their present form. Indeed, the conclusion which follows from this chapter is that the alternatives to globalization here discussed are unworkable economically or politically, and where they are workable they are undesirable, from the point of view of many of the people who support anti-globalization, not to mention the general citizenry. These somewhat severe criticisms are not made in a hostile spirit with the aim of undermining the movement. On the contrary, they are made from the point of view of enhancing the credibility and therefore the political effectiveness of the anti-globalization movement. At least that is the claim.

One of the most important questions facing the anti-globalization movement is the issue of developing theoretically and empirically convincing alternatives to the existing corporate global and political systems. This is a vital matter from several points of view. In the first place, as the movement has grown to the massive size that it has today, with demonstrations regularly reaching the level of over 300,000 persons, it is drawing in persons from ever-wider social strata. These different, often single-issue, groups come to the anti-globalization movement from very diverse viewpoints and experiences. Many are environmentalists, outraged by the threat that greenhouse gases are posing for the environment. Others, moved by the intensifying poverty in the developing world, are advocates of Third World debt cancellation. Yet others are trade union activists from developed countries, concerned that free trade and deregulation are leading to the migration of jobs away from their own members, to lower-wage and less-regulated economies. This diversity is a source of the mass strength of the movement. At the same time it poses serious challenges to the unity of the movement, especially over the longer term. Clearly, if these very diverse perspectives are to maintain their unity over the longer term, then some kind of development of a common theoretical outlook, program and organization, however loosely adhered to, would be beneficial.[1]

Likewise, one must note that the advocates of globalization increasingly place at the center of their criticisms of the movement the claim that the anti-globalizers have no credible alternative to globalization. They argue that the movement has a purely negative program – is simply a form of 'anti-ism' – without having any constructive alternative to offer. The implication of this message is obvious: anti-globalizers are 'adolescent' college students or 'anarchists' whom no responsible member of society could possibly support. The entire point of this argument is to quarantine the anti-globalization movement and to prevent its considerable growth from spreading into the central institutions and pivotal groups of society. In other words, this issue of the presence or absence of a credible anti-globalization alternative is increasingly becoming a central one for the development of the movement and the consolidation of its influence in society.

One should not fail to mention that this question of theoretical clarity and alternatives is not regarded by all participants in the movement as necessarily that important. Indeed, many (especially some in the Italian movement) make the argument that it is precisely this absence of what I am here calling theoretical coherence which is the strength of the movement and the source of its current credibility. Likewise the absence of clear-cut organization. This tendency argues that preoccupation with alternatives was a weakness of past movements in the 1960s and 1970s and leads to sectarianism, bickering and ultimately to disunity. In addition to this pragmatic argument against diverting energies to a search for clear alternatives, there is a more philosophical argument that addresses this criticisms of the globalizers by embracing them. The approach here is to proudly affirm that indeed, one has no 'alternative' and that to posit alternatives is simply to seek surreptitiously to replace the existing system of corporate hierarchy and domination, with another, even more elitist 'vanguardist' one, from the Left. Again, the studied avoidance of any thrust for organizational coherence is often regarded as one of the cardinal strengths of the current movements in contrast to the Stalinist ones of the not so recent past.

This chapter takes another view. It argues that while the anti-globalization movement has grown into an enormous worldwide movement capable of having a powerful influence on the central issues of world society, it still has not moved into the mainstream. Without what I call 'moving into the mainstream', this vast and growing movement will not be able to achieve the objective of meaningful social, economic, environmental and political change. By 'mainstream' I mean the arena of the everyday politics of unemployment, poor education, health care, world poverty and inequality, racism, development, taxation, budget deficits, war and all the other issues that are the bread and butter of the established main political parties and interest groups in civil society. It is in fact the only movement on the horizon that has the potential to bring about positive changes in society at a global level, which is where they are needed. It is therefore a vital matter for this movement to take itself into the mainstream where the central issues that directly affect the lives of hundreds of millions of people are fought over politically. In order to do so, the movement must, like other political forces, artic-ulate some kind of program, however loosely, and develop broad alliances, for example, with trade union and civil rights movements in the developed world and anti-imperialist movements in the developing world – a kind of 'grand alliance'. At least this is the point of view from which this chapter departs. One can be lulled into complacency by the very size of the anti-globalization movement. What participants may forget, however, is that gigantic mass movements from the Left have existed before but petered out. For one reason or another they failed to move into and secure the support of the mainstream on any long-lasting basis.

Many in the anti-globalization movement increasingly recognize this problem which is why the term 'global justice movement' – an inade-quate term, given the inherently limited distributionist content of the concept of 'justice' – is gaining more popularity. The point here is that it is no longer good enough to be simply 'anti'. One now has to start elabo-rating what one is and is not for. Such an exercise carries obvious risks, especially that of generating excessive argumentation, sectarianism and divisiveness in the movement – to the great potential benefit of the sup-porters of globalization. But it can hardly be avoided if the movement is to make that shift into the mainstream that I am arguing is essential.

In this chapter I critique the proposals of one such group in the anti-globalization movement, who have taken up the challenge to develop a credible alternative to corporate globalization. This is the work of Colin Hines and the International Forum of Globalization (IFG) and which refers to itself, accurately in my view, as a 'Localization' perspective. This is basically an Anglo-American group, although it has important representatives from Asia – Vandana Shiva, Martin Khor and Walden Bello to mention a few. No claim is made here that the particular alternatives proposed in their writings are in any way definitive or characteristic of the anti-globalization movement as a whole. However, their perspective is undoubtedly an important one that captures many of the instinctive views of persons who are anti-globalization. Indeed, the arguments presented here apply to many of those in the movement whom Callinicos describes as 'autonomous' and 'reformist' anti-capitalists.[2] The perspectives of IFG and Colin Hines, although containing many differences, in their general shared characteristics provide an opportunity to discuss some of the critical issues which any anti-globalization movement must confront as it seeks to connect with mainstream politics.

## Two Bodies of Experience and Theory

One of the most striking features of this literature on alternatives to globalization is the failure to discuss the considerable body of empirical and theoretical knowledge that has accumulated around the issue of alternatives to imperialism and capitalism in general. I am referring to the vast literature on the problems of central planning and other failures in the Soviet economy, the issues of how to understand the NEP, the failure of the Khrushchev and Kosygin reforms and the failure of *perestroika*. There is an equally vast literature on the roots of the Polish crisis which led to the rise and fall of Gomulka, the Gierek boom and bust crisis of 1971–75, the problems of the Yugoslavian self-management system, the experience with the Hungarian reforms of 1968 and the many attempts to develop a viable economy in the former Czechoslovakia and the former GDR.[3] Likewise, there is no reference to the experiences of China during the 'Great Leap Forward' or the Cultural Revolution and the movement to market relations and globalization after the 1979 reforms – arguably the most gigantic and significant act of globalization in the economic realm ever undertaken anywhere in the world. There is no discussion of the experience of Cuba either, and the question of the controlled but unmistakable extension of market relations in that economy. Indeed, the desire of Cuba to integrate itself into the global economy – in effect – to become a part of the process of globalization seldom if ever attracts any comment. Nor is there any exploration of the problematic achievements of the Mondragon Cooperative Corporation (MCC) in the Basque country.[4] There is no reference either to the well-known work of scholars such as Roemer and Schweickart on the development of socialist alternatives to capitalism in the light of the failures of the Soviet model of socialism.[5]

This strange neglect may be explained by the attitude of anti-globalization thinkers to reject the experience of any form of explicit socialism as irrelevant and precisely what they wish to avoid when they attempt to develop an alternative to globalization. As Cavanagh writes:

> Both [capitalism and state socialism] centralized the power of ownership in unaccountable institutions, the state in the case of socialism and the corporation in the case of capitalism. Both worked against the classic liberal economic ideal of self-organizing markets—markets in which communities organize themselves to respond to the local needs within a framework of democratically determined rules.[6]

Such a position may or may not be acceptable but in any event does not answer the point raised here. The reason is that the abortive reforms attempted in state socialist regimes were precisely an attempt, however half-hearted and fraught with insurmountable contradictions, to move *away from the state* aspects of state socialism and to make some kind of space for local autonomy and market relations 'of the classical liberal economic ideal'. One would therefore have thought that a clear-headed evaluation of this experience – after all, the only concrete one in which various alternatives to capitalism were attempted – would provide some invaluable lessons for the anti-globalization movement, of both a theoretical and practical nature.

Even if the experience of state socialist regimes is deemed irrelevant, the same cannot be said of the experience with the Popular Front regime in France between 1936–37 or with the Allende regime in Chile of the 1970s. In both cases, alternative economic arrangements were attempted by regimes which could hardly be characterized as state socialist and in both cases the reforms culminated in collapse, disaster for the popular forces and the capture of power by the extreme Right. Surely such experiences, while no doubt having their unique aspects, have much to tell us not only about the economic feasibility of the alternatives to corporate globalization but about the politics of such a process as well. A careful reflection on the critiques contained in the works of Nove, Sutela or Caldwell, for example, might more than repay the effort.[7]

In fact, one of the striking features of the anti-globalization literature is the almost complete silence on the standard political objections which are made to attempts to regulate capitalist relations of production which is what is explicitly proposed by the IFG group, as shall be seen in a moment. The familiar and time-honored critiques that such changes inevitably lead to a highly controlled and bureaucratic society in which personal autonomy and the rule of law are sacrificed in the name of some social cause – be it the environment, preserving the 'local economy', defending the local culture, reducing social inequality, or whatever – is not even raised, much less discussed. Yet these are real issues which cannot simply be dismissed as neo-liberal propaganda, especially if one claims to be seeking to restore 'the classical liberal economic ideal'.[8]

As is well known, in this tradition, this kind of economy is thought to have a political counterpart in the form of liberal democratic parliamentarianism and the rule of law, the existence of which is not simply a matter of 'bourgeois right'. As we shall briefly see towards the end of this chapter, the political dimension of the alternatives to globalization are certainly referred to but not adequately discussed.

I regard this disconnect between previous theoretical and practical attempts to construct alternatives to capitalism and the current thinking of the anti-globalization movement as one of the most harmful aspects of the present situation. Whether this avoidance (evasion?) is for good tactical and ideological reasons or not, the fact is that the movement will hardly be allowed to get away from the uncomfortable reality of confronting these experiences, nor should it attempt to do so.

## Localization

Hines and the IFG group put forward their position as one of 'localization'. By this they mean that they wish to return to what they describe as 'human-scale' living in relatively small communities and they want to institute an economic and a political system which, they argue, would bring this about. We shall return to the issue of what 'human scale' means and the complex and contradictory attempts to give it substance.

This notion of the alternative follows from the understanding of the problem of 'globalization' to inhere in its global character – its extensiveness and spatial scale, so to speak. According to this view, globalization is imperialist and exploitative in nature – of its own societies, of economies and peoples in the developing world and above all of the global environment.

But at its core this exploitation is thought of as deriving from and expressed primarily in the large-scale nature of much of the contemporary corporate economy from which its oppressive and damaging characteristics are thought to derive. It is this largeness that leads to the vast consumption of natural resources in the production process. It is the same vastness that leads to excessive carbon emissions. It is vastness that leads to and is expressed in global 'long-distance trade'. It is vastness that leads to the huge concentration of wealth in a few hands. And it is vastness that leads to the huge and undemocratic concentrations of corporate power. 'Globalization is de-localization', is the expression used to capture this point.[9]

An important theoretical point arises here. In this line of analysis, the large-scale nature of private and public corporations is not regarded as an outgrowth of other forces, such as inescapable tendencies to bureaucratic rationalization as in the well-known line of thinking of Max Weber on the necessary disenchantment of modernity. Nor for that matter, are the arguments of the reactionary German phenomenology, concerning the inevitable emergence of 'inauthentic *Dasein*', following the replacement of *Kultur* and *Gemeinschaft* by 'bourgeois *Gesellschaft*', accepted. Nor is size seen as a necessary product of the growth of the division of labor and the market as in the civil society tradition running through Adam Smith, Hegel and Marx.[10] Size is not, so to speak, a dependent variable. It is itself causative and *sui generis*. It is willfully chosen as a particular form of economic organization precisely in order to extract super-profits and to plunder the wealth of the entire world.

This idea is best captured in the following statement from Cavanagh:

> In the eyes of citizens movements, these trends [towards large corporations and global trade] are not the result of some inexorable historical force but rather of the intentional actions of a corrupted political system awash with money. They see the World Bank, the IMF, and the World Trade Organization as leading instruments of this assault against the people and the environment.[11]

This rather voluntaristic notion of how and why firms are formed and grow, bears no relation to any of the theories of firm organization such as those formulated in the important work of Williamson. Willfulness, greed and corruption are to be blamed. Given such a naïve consciousness, it then follows that the task is to reduce and eventually to eliminate bigness. Size is the problem, not the relations of production, forces of production, technology or economies of scale. If bigness *per se* is the root of the evil, then clearly smallness must be the solution. If 'globalization is de-localization', then the alternative must be one of 'localization'.

This is the line of thinking that leads to the attempt to propose the breaking up of the contemporary economy made up of large-scale transnational corporations engaging in global trade. This would be converted into a small-scale community-focused economy in which what is called 'long-distance trade' would be confined to a limited set of goods and services and would be carefully controlled.

Such a local economy would try to produce as much as possible for itself from its own resources and would trade mainly locally, except in exceptional cases such as the trading of necessarily large-scale energy supplies. This is called the 'site-here-to-sell-here' policy. This localization of production would also be a localization of consumption. It would therefore get rid of the requirement to ship goods and services over long distances around the world which is undoubtedly one of the main sources of environmental damage in the world today. One result of this, it is argued, would be greater respect for the environment, as it would now be in the clear and obvious interest of the local community to husband its resources. It would also lead to a reduction in excess consumption, especially of luxuries and exotic products. This is because such trade would either be banned outright or taxed at a prohibitive level.

Credit and investment in such an economy would be provided by local banks only and, indeed, there may even be the creation of local currencies that circulate only within the community, side-by-side with national currencies. Necessarily, the labor market policy would also be controlled, with preference given to local labor and with barriers erected to discourage immigrant labor. Labor would have the right to move from one community to another only in exceptional circumstances. In general, a taxation and regulatory policy would be pursued which over time would lead to the break-up of large corporations and their conversion into small and medium-sized business which operated at the local level. Likewise, such policies would inhibit the growth of large corporations in a deliberate move to maintain the 'human scale' of the economy.

In fairness, it should be pointed out that it would not be strictly accurate to characterize these ideas as a proposal for autarky, familiar to *aficionados* of world systems theory from the 1970s. Although without doubt influenced by this body of ideas, this is not a program to 'de-link' from the global economy, as it was fondly called. This is so for a number of reasons that are important to understand.

In the first place, although the IFG group is hostile to what it calls 'long-distance trade', it recognizes that some of this is necessary for a number of reasons. First of all, in the interest of many developing countries that produce, say, bananas, and who depend on the world market production and consumption of bananas for their livelihood. The IFG group is strongly in solidarity with the plight of developing countries and an aggressive advocate of debt cancellation. They recognize that banning such trade would be extremely harmful for the standard of living of millions of people in the developing world and so this is one of the cases of long-distance trade that will be allowed to persist for a considerable period of time. They are also well aware that some goods and raw materials cannot be produced locally, either because they are simply not available or because of the obvious benefits of the economies of scale in the provision of certain goods and services – for example, energy and rail services. The trading of these on a long-distance basis too would be permitted as exceptions. Third, it may be the case that better off groups that have the money may be permitted to purchase luxuries but this would not be common. The point to note in all of this is that the aim is not an absolute ban on long-distance trade now or in the future. The aim is to reduce and limit this trade to the absolutely minimally possible level, taking the above factors into consideration. Thus what is being aimed at is what one might call 'relative' rather than 'absolute' autarky.

This proposal for local production, consumption and trade is also accompanied with a proposal for a generous sharing of information and culture on a voluntary international basis. IFG is not putting forward a purely inward looking not-in-my-backyard approach. What it is seeking to do is to combine a core localism with a voluntarily expansive and internationalist inter-relationship of sharing between communities. Thus, the proposal contains major measures to transfer technology from the developed to developing countries, but this must be appropriate technology which minimizes consumerism and environmental damage.

A critical aspect of the proposals for localization of the economy is that these do not envisage any major changes in property relations. The vision is very much of a dominant private sector made up of locally owned businesspersons and supported where necessary by large-scale trans-local institutions carefully controlled by democratic procedures. The IFG group is clearly aware that this will mean the persistence of some social and economic inequalities at the local level.

This does not mean that no intrusions on private property relations are contemplated, for there is some room left for maneuver. The most explicit statement I was able to find on this ticklish issue was the following:

The current and future well-being of humanity depends on transforming the relationships of power within and between societies toward more democratic and mutually accountable modes of managing human affairs that are self-organizing, power-sharing and minimize the needs for coercive, central authority. *Economic* democracy, which involves the equitable participation of all people in the ownership of the productive assets on which their livelihood depends, is essential to such a transformation because the concentration of economic power is the Achilles heel of *political* democracy, as the experience of corporate globalization demonstratess.[12]

This hints at a lot but does not take us too far explicitly, perhaps with good political reason! What exactly does 'equitable participation' mean and how will it be realized? Which 'productive assets' are being referred to? It seems only those 'on which their livelihood depends'. What exactly does 'livelihood' and 'depend,' mean here? And 'all people?' Will employers and employees be treated in exactly the same manner? All these questions are left up in the air, but of course in real life they will turn out to be absolutely critical.

Although dominated by the communitarian ideal of a well-integrated local community with a common culture that needs to be defended against the intrusions of a shallow cosmopolitanism, the IFG group understands that no such homogeneous community is likely to emerge. Indeed, there is a curious influence of the liberal ideal of a lost golden age of equal enterprises – perhaps in the eighteenth century at the time of Locke or at the time of the Industrial Revolution in the early nineteenth century with Ricardo! In this golden age, enterprises were relatively of similar size, markets were largely local and inequalities relatively small. Heterogeneity and individual difference prevailed. There was perfect competition. This was beneficially re-routed into mutual dependence by the division of labor and the invisible hand, civilized by moral sentiments and the rule of law. Neither the London of Dickens nor the Manchester of Engels existed. Transnational corporations, 'long distance trade' and globalization were unknown. This is one aspect of the 'conceptual history' of anti-globalization.

Thus, the IFG ideal is not a homogeneous Germanic (or Central European) *Gemeinschaft*, anchored by a *Volk* of *Blut und Boden* or by a born-again faith community, or by both. What one is faced with here is the familiar paradigm of civil society, so deeply embedded in the Anglo-American tradition from Harrington, Hobbes and Locke through to Bentham and Mill. This is communitarianism but of the possessive individualism variety.

Where socially necessary and agreed on by all then, changes in property relations could be voted into existence by popular democratic consent. But this would clearly be the exception and is not at all the ideal being proposed. The reasons for this are both economic and political. Economic in the sense that there is no confidence in traditional Marxist analyses which argue that lasting social and economic improvements require socialization of the means of production. Although not explicitly discussed, there is a kind of common-sense Anglo realism that this has simply proved itself unworkable and is somehow beyond the pale. This, indeed, seems to have been a lesson silently drawn from the dismal performance of state socialist economies and their eventual collapse. Nowhere is their any sign of a yearning for social forms of property ownership unless where technical or some other necessity makes this compelling. It is simply taken for granted that 'everybody' knows now that this does not work and is economically a non-starter.

But there are also political reasons for the adherence to the ideal of a local economy composed of privately owned small and medium-sized enterprises. The reason is that the IFG group is resolutely committed to the preservation of liberal notions of personal autonomy and parliamentary democracy. They take it for granted that such systems have demonstrated that they are indispensable for personal freedom and democracy of any kind, including the communitarian one. Although there is much lamentation of external cultural penetration and of the need to preserve community culture, there is no suggestion whatsoever that the community is characterized by some kind of *Geist* or Rousseauian 'general will' which supersedes the simple aggregation of the will of individuals. IFG thinkers (at least those steeped in the Anglo tradition) are well aware where that line of thinking leads politically. An interesting question that this chapter cannot explore is whether this civil society liberal communitarianism is shared by the Asian members, especially those inspired by *Swadeshi* or some concept of an ideal Malay community uncontaminated by the materialistic West.[13]

They likewise understand instinctively that socialization of the relations of production and the resort to central planning and an administered economy, necessarily have political consequences. Economic administration requires strata of administrators and political power necessarily accrues to these groups simply in the normal course of the discharge of their administrative duties. It is therefore taken for granted that small and medium-sized property 'regulated' largely by the market is a necessary precondition for the individual political freedoms and personal autonomy which is obviously very highly valued in this group. What this alternative seeks to do therefore is not to eliminate market relations but to confine them as far as possible to the local level. It is strictly a program for localization.

The issue therefore arises as to what exactly is regarded as local and how this term is concretely specified. Because of the emphasis on the reduction of size and the return to 'human-scale' living, this is a crucial question. Unfortunately inconsistent and variable answers are given. The local is said variously to be the local (rural?) community; an association of adjacent communities – a regional community; or even at times the nation. Indeed, the authors speak repeatedly about obtaining assistance from the European Union and obviously take it for granted that this regional bloc of nations will continue to exist and grow. Likewise, allowance is made for the fact that developing countries may themselves need or wish to come together in a larger economic bloc, for similar reasons as the nations of Europe. Clearly this is conceptually very untidy. After all, if the area from Limerick to the Elbe can be regarded as 'local', then in the same manner NAFTA must also be local, at which point the entire model falls apart. This issue is never satisfactorily resolved but the authors do make an attempt to deal with this objection.

The concept used to address this problem is the notion of 'subsidiarity' developed in relationship to attempts to democratize the mechanisms of the European Union.[14] What this is supposed to mean is that anything which can be better done at the local level should be transferred, say, from Brussels to the nation–state level, from the nation to the region and from the region to the local community as necessity dictates. The notion as it is interpreted here is one of the subordination of central organs to the local ones. Power should flow upwards from the local to the central. Indeed, whatever powers the center exercises in the ideal version of this model are residual ones left over after local authorities have acted. In other words, this is almost a complete reversal of the notion of delegation of power from the center to the region and downward – the traditional notion of sovereignty long characteristic of the nation–state. Subsidiarity, in this particular unique sense, is not a case where the center lays down and maintains overall rules and procedures and then delegates specifics to regional and local bodies, as in the proposals for constitutional reform of the welfare state developed by Maus.[15] It is more ambitious even than a federal system in which 'states' rights' dominate. For here 'community rights' would trump even 'states' rights'.

Thus, even if a nation–state persists economically and politically and also regional blocs of one sort or another, these will still be subordinated to local communities by resorting to the kind of constitutional and political relationships discussed above. What is envisaged is 'a planetary system of economies made up of locally owned enterprises accountable to all their stakeholders'.[16] How realistic this or any of the other arrangements would be is another matter, to which we shall now turn.

## Feasibility

I will now turn to the discussion of the general feasibility of the alternative proposals and how this feasibility could be enhanced, if possible. The first issue that confronts us in this proposal for a community economy is that of the relationship between size, the growth of the division of labor, and trade. The proposals contained in the IFG documents assume that size can be reduced and trade curtailed to local trade without any significant repercussions in the standard of living of the community and in the overall well-being of a nation. The thinking is not that there will be no repercussions at all but that these will not be drastic. They will be confined to superfluous aspects of consumerism without significantly affecting what people really need and want to produce and consume. If such reductions occur, then they would be a good thing because this in turn would reduce resource consumption and help to protect the environment, especially from the pollution by motor vehicles and from excessive consumer waste. Apart from this kind of reduction in consumption, it is fair to say that IFG does not anticipate a huge reduction in the standard of living of communities in the developed world.

They could hardly do so because they clearly assume that substantial funds will be available for research, for spending on environmental protection, public health and social welfare as well as substantial sums available to finance the cancellation of Third World debt and to provide generous development assistance to the needy in Africa, Asia and Latin America. In other words, all this assumes a highly productive economy generating a substantial surplus, leaving enough for re-investment and generous public programs. This surplus would have to be generated somewhere and the question would then have to be, given an economy of small and medium-sized community enterprises, how would such a substantial surplus be generated?

But this issue of how a social surplus would be generated is, in the final analysis, a secondary question. The more important issue is the vision of a community economy 'of the classic liberal sort' made up entirely of small and medium-sized firms serving the local community.

This is a fundamental misconception of the modern economy and the role of small and medium-sized firms in it. In a country such as Britain, for example, the inputs for most small and medium-sized business are obtained from all over Europe. and the world. Some machinery is obtained from Italy (for example, in high grade ceramic tile manufacturing), others from Sweden (ball bearings), much from France and Spain, a vast quantity from Japan and an increasing quantity from China, Malaya, Brazil and from all over the world. In turn, these small and medium-sized firms export their products all over the world, especially back to a number of countries in Europe. In the case of Germany, the technical strength of the German export economy is often said to rely on the *Mittelstand*, that mass of medium-sized community-level firms who, for example, controlled the world market in precision machine tools, until Japanese transnational competitors relieved them of it.

In other words, successful small and medium-sized firms in Europe are major importers and exporters themselves. This is so because many of these small and medium-sized enterprises, if they do not import and export directly, are sub-contractors to transnational corporations that do.[17] They are also sub-contractors to the sub-contractors and so on down the line. The most efficient and profitable ones are also very specialized and have a high technical level in employees as well as equipment. Indeed, with the increasing tendency to just-in-time production, quality management, flexible specialization and management information systems – including integrated electronic warehousing and management systems, and enterprise management systems – 'network management' of what are in effect very complex and sophisticated enterprise zones has proliferated. All these systems have grown enormously in the world economy in recent decades, especially in the developed world. Millions of products and services are involved daily in the extremely complex exchanges involving these relatively small firms.

Although transnational corporations have the lion's share of international trade by far, it is a misconception to think that the leading small and 'human-scale' firms that currently exist are operating mainly within local markets. This is far from being the case. In fact, through an extremely complex commodity chain, they are just as much involved in 'long-distance trade' as any transnational corporation. Moreover, given the proliferation of the networks described above, how would one separate small, medium and large firms from transnational corporations? Contrary to what Hines and the IFG write, these practices spring not from theories of comparative advantage. They derive rather from the much more flexible doctrine of 'competitive advantage' and regional economies of scope and scale put forward first by Alfred Marshall and more recently by Michael Porter.

If this is the case, it means that any attempt to reduce long-distance trade to a prescribed minimum would not only be a matter of restricting the operations of transnational corporations as the IFG group seems to imagine. It would just as much require action against the operations of the very small and medium-sized business that they are championing. I set aside for later the discussion of who would determine what level of trade is allowed, in what goods and services (there are millions of them – inputs, inputs to inputs, inputs to inputs to inputs, and so forth) in which firms; and what method could conceivably be devised to manage all of this, even at the community level. How small would one have to be not to qualify as a transnational corporation and who would establish and police this 'maximum'? We shall come to these issues later.

For the moment, let us simply note that it would be necessary not only to re-orient transnational corporations. They would also have to be a radical disruption in the operations of the most profitable and efficient small and medium-sized business – often the ones which are environmentally most friendly and who are most likely to support groups such as IFG at the moment! Again, such a program is fraught with dire political implications, as the experience of Léon Blum in France and Allende in Chile teaches us.

For the existing supply lines of these small and medium-sized business would have to go. Their markets would have to change. They would be required by some form of export controls and quantitative restrictions to use local raw materials, equipment, services and labor, irrespective of the efficiency gains or losses. This is, after all, an alternative that claims to put 'life' before 'money' and to put the 'democracy of people' before the 'democracy of money' – all of which are highly questionable oppositions within the materialist tradition.[18] What then would happen to their costs? Could they even break even, much less make a profit? Could they continue to operate at all? What then would happen to the people currently employed by them? What would happen to the genuinely local small business services (the local corner shop) that depended on demand from these 'long-distance' small business for their markets? What then would happen to the local standard of living? What would happen to the 'local culture' and 'economic democracy', not to mention 'political democracy'? The matter of the relationship between size and international trade is hardly as simple as the anti-globalization movement tends to present it.

Let us assume that this radical re-orientation not only of large corporations (many would have to be closed) but also of small and medium-sized business to the local community or region is achieved by some Herculean political effort. These firms now begin to compete in the market as is envisaged, albeit a local market. Some firms turn out to be more efficient than others. They innovate. They sell more and seek to produce more. They make more profit. Their owners are thus able to remunerate themselves more than is the case with less successful small firms. They naturally seek to reinvest these profits and to expand their 'productive assets'.

On the other hand, other firms do less well. For whatever reason they are not able to compete as efficiently. They are less profitable and may even lose money. After all, this is a market economy. At this point, it is worth noting that one of the main sources of economic inequality after the relatively successful Hungarian reforms of 1968 was the rise of efficient, highly successful small firms, often operating in the service sector. Clearly, the normal operations of the market, even the local market, will over time undermine the lofty sentiments expressed in the statement on economic and political democracy quoted above. Of course, it could be that the IFG group has in mind the idea that they would not allow bankruptcies. That they would offer subsidies in the cause of keeping the local community firm alive. But experience teaches that this cure may be worse than the disease!

First, whence the surplus to finance these subsidies? Large corporations generating super-profits and making hefty contributions to the tax base (they also massively avoid taxes, of course – not being denied) would have been abolished. The taxes would now have to come from the successful small firms – likely to be the minority. Setting aside the impossible politics of such a tax policy (it brought down Allende and helped to put Pinochet in power), will sufficient funds even exist at all? Then there is an even more important question. If there is no penalty for failure, why bother with success? Surely any sensible person in the successful firms would look around and notice that economic and social reward was independent of profitability and economic success, at least as measured by the market. So why bother? What then would happen to the successful firms? This is the well-known problem of incentives in a situation of market constraints. Those who think this is a theoretical issue or one to be resolved by the creation of 'the new socialist woman' should take a closer look at the history of Cuban and Eastern European (especially Polish) productivity or rather the lack thereof.

What is more, the efficient small business may want to expand. It has identified cheaper and higher quality raw materials in Romania. It has found better machinery in Brazil and some phenomenally attractive packaging in China. Actually the firm in China is really a subsidiary of a German company that relocated to Mississippi, attracted by low taxes, the lax labor code and the non-existent environmental regulations. It says it imports its raw material from Malaya but there is good reason to believe that it is really smuggled in from Indonesia by a company which has violently fended off investigations from Greenpeace for years. The British firm, which is participating wittingly or unwittingly in this complex web, wants to use French engineering services and a suave Italian marketing firm. It even seeks to use immigrant labor from Jamaica, promising, hypocritically of course, to observe the labor code and to pay high wages. It needs to practise the dreaded 'long-distance' trade. But this is a no-no. The local authorities simply refuse to permit it on both economic and cultural grounds. It must stay as it is, and plod on with 'local' raw materials, services, equipment and labor. It must confine its horizons to the local community. But local demand is not large enough to support such a firm. Under the circumstances it must wither and eventually die. This will have not only serious economic consequences. It will also create a political crisis.

Supporters of the IFG position could well retort that this is an overly gloomy picture of the economic prospects of firms in a local economy. After all, there will still be a regional and a national economy to appeal to for assistance. It is even envisaged that there would still be a European Union, euro and all, and perhaps even a European Central Bank, perhaps no longer housed in an elegant futuristic skyscraper. There would still be a London and a Paris and a Frankfurt; and, of course, a Brussels (the French would insist on the preservation of the EU bureaucracy). We could do without Geneva (away with the WTO) but not Zurich (everyone would insist on the preservation of the Swiss banks). There would also still be a New York, because, although we won't need the abominations of Wall Street, Times Square and Madison Avenue, we want to keep the UN! But would these 'spaces' be so easily converted into 'places' as the localizers imagine? Let us follow the logic of the argument.

What causes these huge modern cities to exist? What is the source of their size and complexity? It is hardly news that this is due to their role in a centuries-old global division of labor, including the regulation of global production, finance, trade and communication and global governance, such as it is.[19] London in particular is a city that developed very early as a city of merchants and financiers and of the governance of the domestic and overseas empire. Think of a man like Martin Noell who founded the Bank of England and who, along with others, egged Cromwell on to seize Jamaica from the Spanish Crown and develop plantations and the slave trade after 1655.[20] This was 'long-distance trade' with a vengeance and God's Englishman needed precious little egging. The deep embed-dedness of London in international finance and politics is thousands of times greater today. Cut away this trade and the London which we currently know, and which anti-globalizers seem to think will simply suffer a little tinkering here and there, will cease to exist. No more Whitehall. No more City. No more Oxford Street. No more West End theatre. No more Brixton either.

The same is the case for the economy called 'Britain'. This is after all your original 'long-distance' trading economy, perhaps going back to Roman times. And one must not forget Amsterdam and Antwerp and the smug Dutch and Belgian bourgeoisie. Where would those economies and those cities be without 'long-distance' trade? I will not even bother to mention cities such as Hong Kong, Shanghai, Tokyo, Mumbai, São Paulo and Mexico City. Nor would there be any economy to unite with in any 'European Union' if long-distance trade was curtailed. The localizers can-not have their cake and eat it. If one says 'community economy', one can-not at the same time assume the persistence of a strong national economy and of powerful regional economic blocs. These blocs are expressions of the fact that the economy is no longer 'local'. It would be more consistent to propose the dismantling of the nation and of the region and the estab-lishment of an 'anthropologically' restricted exchange and periodic market, linking essentially autarkic local economic communities. This is what anthropologists who are also anti-globalizers, such as Graeber, could be interpreted as proposing.[21]

Economies ceased to be 'local' thousands of years ago, long before the emergence of capitalism. The very existence of the national economy and the formation of the nation politically and culturally is an expression of the fact that 'self-sustaining' local economies no longer exist, if they ever did. It would not therefore be a matter of 'going back' to some non-existent liberal golden age as seems to be imagined. It would be a matter of 'going forward' to something not existing in human history for thousands of years. Dismantle the economic ties which constitute the national and regional economy and you dismantle the nation and the region. The same of course applies to the global economy. I leave it to the reader to judge the feasibility of such ideas.

Big corporations arise out of the growth of the division of labor, which is what leads to the extent and spread of market relations. Adam Smith made this elementary point in 1776. Hegel took it up and devel-oped it in 1816.[22] *Pace* Smith, Hegel pointed out that civil society was not as happily regulated by the invisible hand as Smith imagined. With characteristic far-sightedness Hegel wrote the following, concerning the claims of harmony put forward by Adam Smith for the bourgeois social order:

> Particularity by itself, given free reign in every direction to satisfy needs, accidental caprices, and subjective desires, destroys itself and its sub-stantive concept in the process of gratification. At the same time, the satis-faction of need, necessary and accidental alike, is accidental because it breeds new desires without end, is in thoroughgoing dependence on caprice and external accident, and is held in check by the power of uni-versality. In these contrasts and their complexity, civil society affords a spectacle of extravagance and want as well as the physical and ethical degeneration common to them both.[23]

Because of the growth of the division of labor and therefore of 'long-distance trade', great hardships followed unjustly for workers in one part of the world because of recession in another part. Civil society was, according to him the 'animal kingdom of mankind'. The state had to step in (the *Beamte* – the universal class!), regulate the economy and protect the vulnerable. Special steps had to be taken to draw citizens into public life if the natural inclination of bourgeois society to propagate a narrowly self-centered private existence was to be countered. In Hegel's schema, 'Corporations' were allocated the task of achieving this feat – of restoring the public civility of classical Greece to modern bourgeois civil society. But nothing could be done about competition, the inescapable swings of the market and the inevitable rise of large enterprises. Attempts to elimi-nate inequality, as in the French Terror, were fundamentally misconceived and doomed to fail. This was the source of his simultaneous admiration for and alienation from the French Revolution.

Durkheim, as is well known, transformed these notions into an argu-ment for something that he called *Solidarité* ('organic', he claimed), with this same division of labor that both Adam Smith and Hegel had deplored, now serving as the source of a beneficial national integration. Again with a little help from the state. Weber, with characteristic Germanic pes-simism, rejecting reactionary anti-capitalist Romanticism (although obvi-ously drawn to Nietzsche) also taught that 'disenchantment' and rationalization were inexorable realities of the modern world and had to be borne stoically. One would have to do one's best to preserve the rule of law but Lockean illusions of a natural law foundation for modern jurisprudence were simply too laughable for words. An attitude of resigned twentieth-century bourgeois subjectivity – the so-called 'Schopenhauerian attitude' – depicted in so many of the works of Thomas Mann – is the only possible one – that is the Weberian message. Globalization is simply the iron cage of our times. Foucault went further and Koselleck the furthest.[24] This whole optimistic liberal civil society line of thinking is an elaborate modernist power play. Weber was not too pessimistic: he was not pessimistic enough! We must plunge into the nihilism of discourse analysis and *Begriffsgeschichte*, setting both globalization and localization aside. *Pace* Weber, Marx claimed to offer a way out the dead end. We shall try to address this issue very briefly.

## Political Issues (Briefly)

Since localization proposals first of all raise economic issues, this chapter focused on those. However, as alluded to above, there are clearly major political problems with the IFG proposals as well. Here I am not referring to the challenges that winning political support for such a program would entail, nor to the politics of the actual transformation process – daunting as both would be. I make the more generous assumption that these political challenges have been successfully seen off and the question before us now is the one of the system of political governance of a world of local economies. It is important to reiterate here that the ideal of the IFG group (at least the Anglo section) is clearly that of liberal democracy of the type familiar in the Western parliamentary system.

If so, there is a problem. This is because it should be clear by now that a local community society will require extensive intervention from the 'community state' in the affairs of the 'community economy'. Some body has to regulate the size of firms. Some other body has to deal with the regulation of inputs, and outputs – ensuring that they are confined to the local community. Indeed, relations with the 'outside world' will need constant and vigilant regulation, in order to make short work of any tendency to over-involvement in 'long-distance trade'. Some body has to regulate prices – to control them in the name of community equity and harmony. Some body has to regulate labor market practices to ensure that there is no exploitation and that local labor has the first choice of jobs. We have not even come to the environmental regulations yet and the provision of public services. It is clear that these too will occasion the formation of a significant number of local committees. In the Soviet case, it used to be said that the attempt to centrally plan the entire economy generated about 4 billion 'indicators' to be optimized by electronic computer routines! One does not anticipate such a load for a local community economy. But it would be a grave mistake to imagine that the work involved in price and economic regulation on even this community scale would be a light one.

In addition, major political, legal, constitutional and practical problems arise around implementing the notion of 'subsidiarity', as here understood. One assumes that there will be some kind of separation of powers. One assumes that there will be some kind of executive, although pompous titles like 'Prime Minister' and 'President' may be deflated appropriately. But the whole system of governance is unspecified even in outline.

Will there be an independent judiciary and what powers will it have to review legislation, especially social and regulatory legislation? The mind boggles at the number and range of disputes that would arise in the course of this comprehensive regulatory regime. What about the infamous problems of 'telephone justice' prevalent under state socialism?[25] How would legal determinacy and the rule of law survive the plethora of special case interventions in economic and social life?[26] Clearly the solution to the problem of legal deformation proposed by Maus with respect to German environmental law would face some major obstacles in the event of 'localization'. Maus has made the astute observation that the problem of indeterminacy in welfare, environmental and anti-trust law (state intervention in the economy in general) springs from concessions to the special interests of one privileged group in the society or the other (usually transnational corporations). This leads to numerous special exceptions in legislation (think of anti-trust law) and therefore broad room for administrative discretion under omnibus 'in the public interest' clauses. This is a major source of legal deformation and the undermining of the rule of law by special interest groups.[27]

How will ideals of personal autonomy survive such a committee-rich environment? What will prevent further legal deformation and the inroads against 'bourgeois right' that they inevitably produce? Clearly, with the proposed comprehensive intervention of the 'community state' in the 'community economy', localization would create formidable challenges to legal determinacy. Of course, one could take the position of Unger and argue that legal determinacy is merely another bourgeois illusion and one is well rid of it.[28] But such a line is not open to those who obviously base their claims on a liberal foundation. The way to resolve these bourgeois departures from bourgeois law (driven by special interests, but would these vanish with localization?), and to re-assert a substantive rule of law, according to Maus, is first to abandon the blanket clauses.

But the other key part of Maus's theory could not be applied in the localization case. This is the proposal to make administrative welfare agencies subject to local legislatures which would, for example, have the consequence of placing state social work agencies under the democratic oversight of their clients. Maus points out that the clear precondition for this would have to be the maintenance of the sovereignty of the central legislature over these local legislatures that would exercise a derivative and in the end a delegated authority. This would be vital for sovereignty purposes as well as to ensure that standard procedural rules were preserved and practised at the local level.[29] In other words, the supremacy of the central legislature cannot be challenged without endangering the rule of law, including the welfare rights of the working citizen.

The IFG group seems oblivious to such extremely critical issues of 'bourgeois right.' Subsidiarity, which is the opposite of the Maus perspective (the central is 'subsidiary' to the local and derives its authority from it) would clearly pose a major challenge in this critical respect. Although this is exactly what is not intended, the political consequence of the IFG program would be the stifling of personal autonomy by an ever-present committee system.

In conclusion, the IFG group seems oblivious of such extremely critical issues of 'bourgeois right.' Subsidiarity, which, in the current conception as well as practice of the European Union, makes the local subsidiary to the central, would clearly pose a major challenge to the decentralization notions of the IFG program. When looked at carefully from either the economic or political perspective, the existing economic alternatives of the global justice movement appear ill-thought out and deeply contradictory. Anti-globalizers want to have their cake and eat it in the economic sense. On the one hand, they want to preserve private property and the market and at the same time they wish to restrict these to the local level. They wish to curb the operations of large transnational corporations without affecting the viability of many small and medium-sized business which often depend on these very same transnational corporations for their prosperity. They want to maintain the basic standard and quality of living enjoyed by many in the developed world and to do improve standards in the developing world, while proposing measures which would in practice undermine the global standard of living. They propose localization in the sphere of the economy and at the same time assume that this would have little impact on the national, regional and international economic and political institutions which they favor. In the political sphere, they drastically underestimate the degree of bureaucracy entailed in the implementation of their proposals and do not see that these have the potential to raise serious challenges for the liberal parliamentary democracy which they hold dear. Their political proposals in fact raise fundamental questions for the rule of law but they seem blissfully unaware of this reality. In short, the inconsistencies in the positions put forward by the anti-globalizers are so great that it is difficult to take them seriously.

# EIGHT Alternatives

## A Global Approach to Anti-Globalization

This analysis appears to leave us with a dismal set of conclusions. The globalizers seem to be right: there is no credible alternative to globalization. Weber was not pessimistic enough. But do such conclusions follow?

What these problems emphasize is the urgent need for greater economic knowledge within social and cultural theory and a bringing together of the large literature analyzing socialist alternatives to capitalism with the anti-globalization critiques. There is today, partly as a result of revulsion at neo-liberalism and capitalist globalization and the persistent culturalism criticized in this book, a profound lack of appreciation of market mechanisms on the left of the political spectrum. Here, it is often taken for granted that the market is simply a capitalist institution and that 'commodification' will have no role in a socialist economy. Sloganeering against 'commodification' abounds. Yet all the experience of socialist economic reforms in the twentieth century, whether it be the Soviet Union, Hungary, Yugoslavia, China or the Mondragon cooperative in Spain, conclusively establishes that the market – both national and international – must play an essential role in any realistic alternative to capitalism.[1] What is more, following on from the very conception of universality first developed by Hegel and adapted to materialism by Marx, the inter-dependence created by a global division of labor is the necessary foundation for the realization of the possibilities of the individual on the broadest possible scale.[2] Current attempts to revive 'historical materialism' which inveigh mindlessly against 'economism' weaken social and cultural theory further.[3] We need more 'economism', not less.

The difficulties of developing a feasible and viable alternative to monopoly capitalism should not be under-estimated. It is by no means a simple task, as the innumerable analyses of the failure of socialist policies and projects amply demonstrates.[4] The lessons of these failures must be faced up to and learned, not swept under the carpet by populist or culturalist rhetoric. Anti-capitalism is not enough. The notion that central planning is a cure-all for the contradictions of capitalism has been shown to be gravely mistaken. Likewise, naïve faith in 'market socialism' and worker self-management which ignores the necessity for central coordination and planning at both the national and international levels derives from a failure to positively appreciate the enormous benefits of a globally integrated economy and society. It too is not helpful. It is in fact a step backward in comparison to what capitalism has developed today in the International Monetary Fund, the World Bank and the World Trade Organization and, especially, to the proposals of John Maynard Keynes at Bretton Woods, the most progressive of which were never accepted.[5] Without paying far closer attention to economics – without bringing the economy back in – those who are serious about overcoming the failures of capitalism will find themselves confined to an anti-capitalist passion which is incapable of gaining wide public support.

We must start from the view that the problem of global oppression is not size as such, but who owns and controls this 'size' and who benefits from it. Thus, the issue is not the spatial spread of corporations, long-distance trade and the global economy. Nor is the issue 'commodification' or 'exchange'. In a sense the problem is not globalization at all. It is matter of private owner-ship of the means of production and of monopoly capital and the inherent challenge of restoring individual and social control over a process based on the division of labor on such an internationally vast scale.

The large size of corporations is simply a reflection of the high level of contemporary forces of production. It simply reflects the growth of an international division of labor on a grander scale. This is a good, not a bad, thing, economically, culturally, socially and politically. Yes, there are diseconomies of scale and monopolies and these must be prevented. But this is to look at the matter from the point of view of the trees and to miss the wood. What follows from this is that the development of alternatives to capitalism must base itself on the social-economic foundations which have already been developed within the global capitalist system. Any alternative to the existing system of global monopoly capitalism must build on, indeed, *extend this globalization*. All attempts to revert to one form or the other of communalism or localism must be firmly rejected. For example, a lingering communalism – in which labor mobility is restricted and community banks control substantial amounts of investment funds – is a weakness of the economic democracy and self-management alternatives advocated by Howard and Schweickart.[6]

Once the division of labor has reached its current level, it is not possible for value to be realized on other than an international scale. Markets or exchange relationships on a global scale are an expression of this division of labour not the cause of it. It is also the case, that without such global markets it would be impossible to distribute savings and investment across the various branches of the worldwide economy. Any feasible socialist alternative would in fact require the extension and intensification of global exchange relations. For the foreseeable future, the bulk of this global exchange deriving from the global division of labor would be market exchange, although not all of it. Some parts of global exchange needs to take the form of directly administered exchange. Moreover, it is abundantly clear that global market exchange is in need of public control and regulation if current inequities and volatility are to be reduced.

The case of the powerful Chinese impact on world markets clearly demonstrates that the reduction of poverty in the world cannot be achieved otherwise than by large increases in human productivity. Human productivity in India and China cannot be increased without their current access to the world market. This is the only way to provide the global effective demand (world markets) on the scale required to absorb the productivity increases. The same is true for Africa. Africa too needs to be more fully integrated into this selfsame world market in much the same way that China and India are coming into their own, for these same reasons. At the same time, access to the vast markets of Europe, the United States, China and India (and, in the near future, Latin America and Africa) is vital to reduce poverty in all parts of the developing world. The accumulation of huge trade surpluses in countries aggressively pursuing export-led development has extremely serious implications for high rates of global unemployment and lack of liquidity in the international financial system.[7] The development of a much more balanced global trading regime is essential. That this has major implications for the privileged position of the populations in the currently developed economies, goes without saying. That it also has major ecological implications is incontestable. But solutions to both of these problems can be found which are mutually beneficial. One thing seems undeniable: large-scale reductions in human poverty require large-scale increases in human productivity which, in turn, requires further development of the division of labor on an international scale. There is no other way. One should forget about any localization program that attempts to abolish exchange relations or the market. How we have to approach these issues is not from the viewpoint of negation but with a view to the 'sublation of bourgeois *Gesellschaft*'.[8]

147

The reality of this international division of labor developed by global monopoly capitalism places some real constraints on the development of credible anti-globalization alternatives. What it suggests is that those who go another route – seeking international solutions to global problems – are the ones heading in the direction that we need to go. This approach – the development of a 'global' instead of a 'local' alternative to globalization – will not be easy, for many of the reasons alluded to above. But this is the challenge presented which has to be met.

Critical work in this area has been done by the well-known studies by Eastern European scholars and of seminal texts such as Nove's – whose ideas have played a central role in my conceptions.[9] More recently, authors such as Schweickart and Lawler have debated Ollman and Ticktin on the critical issues.[10] The general conclusion which I draw from this body of work is that neither self-managed market socialism of the Yugoslavian variety nor centrally planned socialism of the Soviet type is feasible or desirable. What is needed is some (difficult to specify) combination of 'plan' and 'market'. In this connection, it is important to recall that, as mentioned before, important scholars and policy-makers such as Brus and Kornai have moved from an earlier reluctant endorsement of this 'plan and market' model to a firm conviction that it is unviable and that only a free market economy is capable of operating efficiently.[11]

Nonetheless, most of these authors, especially Schweickart, put forward the alternative of a market socialism comprised of self-managed, worker-controlled enterprises. This alternative, heavily influenced by a perhaps too positive assessment of the Yugoslavian self-management experience as well as of the Mondragon cooperative conglomerate in the Basque region of Spain, is a useful point of entry into a brief exploration of the features which constitute a realistic alternative to global monopoly capitalism. What follows is an outline of an alternative to monopoly capitalist globalization without discussing the many detailed and complex problems which any such alternative raises.

The first point to make clear is that a fully centrally planned economy will not work for both economic and political reasons. On the political side, it should be obvious that such an economy, in which all outputs of goods, services and investment are specified in detail in a single comprehensive plan which is then administered by a set of central planners, requires political centralization as well. One cannot have democracy under such circumstances. The objections on the economic side are equally formidable. The number of prices and outputs in any modern economy run into the millions and even if these were specifiable by computerized routines, there is no way for consumer preferences (price, quality, variety, quantity) to be efficiently and effectively specified *ex ante* by a central planning agency. It is only in the actual act of buying and selling by free consumers and producers that the social value attributed to particular goods and services emerges, *post hoc*. Once the inequities and gross maldistribution of incomes typical of monopoly capitalism are corrected, socially necessary production can only express itself in the actual sale and purchasing decisions of millions of individual consumers and producers. Therefore, socialization of the means of production – essential for the solution of the contradictions of capitalism – must at the same time operate through a partially socialist market.

In the conditions of the modern world where there are giant transnational corporations and banks, this issue is posed not simply at the national but at the international level. A vital question therefore is not primarily the issue of 'trade' which often exercises the anti-globalization movement. It is the issue of what is to be done with these huge global concentrations of capital which are the root of the economic and political problems of the world. As economists such as Bagwati have insisted, one must distinguish clearly between free trade in goods and services and free movement of capital.[12] The first does not imply the second. Indeed, the second often undermines the potential benefits of the first.

I approach the problem of developing an alternative to the present global economy in a two-stage manner – a minimum and a maximum program. Contrary to what Callinicos seems to suggest, such a minimal program would be anti-imperialist, not anti-capitalist.[13] I do not discuss the politics of these programs although this, to say the least, is an absolutely vital question. My only comment on the political feasibility question is to observe that proposals which often seem far-fetched in one social and economic context are precisely the ones which come to the fore in another. If one seriously holds to the view that present global economic and political systems are not sustainable, then this by itself suggests that, as events unfold, this unsustainability will show itself in crises of one sort or another. The time to develop alternatives in anticipation of such crises is now, not when the crises are upon us. What political solutions emerge from any given crisis depend on human agency and are inherently unpredictable. One thing, however, is certain: if one has not thought about and discussed alternatives before, by this fact alone, one nullifies one's possibilities for agency in any given crisis situation in the future.

The first issue that arises therefore in formulating an alternative to global monopoly capitalism (minimum program) is for there to be a restoration of exchange controls. The imposition of a Tobin Tax on global currency or stock market transactions is a problematic proposal which could have perverse effects as Davidson has pointed out, but is, in any event insufficient.[14] It potentially can provide funds for developmental purposes and for increased social and environmental purposes but it does not address the fundamental issue of speculative capital movements – 'hot money' – undermining the economy of particular countries. This can only be addressed by a return to a comprehensive global system of exchange controls which allows for capital to move to areas in which it is needed but also allows for this to be done on a stable and equitable basis. Arrangements must also be made – as in Davidson's resurrection of Keynes' proposal – for creditor rather than debtor nations to bear the burden of the costs of structural adjustment.[15] This is essentially the current system of IMF special drawing rights, minus the conditionality and with the burden of adjustment shifted away from the debtor to the creditor nations. All these issues are not just matters for developing economies but are vital ones also for Europe and especially the United States in which export of capital and the neglect of investment in domestic social and physical infrastructure as well as manufacturing, are major issues. The restoration of exchange controls is therefore an area in which both developing and developed countries have a common interest. It should be accompanied by – indeed, makes no sense without – the cancellation of the debt of the developing countries.

In general, an entirely new set of international financial institutions need to be created. In other words, an international economic agency will have to be formed which is not only responsible for international macroeconomic management in the manner of the International Monetary Fund (IMF) and whose powers and functions go beyond the International Clearing Agency proposed by Davidson. This is because any restructuring of international public financial institutions must bring to the fore that part of the system which provides development funds (not just balance of payments support) to the developing countries on a substantial and long-term basis.

In any serious alternative to contemporary capitalist globalization, therefore, it should be obvious that entities such as the IMF, far from being abolished, will become more important and powerful than ever. This is because it will be of the utmost importance and very much in the interests of ordinary working people, to manage international and national inflation and the global movement of capital and exchange rates. Failure to maintain, indeed expand, this international macroeconomic management will lead to the persistence of global unemployment, the sluggishness in global growth, currency instability, sudden flows of hot money from one economy to another and profound dangers of depression to the global economy. A real global central bank of some kind will therefore be essential. The issue is not to abandon such centralizing institutions and to retreat to some kind of local or even national economic arrangement. Such a move would in fact preserve and increase global poverty, not reduce it. Such a retreat would have devastating consequences, given the scale of the currently existing productive forces and the huge pools of capital which already have been created. The real political challenge is how to democratize such centralizing institutions and to devise ways to ensure that they operate with fairness and democratic accountability. The real economic issue is how to ensure that these institutions act to maintain a global economic balance (low inflation, control of so-called 'hot money', international trade and currency stability) while channeling substantial resources into productive investment in both the developed and developing countries.

This is not the place to go into detail on the formidable institutional challenges which such issues present. These problems certainly will be difficult but not insurmountable. In general, the solution lies in specifying democratic voting rights for member states, mechanisms of transparency and access to information, regular, independent public review and auditing, worker participation mechanisms to ensure accountability, as well as enhanced systems of anti-trust and anti-competitive oversight and regulation. Once it is understood that, contrary to what many may think, overcoming the problems of globalization means more globalization not less, then this issue of how to democratize public international and national institutions – economic as well as political – necessarily becomes the crucial one in the formulation of any realistic alternative to capitalist globalization practices.

The purpose of the restoration of exchange controls and the considerable expansion of the soft loan window of international public financial institutions is two-fold. On the one hand, the accumulation of huge balances of trade surpluses in a handful of economies at the expense of the global economy as a whole would be addressed. On the other hand, a mechanism would also be established for the orderly transfer of the vast pools of existing investment funds to be channeled to where they are needed in a relatively orderly manner. It should be fairly obvious that accompanying this global re-structuring would be an enormous 'peace dividend'. Defense budgets would have to be cut on all sides and the funds released re-directed to the re-development of the productive forces and the provision of substantial social benefits in both the developing and the developed countries.

In this connection, it seems essential to me that the proposal, most extensively argued for by Parijs, for a substantial annual basic income for all, be implemented on a phased basis in the developed capitalist societies which can afford it, has great merit.[16] The point is that, in the context of existing trends towards automation and productivity growth, it is difficult to see how huge increases in the provision of employment opportunities will arise in either the public or the private sectors of the highly developed countries. I would argue that this will be the case even if more balanced trade and financial policies are pursued and there is a substantial increase in the investment in national social and physical infrastructure. The reservations to an annual basic income expressed by Gorz and discussed by Howard – that this will cut the link between work and income, lead to a decline of the work ethic and create serious divisions in society between those who work and those who receive public support – are important ones but not, in the end, convincing.[17] This is because, in the first place, the provision of an annual basic income would be universalized to all citizens as an entitlement, irrespective of socio-economic status. Second, the day when modern capitalist society depended on the work ethic to function has long passed. Moreover, the argument of Gorz that 'You cannot become a member of any community if you have no obligation whatsoever towards it. Being a member of a group means that you can rely on the others, but also that they can rely on you' is true but hardly conclusive.[18]

One could argue that the entire jet-setting global *rentier* class which is larger than ever in capitalist society and central to its narcissistic cosmopolitan culture, gives the lie to this rather old-fashioned Protestant idea. Further, there is nothing which says that one's contribution to society must take the form of wage labor. On the contrary, the goal of the entire socialist tradition is to emancipate people from the constraints of wage labor and to enable them to develop themselves in a many-sided way, outside of the necessities which earning a living inevitably impose. It is hard to see how the traditional socialist ideal of the cultured and many-sided individual who overcomes the division of labor could be accomplished unless some kind of basic annual income becomes a reality wherever it is economically feasible. In any event, a critical part of the minimum anti-globalization program must be the thorough overhaul of the system of social provision, to restore universal health care and re-finance public education at the high levels of funding which it requires.

In terms of a maximum program, the proposal would be for the development of a mixed economy, with the state controlling the main financial institutions on which both public and private investment would depend. Many of the largest enterprises in a developed economy would have to be placed under public ownership. Medium-sized and smaller firms would remain privately owned as would the bulk of professional and personal services, food establishments and many retail entities. Both public corporations and private firms would produce for exchange and allocate resources – producer and consumer goods – through a market exchange mechanism. If, therefore, the individual and society are to have some control over these activities, a significant degree of central planning, coordination and macroeconomic management will be essential. But this would largely take the form of indicative and investment planning. In other words, what is envisaged in a maximum program is a combination of plan and market in which maximum efficiency is combined with social justice goals. In this model, any re-allocation of investment funds to regional and community banks in the sense proposed by Schweickart would be avoided because of the dangers of inefficiency, duplication, unemployment and macroeconomic instability which, based on the Yugoslavian experience, these kinds of arrangements tend to produce.[19]

That such a program poses serious challenges for the preservation and expansion of democracy should be obvious. Worker self-management for all public entities is one proposed solution to the lack of democracy but experience in both Yugoslavia and at Mondragon has shown that this is by no means unproblematic. Serious dangers of lack of innovation, high unemployment, duplication of investment and oligarchic management often develop hidden within the self-management framework.[20] In addition, there is the huge problem of irresponsible monetary policy which can have devastating inflationary, foreign trade and currency instability consequences. It is probably more effective to rely on other means of public oversight and scrutiny, including independent auditing, transparency, anti-monopoly legislation and oversight, access to information, and a well-defined system of incentives and penalties.

A most interesting but seldom discussed question is that of what is to be done about the large transnational corporations which today dominate the world economy. In any maximum plan of the kind being outlined here, it is clear that the national operations of these large monopolies would become public property. The key question, however, is what is envisaged for their currently substantial transnational operations. One solution, proposed by Schweickart, is for control (but not ownership) of the foreign divisions of these firms to be turned over to the workers in the overseas countries in which they operate. This way, net profit from local operations would accrue to the workers at the various localities while, over time, full ownership of these branch plants would be turned over to local workers.[21]

No doubt some transnational corporations can be effectively dismantled into national operations in this manner. But this is unlikely to be the case for many without a serious loss of productivity and other efficiencies. The problem with Schweickart's idea is that it will have the effect of fragmenting the operations of these large corporations, many of which operate most efficiently and productively as integrated global entities. In other words, there are good economic reasons, independent of monopoly capitalism for these corporations to remain as internationally managed and coordinated entities. This may have to do with technological, cost or informational efficiencies. Breaking these enterprises up into local branches will therefore lead to a loss of these efficiencies which will not be available to the separated divisions. The challenge really is how to capture what one may call these international externalities for the global good.

If one thinks about this problem seriously, the only feasible solution is one which it is difficult but necessary to envisage as a practical reality. The solution which comes to mind is that many of these transnational corporations, especially the huge Japanese, American and German banks with their trillion dollar assets, will have to be transformed into international mixed public–private entities. This is a question which requires much more careful study than has hitherto been accorded to it. If such large public–private investment banks were to emerge, how would they operate? How would they be regulated? What implications would they have for the stability of the international monetary system? How would they affect the flow of hot money and irresponsible loans to weaker economies? These and many more questions arise in such a proposal and cry out for further study.

The difficulty in developing a feasible alternative to currently existing globalization arises from the following contradictory factors. The elimination of global poverty, indeed human progress as a whole, requires the further extension of the global division of labor. But such an extension means in reality an even greater loss of power for individuals, communities and nations than currently exist under monopoly capital. At the same time, the very scale of the division of labor, for it to work at all, demands that these far-flung processes of production which are, in fact, mutually dependent, be coordinated and centralized at a higher level. Under monopoly capitalism, this coordination is provided by the head office of the firm, its executive vice-presidents and board of directors. It is an illusion to think that Wal-Mart's vast marketing operations coordinate themselves, without huge human, financial and technical resources actively managing this coordination.

Under any conceivable alternative to globalization, this coordination and centralization *will have to be preserved*. Indeed, it will have to be increased, since the goal is to establish a system whereby ordinary individuals and society as a whole will have some control over this vast production apparatus *ex ante*, and not simply be at the mercy of market outcomes, *post hoc.* What this will certainly mean, as all experience confirms, is great power for the central planners. In the past, this has meant bureaucratic socialism, one party dictatorship, Stalinism – a political, economic and human disaster. I doubt that measures such as 'participatory planning' are really likely to make any real impact on this profound dilemma. This is because the problem of centralization inheres in the scale on which the division of labor has been developed. Only when and as this division is overcome, can one foresee an elimination of the need for some centralization.

Yet, as implied above and by the general structure of the argument of this book, this centralization which cannot be wholly avoided, must be minimized. The old libertarian traditions of socialism which foregrounded the withering away of the state, must be restored. This is essential if one envisages a socialism which enhances and does not suppress the liberties of the individual which bourgeois society has undoubtedly developed, albeit more at the formal level and for the rich, than in reality for all. This political principle, as much as the economic arguments, is the reason why detailed planning of the Soviet type must never be established. It is the reason why planning should take an indicative form and the form of macro-economic management, and why the market, far from being eliminated in any alternative, must be regulated and utilized.

# NINE Conclusion

## The Noisy Sphere and the Hidden Abode

> The consumption of labour power is completed, as is the case of every other commodity, outside the limits of the market or of the sphere of circulation. Accompanied by Mr. Moneybags and by the possessor of labour-power, we therefore take leave for a time of this noisy sphere, where everything takes place on the surface and in view of all men, and follow them both into the hidden abode of production, on whose threshold there stares us in the face 'No admittance except on business.' Here we shall see, not only how capital produces, but how capital is produced. We shall at last force the secret of profit making.[1]

This work has argued for the restoration of the understanding of the complex connection between 'this noisy sphere' – the sphere of the market and spontaneous public culture and 'the hidden abode' – the sphere of production. I argue that this double impact of originating and obscuring, or Marx's conception of the cunning of the capitalist production process, provides a profound and original explanation of the possibilities and limits of popular forms of consciousness and life. It is the only convincing explanation of the means by which ideologies of false consciousness arise and are sustained and, most important of all, how such limitations can be overcome and social relations transformed to establish equality. Or at least, that is my argument.

Contrary to what has been assumed in both cultural and sociological theory, the severing of this materialist determination was not essential to the recovery of human agency, intellectual autonomy and freedom. On the contrary, the anchoring of the realm of consciousness and everyday social relations in the relationship of different realms of material reality to each other establishes a particularly powerful role for human agency and intellectual activity. My argument has been that cultural and sociological theory does not simply ignore the economy – often they do not – but they confine themselves to the noisy sphere of the lifeworld – the profusions of the developed capitalist marketplace. The key to understanding the problems of consciousness and everyday life lies in understanding pro- duction, as Hall inadvertently recognized when, in an aside, he criticized the tendency in Marx 'to insist on the prior analytical value to be accorded to the relations of *production'* which he argues has led some Marxists into a 'productivist' error.[2]

This work has also attempted to show that one of the most vexed the- oretical and practical problems which plagues modern social, cultural and political life – the relationship between race and class, between identity politics and class politics, arises from the theorizing of the cultural sphere or the market as autonomous from production. In these viewpoints, race is seen to arise from a deeply experienced historical inter-subjectivity, from the famous Hegelian 'recognition' explicated by Charles Taylor and Nancy Fraser or from a simple historical inertia persisting from the days of plantation slavery and not from material production, not from imperi- alism as in the work of Lauren and Tabili.[3] Thus, race and class, 'identity' and class politics deriving from different sources – one about culture and respect and the other about distributive economic justice – are necessar- ily conceived of as separate. Any enlightened person would, of course, attempt to join the two in practice, but this is a pragmatic humanistic and ethical act not a logically necessary one.[4] The two are not inherently joined in theory and therefore do not *have to be* joined in practice. But what if 'identity' is not primordial but is, on more careful analysis, a ratio- nalistic form of *consciousness*? What if identity, like class, has a material foundation? What if class is not at bottom a matter of distributive economic justice but of the relations of production in the hidden abode?

My argument has been that this apparent contradiction can only be adequately resolved if the, by no means obvious, nexus between the noisy sphere and the hidden abode is restored in critical analysis. The same applies to the debates over hybridity, creolization and diasporic public spaces, all of which are various attempts both to understand the chief characteristics of the monopoly capital globalization process as well as to escape from purist concepts of culture as overly integrated. Here we are paying a high price, not only for the abandonment of Marx but also for the rejection of Hegel, again a common feature of cultural studies and post- modernism. Because, despite his many well-known limitations – to which list we can add racism and sexism – Hegel's notion of development necessarily taking place through contradictions – a vale of tears – but with humanity eventually emerging in rationality on the other side, is the one which best allows us to disentangle some of these critical confusions of our time. It is Hegel who helps us to understand the underlying cultural similarity amidst difference which has always existed in the world ('concrete universal'); the many-sided, mixed and contradictory character of cultural integration in the most united of nations (a 'unity of opposites' – one thinks immediately of 'the United Kingdom'); and the dynamic, always impure and ever changing manner through which all cultures develop (aufheben). In other words, Hegel's thought is the antidote to 'alterity', an antidote which we avoid at great peril, especially in these current conditions of advanced capitalist globalization.

The argument of the book has been pursued through a critique of the foundational theories of Stuart Hall, Anthony Giddens, Scott Lash and John Urry, and Manuel Castells whose work has played the main role in shaping cultural studies, structuration and network society theory in the past 20 years and more. The emphasis of these authors on autonomy and their rejection of Hegel, albeit from different angles, is well established in the literature.

I have also examined the work of Paul Gilroy who, in my opinion, exemplifies some of the dangers and confusion of the application of the concepts of cultural studies to the issue of identity, in particular, to race. I tried to show that his is a prime case of the tangle which ensues when one sincerely adheres to an abstract humanistic ethics. This leads one to yearn for a universalistic world rid of all essentialisms – for Gilroy's 'planetary humanism'.[5] But one has little notion of the rootedness of 'identities' in the constitution of the hidden abode. In the given case of racism, one fails to grasp how racism is not simply rooted in the consequences of the past but in the very present system of imperialism and neo-imperialism which, at its core, is a system for the production and export of finance capital.

## The realms of consciousness and the realms of the economy

In these concepts of 'the noisy sphere' of the market and 'the hidden abode' of production Marx developed one of the most profound insights into the relationship between culture and the process of economic exploitation under capitalism. Marx's point in the passage quoted at the beginning of this chapter was that political economy had a double impact on that noisiest of spheres – the zone where public consciousness was formed under capitalism. This sphere of distribution and exchange – the market – first gave rise in people's minds to spontaneous ideas about how the system functioned which, while reflecting real everyday experiences, were nonetheless sustaining of the system, even while vigorously opposing oppressive outcomes. But second, and perhaps more important, the economic system operated not only to produce a false picture of how it worked, but also to conceal the true mechanism by means of which it actually worked – a secret hidden from the public view in the sphere of production by the dazzle of the marketplace and everyday life.

Elsewhere, Marx makes the point that this ideological cunning reflects a real cunning and is a unique characteristic of the capitalist mode of production. He argued that the hiding achieved by the abode of capitalist production is a subtle one, easily missed even when the sphere of production is itself observed. For, unlike capitalism, in other modes of production the real sources of exploitation are much more visible. In slavery, where the slavemaster takes *the entire* product from the slave who is herself property, exploitation is obvious. In feudalism, in which the peasants worked for themselves for some of the days of the week and then on other days of the week provided bonded unpaid labor on the land of the 'lord' of the land, it was also difficult for exploitation to be hidden: the surplus labor for the lord was distinguished from work for themselves by being located in a separate place and by being performed at a different time. In other forms of exploitation such as tributary systems, the abode of exploitation is also visible, since the exploited party has to hand over physically a given sum of produce or service or cash and valuables to the exploiter. For this reason, public consciousness seldom fails to grasp the reality of exploitation, only whether and how this exploitation is ordained.

Not so in capitalism. Here the official ideology, accepted by the mass, is that equality, justice and freedom reign and, where they do not, this is an adventitious failure, not coming from within, not systemic. This illusion is maintained because here, in the hidden abode itself, there was no distinction in place and time between work done by workers to support themselves and work done for the exploiter – the two were merged into a single working day. Here there was no separate physical product, part retained by the workers for themselves and another part transferred by them to the capitalist. Here the worker never had control over the physical product at all – it belonged as always to the owner of the means of production – the capitalist. Here the worker received a money wage, apparently in return for the entire day's work. Thus the telling reality was revealed that the crux of exploitation under capitalism was not 'low' wages which popular consciousness (and trade unionism) to this day assumes to be the case. 'High' wages could be even more exploitative. The heart of the matter was that any level of wages which the worker received under capitalism, whether high or low, always represented only part of the value of the commodity produced. The rest was appropriated in various proportions by different sections of the capitalist class as a whole. Yet the worker was paid for her labor-power, only not for her labor time. Thus the hiding achieved in the hidden abode is no simple matter and is not readily obvious to any observer. On the contrary, it is only by overcoming the limited conceptions – the false consciousness – generated at the popular level in the noisy sphere and by careful study of the hidden abode, that the secrets of the capitalist mode of production could be revealed. One has to rehearse these hoary truths of the labor theory of value if the issues before us are to be resolved.

Marx reverts to the ancient traditions of Jewish mysticism – the hidden abode where God (*Eyn Sof*) resided – alluding to a metaphor borrowed from the Kabala in order to ironically emphasize his point. The point being emphasized by Marx's use of this metaphor is about the effort, intellectual and political, which was required to penetrate this inner sanctum of capitalist production analytically. For in the Kabala, the ascent to God sitting on his throne in his hidden abode is the most arduous and testing of ordeals, fraught with every conceivable trial and tribulation. It is only after pronouncing the seven seals that the adept is allowed to pass through the fiercely guarded gates of the seven heavens and finally to come before and to 'know' *Eyn Sof*. Only a privileged few theurgs would acquire knowledge of the *voces magicae* which would finally open the gates to this hidden abode where He sat on His Throne. With such an analogy at the back of his mind, one gets a sense of the point Marx is trying to make by the use of this metaphor about the vital and indispensable role of exacting and rigorous intellectual analysis.

According to this analogy, the ascent to the hidden abode of the capitalist system was a long and arduous intellectual and political journey, requiring persistence, intense and prolonged commitment and great moral courage. Only after this struggle, in which one had to overcome numerous obstacles, could one arrive at class consciousness and a truthful understanding of reality. Thus, the limits of popular consciousness did not arise from the deception of the priests – an idea arising from the traditions of French anti-clerical rationalism and which was incompatible with Hegelian notions of dialectical reason, let alone with historical materialism. Nor did the limitations of popular consciousness arise from ignorance or any intellectual limitations of the people, although there was ignorance aplenty under slavery, feudalism and capitalism. Neither the truths nor falsehoods of ideology had an abstract rationalist and intellectualist origin, in 'discourse' or 'discursive formations'. Such thinking may be found in Feuerbach but not in Marx. The limits of popular consciousness arose from the structure of reality itself. According to Marx, false consciousness had a deep root, arising necessarily out of the actual complexity of the relations of political economy themselves.

For this very reason, the effort required to force the secrets of reality into the open was no mean feat. Deceptive appearances arising from spontaneous forms of consciousness had to be overcome and hard, time-consuming and difficult study was required to penetrate to these truths, the more so as now there were no mystical theurgical formulae, no *nomen barbarum* to which one could resort. Only hard and critical intellectual and political struggle could yield useful results. Left to itself, the mechanisms of exploitation would never reveal themselves spontaneously to popular consciousness. This cunning of production and these deceptions of popular consciousness, derived neither from a semiotic nor from a psychological source, as many in cultural studies and postmodernism assert. 'Multi-accentuation' *à la* Bakhtin is but a mechanism through which cunning sometimes operates, not its source. They derived from reality and thus were ideologies, not just 'discourses' or 'discursive formations'. It is apparent that what we have here is a theory which posits that what is spontaneously reflected in popular consciousness, moving and profound as it may be, is necessarily limited and often deceptive and that the real truths of life are, for this very reason, never spontaneously reflected but are concealed. Hence the crucial role of intellectual (and political) agency and the critical contribution (or harm) which such persons could make to human development.

But there is a further implication of Marx's conception of the double impact of reality. Since, as has been pointed out, reality is hidden, it has to be forced into the open by intellectual analysis combined with political struggle. But since false consciousness is anchored neither in semiotics nor in 'misunderstanding' but in political economic reality, intellectual exposure and critique by themselves do not alter the fact that the system of exploitation continues to persist in reality. Therefore, even the act of intellectually forcing open and exposing this hidden abode cannot dispel the complex influence of the noisy sphere on popular consciousness. After writing or reading *Capital* and accepting its critique, capitalism continues to flourish, perhaps more powerfully than ever. Human development has to be accomplished in reality and not just literarily and it takes a great deal more than an intellectual or emotional act of expressive culture to achieve this goal.

Thus, as is well known, to Marx, religious distress was the expression of real material and personal distress. By itself, theoretical criticism exposing religion as a form of false consciousness, no matter how penetrating nor how forcefully, lucidly or eloquently expressed, whether in words or evoked in song, could never lead to the decline of religion. Nor could exhaustive accounts of how prisons or clinics came about significantly affect their persistence in real life. It would seem obvious that it was not the power of discourses, of 'dividing practices' – not the power of the word – which led to the development of prisons and clinics. Rather, it was the requirements of reality itself which gave power to these words. Autonomous discourses by themselves, no matter how insightful, could never achieve such an outcome. On the contrary, for cultural criticism to have any lasting effect, it had to be united with real struggles to eliminate the actual material conditions of distress. Thus, the distinction between the two spheres not only provides the theoretical justification for the essential importance of intellectual work, it also explains why theory needs to be united with practice *if theory itself is to have its theoretical effect*, let alone if our goal of the permanent end to the systemic bases for exploitation and human misery is to be achieved.

Both cultural as well as sociological theories have, in differing ways, broken the link between the noisy sphere and this hidden abode. For the fundamental theoretical assumption of both outlooks is that the cultural sphere and the sphere of everyday life, although having a powerful political effect, are either autonomous or where determined by political economy at all, this is a political economy of the market abstracted from the relations of production out of which it arises. This has culturalized and sociologized both fields, making them unable to propose viable solutions to the most burning problems of contemporary culture or economics. It is also responsible for creating false oppositions between identity politics and class politics which profoundly weakens both.

There is thus a need to bring political economy back in. First, in order to focus analysis and thinking on just and workable solutions to the acute economic problems facing the vast majority of peoples in both the developed and developing parts of the world. Second, it is for the purpose of developing a more effective cultural and sociological criticism: to be able to penetrate to the core of the cultural prejudices and relations of production which imprison hundreds of millions of people. This mental slavery makes them vulnerable to political manipulation for anti-human ends or unable to realize their full human potential. This work is a step in this direction. By critiquing cultural and sociological theory for separating culture and society from the material foundations from which they arise and by explaining what has been lost by this sundering from the production relations of political economy, this work hopes to contribute to the recovery and strengthening of that tradition which links intellectual activity firmly to the task of enhancing human development.

# Notes

## Introduction

[1] Richard Ashcraft, *Revolutionary Politics and Locke's Two Treatises of Government*. Princeton, NJ: Princeton University Press, 1986; G.W.F. Hegel, *Philosophy of Right*. Trans. T.M. Knox. New York: Oxford University Press, 1967; Christopher Hill, 'James Harrington and the people', in C. Hill (ed.) *Puritanism and Revolution: Studies in the Interpretation of the English Revolution of the 17th Century*. New York: St Martin's Press, 1997 pp. 269–86. Christopher Hill, 'Thomas Hobbes and the revolution in political thought', in C. Hill (ed.) *Puritanism and Revolution*. New York: St Martin's Press, 1997, pp. 248–68.

[2] Franz Neumann, *Behemoth: The Structure and Practice of National Socialism 1933–1944*, Second edn. New York: Oxford University Press, 1944.

[3] Ronald Dore, *Flexible Rigidities*. London: The Athlone Press, 1986; Ronald Dore, 'Goodwill and the spirit of market capitalism', *British Journal of Sociology*, 34(4) (1983): 459–82.

[4] William E. Scheuerman, *Between the Norm and the Exception: The Frankfurt School and the Rule of Law*. Cambridge, MA: The MIT Press, 1997; William Scheuerman, *Carl Schmitt: The End of Law*. Lanham, MD: Rowman & Littlefield Publishers, 1999.

[5] George Monbiot, *Captive State: The Corporate Takeover of Britain*. New York: Pan Books, 2001.

[6] Vladimir Lenin, 'Imperialism: the highest stage of capitalism', in H.M. Christman (ed.) *Essential Works of Lenin: 'What Is to Be Done?' and Other Writings*. New York: Dover Publications, [1916] 1987; Rudolf Hilferding, *Finance Capital: A Study of the Latest Phase of Capitalist Development*. London: Routledge & Kegan Paul, 1981; Carl Schmitt, *The Crisis of Parliamentary Democracy*. Trans. E. Kennedy. Cambridge, MA: MIT Press, 1985.

[7] Carl Schmitt, *The Concept of the Political*. Trans. G. Schwab. New Brunswick, NJ: Rutgers University Press, 1976.

[8] C.B. Macpherson, *The Political Theory of Possessive Individualism: Hobbes to Locke*. Oxford: Oxford University Press, 1962.

[9] Mary Kaldor, Helmut Anheier and Marlies Glasius (eds) *Global Civil Society 2003*. Oxford: Oxford University Press, 2004.

[10]Ulrich Beck, 'The analysis of global inequality: from national to cosmopolitan perspective', in M. Kaldor *et al. Global Civil Society 2003*, pp. 45–55.

[11]Wolfgang J. Mommsen, 'The antinomical structure of Max Weber's political thought', in Wolfgang J. Mommsen (ed.) *The Political and Social Theory of Max Weber: Collected Essays*. Cambridge: Polity Press, 1989, pp. 24–43.

[12]Wolfgang J. Mommsen, 'Capitalism and socialism: Weber's dialogue with Marx', in W.J. Mommsen, *Political* and *Social Theory*, pp. 53–73.

[13]Yahia Said and Meghnad Desai, 'Trade and global civil society: the anti-capitalist movement revisited', in M. Kaldor *et al. Global Civil Society 2003*, pp. 59–85.

[14]David Schweickart, *After Capitalism*. New York: Rowman & Littlefield Publishers, Inc., 2002.

# 1  Bringing the Economy Back In

[1]Mark Rupert and Hazel Smith (eds) *Historical Materialism and Globalization.* New York: Routledge, 2002.

[2]Anthony Giddens, *Runaway World: How Globalization Is Reshaping Our Lives.* New York: Routledge, 2000.

[3]Stuart Hall, 'New Labour has picked up where Thatcherism left off', *The Guardian*, 6 August 2003.

[4]Robert J. Samuelson, 'The creaky job machine', *The Washington Post*, 17 September 2003, A27.

[5]G.W.F. Hegel, *Philosophy of Right*. New York: Oxford University Press, 1967.

[6]Karl Marx, *Grundrisse: Foundations of the Critique of Political Economy (Rough Draft)*. Trans. M. Nicolaus, ed. by Q. Hoare. Harmondsworth: Penguin Books, 1974.

[7]Ibid.

[8]Ibid.

[9]John Gray, *False Dawn: The Delusions of Global Capitalism.* London: Granta Books, 1998.

[10]Emile Durkheim, *The Division of Labor in Society.* Trans. G. Simpson. New York: Free Press, 1947.

[11]Peter S. Goodman and Philip P. Pan, 'Chinese workers pay for Wal-Mart's low prices', *The Washington Post*, 8 February 2004, A01.

[12]Peter Dicken, *Global Shift: Reshaping the Global Economic Map in the 21st Century*, Fourth edn. New York: The Guilford Press, 2003.

[13]Juliet Eilperin, 'Homemade-titanium rule creates defense squabble', *The Washington Post*, 24 June 2003.

[14]Leslie Wayne, 'Butting heads with the Pentagon', *The New York Times*, 23 July 2003.

[15]Giddens, *Runaway World*; Scott Lash and John Urry, *Economies of Signs and Space*. London: Sage Publications, 1994.

[16]Alec Nove, *The Economics of Feasible Socialism*. London: Unwin Hyman, 1983; Pekka Sutela, *Economic Thought and Economic Reform in the Soviet Union*. Cambridge: Cambridge University Press, 1991.

# 2 Politics as Culture: Stuart Hall

[1]Lawrence Grossberg, 'On postmodernism and articulation: an interview with Stuart Hall', in D. Morley and K.-H. Chen (eds) *Stuart Hall: Critical Dialogues in Cultural Studies.* New York: Routledge, 1997.

[2]Stuart Hall, 'The problem of ideology: Marxism without guarantees', in ibid., pp. 25–46. p. 41.

[3]Colin Sparks, 'Stuart Hall, cultural studies and Marxism', in ibid., pp. , p. 97.

[4]Stuart Hall, 'The problem of ideology'.

[5]Hegel, *Philosophy of Right.* p. 10.

[6]Ludwig Feuerbach, *The Essence of Christianity.* Trans. G. Eliot. New York: Harper Torchbooks, 1957.

[7]G.W.F. Hegel, *The Phenomenology of Mind.* Trans. J.B. Baillie. New York: Harper Torchbooks, 1967. p. 75.

[8]Georg Lukács, *The Young Hegel: Studies in the Relations between Dialectics and Economics.* Trans. R. Livingstone. Cambridge: MA: MIT Press, 1976. pp. 454–457.

[9]Hegel, *Phenomenology.* p. 75.

[10]Shlomo Avineri, *Hegel's Theory of the Modern State.* Cambridge: Cambridge University Press, 1988. p. 68.

[11]Hegel, *Philosophy of Right.* p. 12–13.

[12]Stuart Hall, 'The problem of ideology'. p. 45.

[13]Ibid. p. 45.

[14]Ibid. p. 27.

[15]Stuart Hall, 'What is this "black" in black popular culture?,' in D. Morley and K.-H. Chen, *Stuart Hall,* pp. 465–75. p. 470.

[16]Hall, 'The problem of ideology'. p. 40.

[17]Colin Sparks, 'Stuart Hall, Cultural Studies and Marxism.' p. 95.

[18]Hall, 'New Labour'.

[19]Hall, 'What is this "black"?'.

[20]Ibid. p. 473.

[21]Hall, 'The problem of ideology', p. 30.

[22]Stuart Hall, 'Gramsci's relevance for the study of race and ethnicity', in Morley and Chen, *Stuart Hall,* pp. 412–40.

[23]Hall, 'What is this "black"?' p. 472.

[24]Hall, 'Gramsci's relevance'. p. 418.

[25]Hall, 'The problem of ideology'. p. 26.

[26]Ibid. p. 44.

[27]Anne Showstack Sassoon, *Gramsci's Politics,* Second edn. Minneapolis: University of Minnesota Press, 1987. pp. ix–x.

[28]Ibid. p. 252.

[29]Ibid. p. xiii.

[30]Ibid. p. 192 emphasis in original.

[31]Ibid. p. 187.

[32]Alec Nove, *The Economics of Feasible Socialism,* London: Unwin Hyman., p. 198.

[33]Stephen F. Cohen, *Bukharin and the Bolshevik Revolution: A Political Biography, 1888–1938.* New York: Oxford University Press, 1980. pp. 160–212.

[34]Hall, 'Gramsci's relevance'. pp. 419–420.

[35]Sassoon, *Gramsci's Politics*, p. 93.

[36]Ibid. p. 93 emphasis in original.

[37]Hall, 'What is this "black"?' pp. 465–472.

[38]Ibid. pp. 472.

[39]Ibid. pp. 474.

[40]Stuart Hall, 'New ethnicities', in D. Morley and K.-H. Chen (eds) *Stuart Hall: Critical Dialogues in Cultural Studies*. New York: Routledge, 1997, p. 447.

[41]Hall, 'What is this "black"?' p. 471.

[42]Don Robotham, 'Pluralism as an ideology', *Social and Economic Studies* 29(1) pp. (1980): 69–89.

[43]Don Robotham, 'Blackening the Jamaican nation: the travails of a black bourgeoisie in a globalizing world', *Identities: Global Studies of Culture and Power* 7(1) (2000).

[44]Don Robotham, 'The development of a black ethnicity in Jamaica', in R. Lewis and P. Bryan (eds) *Garvey: His Work and Impact*. Kingston: ISER, University of the West Indies, 1989, pp. 23–38.

## 3 Gilroy: Neither Black nor Atlantic

[1]Paul Gilroy, *Against Race: Imagining Political Culture Beyond the Color Line*. First edn. Cambridge, MA: Harvard University Press, 2000; Paul Gilroy, *The Black Atlantic: Modernity and Double Consciousness*. Cambridge, MA: Harvard University Press, 1993.

[2]David Harvey, *The New Imperialism*. Oxford: Oxford University Press, 2003.

[3]Paul Gilroy, 'The organic crisis of British capitalism and race: the experience of the seventies', in *The Empire Strikes Back: Race and Racism in 70s Britain*. Birmingham Centre for Contemporary Cultural Studies (eds) London: Routledge, 1970.

[4]Sharon J. Daye, *Middle Class Blacks in Britain: A Racial Fraction of a Class or a Class Fraction of a Racial Group?* London: St Martin's Press, 1994.

[5]Paul Gilroy, 'Police and thieves', in Birmingham Centre for Contemporary Cultural Studies (eds) *The Empire Strikes Back*, pp. 95–142.

[6]Ibid. p. 143–181.

[7]Paul Gilroy, 'Steppin' out of Babylon: race, class and autonomy', in BCCCS, *The Empire Strikes Back*, pp. 276–314.

[8]Ibid. p. 284.

[9]Ibid. Gilroy's italics. p. 281.

[10]Gilroy, *Black Atlantic*. pp. 3–15.

[11]Friedrich Engels, *Ludwig Feuerbach and the Outcome of Classical German Philosophy*. New York: International Publishers, [1888] 1970; Ludwig Feuerbach. *The Essence of Christianity*. New York: Harper Torchbooks, 1957.

[12]Gilroy, *Against Race*. pp. 127ff.

[13]Frank Furedi, *The Silent War: Imperialism and the Changing Perception of Race*. New Brunswick: Rutgers University Press, 1998; Paul Gordon Lauren, *Power and Prejudice: The Politics of Diplomacy and Racial Discrimination*. Boulder, CO: Westview Press, 1988.

[14]Neil MacMaster, *Racism in Europe: 1870–2000*. London: Palgrave, 2001.

[15]Gilroy, 'Steppin' out of Babylon'. pp. 277 & 283.

[16]MacMaster, *Racism in Europe*. p. 69–70.

[17]Robert Brenner, *The Boom and the Bubble: The US in the World Economy*. New York: Verso, 2002.

[18]Wilson Jeremiah Moses, *Afrotopia: The Roots of African American Popular History*. Cambridge: Cambridge University Press, 1998. pp. 35–38.

[19]Ibid. p. 190.

[20]Gilroy, *Black Atlantic*. p. 1–40.

[21]Ibid. p. 23.

[22]Ibid. p. 27.

[23]Moses, *Afrotopia*. p. 78–79.

[24]Ibid. p. 79.

[25]Wilson Jeremiah Moses (ed.) *Classical Black Nationalism: From the American Revolution to Marcus Garvey*. New York: New York University Press, 1996. pp. 19–20.

[26]Gilroy, *Black Atlantic*. p. 25.

[27]Ibid. p. 26.

[28]Ibid. p. 25.

[29]Ibid. p. 26.

[30]Moses, *Classical Black Nationalism*, pp. 22–28; Moses, *Afrotopia*. pp. 77–79, 104–105, 196–198.

[31]Moses, *Classical Black Nationalism*, pp. 101–104; Moses, *Afrotopia*. pp. 77–104.

[32]Gilroy, *Black Atlantic*. p. 27.

[33]Ibid. p. 29.

[34]Ibid. p. 27.

[35]Ibid. pp. 34–35.

[36]Ibid. p. 29.

[37]Ibid. p. 32–36; Hall, 'New ethnicities', pp. 441–449.

[38]Gilroy, *Black Atlantic*. p. 32.

[39]Ibid. p. 37–38, pp. 112–113.

[40]Ibid. p. 37.

[41]Ibid. p. 120.

[42]Ibid. p. 122.

[43]Ibid. p. 127.

[44]Ibid. p. 144.

[45]Ibid. p. 37.

[46]Ibid. p. 37.

[47]Ibid. p. 39.

[48]Ibid. p. 126.

[49]Ibid. p. 112.

[50]Moses, *Classical Black Nationalism*.

[51]Herbert Hill, Horace Cayton, Arna Bontemps and Saunders Redding, 'Reflections on Richard Wright: a symposium on an exiled native son', in D.B. Gibson (ed.) *Five Black Writers: Essays on Wright, Ellison, Baldwin, Hughes, and Leroi Jones*. New York: New York University Press, 1970, pp. 58–69, p. 66.

# 4 Globalization and Risks

[1]Anthony Giddens, *Runaway World*, New York: Routledge, 2000.

[2]Ibid. p. 62–63.

[3]Ibid. p. 68.

[4]Ibid. p. 91.

[5]Ibid. pp. 91–93.

[6]Ibid. p. 91.

[7]Ibid. pp. 94–95.

[8]Alec Nove, *The Economics of Feasible Socialism*. London: Unwin Hyman, 1983.

[9]Anthony Giddens, *Beyond Left and Right: The Future of Radical Politics*. Cambridge: Polity Press, 1994. pp. 74–75 & 156–57.

[10]Ota Sik, *The Third Way: Marxist-Leninist Theory and Modern Industrial Society*. London: Wildwood House International Arts and Sciences, 1976.

[11]Wlodzimierz Brus and Laski Kasimierz, *From Marx to the Market: Socialism in Search of an Economic System*. Oxford: Clarendon Press, 1996; Janos Kornai, *Contradictions and Dilemmas: Studies on the Socialist Economy and Society*. Cambridge, MA: MIT Press, 1986.

[12]Giddens, *Beyond Left and Right*. p. 126.

[13]Ibid. pp. 40–41.

[14]Giddens, *Runaway World*. pp. 97–99.

[15]Ulrich Beck, *The Brave New World of Work*. Trans. P. Camiller. Cambridge: Polity Press, 2000; Anthony Giddens, *The Third Way: The Renewal of Social Democracy*. Cambridge: Polity Press, 1998.

[16]Julian Le Grand and Will Bartlett, *Quasi-Markets and Social Policy*. London: Macmillan, 1993.

[17]Robert Wade, 'Globalization and its limits: reports of the death of the national economy are greatly exaggerated', in S. Berger and R. Dore (eds) *National Diversity and Global Capitalism*. Ithaca, NY: Cornell University Press, 1996, pp. 60–88.

[18]Peter Dicken, *Global Shift*. New York: The Guilford Press. p. 35.

[19]Ibid. p. 52.

[20]Ibid. p. 230.

[21]Ibid. p. 452.

[22]Alexandra Frean, 'Huge increase in poor families', *The Times*, 14 June 2000; Peter Riddell, 'Labour fails to bridge the class divide', *The Times*, 29 June 2000, 1; Patrick Wintour, 'Class-riven UK exposed in new study', *The Guardian*, 12 July 2000.

[23]David Walker, 'Brown's beneficence', *The Guardian*, 17 July 2000.

[24]Giddens, *Runaway World*. pp. 38–53.

# 5 Capitalism Organized and Disorganized

[1]Rudolf Hilferding, *Finance Capital*. London: Routledge & Kegan Paul, 1981; Scott Lash and John Urry, *Economies of Signs and Space*. London: Sage, 1994; Scott Lash and John Urry, *The End of Organized Capitalism*. Madison, WI: University of Wisconsin Press, 1987.

[2]Manuel Castells, *The Power of Identity*. Vol. II, *The Information Age: Economy, Society and Culture*. Oxford: Blackwell Publishers, 1997; Manuel Castells, *The Rise*

*of the Network Society.* Vol. I, *The Information Age: Economy, Society and Culture.* Oxford: Blackwell Publishers, 1996.

[3]Manuel Castells, *End of Millenium.* Vol. II, *The Information Age: Economy, Society and Culture.* Oxford: Blackwell Publishers, 1998; Castells, *Power of Identity*; Castells, *Rise of Network Society.*

[4]Mike Featherstone, *Undoing Culture: Globalization, Postmodernism and Identity.* London: Sage Publications, 1995; Mike Featherstone (ed.) *Global Culture: Nationalism, Globalization and Modernity.* London: Sage, 1990.

[5]Lash and Urry, *Economies*, pp. 285–286; Dicken, *Global Shift.* pp. 464–465.

[6]P.J. Cain and A.G. Hopkins, *British Imperialism: 1688–2000*, Second edn. London: Longman, 2002.

[7]Lash and Urry, *End of Organized Capitalism.* pp. 270–279.

[8]Lash and Urry, *Economies.* p. 3.

[9]Georg Lukács, 'In search of bourgeois man', in G. Lukács (ed.) *Essays on Thomas Mann.* New York: Grosset & Dunlap, 1965. pp. 21–22.

[10]Lash and Urry, *Economies.* pp. 32–59.

[11]Wolfgang Mommsen, 'Capitalism and socialism', in W.J. Mommsen (ed.) *The Political and Social Theory of Max Weber.* Cambridge: Polity Press, 1989, pp. 53–73.

[12]Ibid. p. 59.

[13]Hans Mommsen, *The Rise and Fall of Weimar Democracy.* Trans. E. Forster and L. Jones. Chapel Hill, NC: The University of North Carolina Press, 1989; Franz Neumann, *Behemoth.* New York: Oxford University Press, 1944. pp. 15–16, 32, 210–228.

[14]Wolfgang J. Mommsen, *The Political and Social Theory of Max Weber: Collected Essays.* Cambridge: Polity Press, 1989.

[15]Lash and Urry, *Economies.* pp. 49–54.

[16]Anthony Giddens, *A Contemporary Critique of Historical Materialism: Power, Property and the State.* 2 vols. Vol. 1. Berkeley, CA: University of California Press, 1981.

[17]Lash and Urry, *Economies.* p. 315.

[18]Gray, *False Dawn.*

[19]Lash and Urry, *End of Organized Capitalism.* pp. 283.

[20]Lash and Urry, *Economies.* p. 3.

[21]Castells, *Rise of Network Society*; Lash and Urry, *Economies.* pp. 94–104.

[22]Lash and Urry, *Economies.* pp. 4–5.

[23]Steven Lukes, *Individualism: Key Concepts in the Social Sciences.* Oxford: Basil Blackwell, 1973. pp. 38 & 157.

[24]Lash and Urry, *Economies*, p. 11.

[25]Lukes, *Individualism.* p. 55.

[26]Ibid. pp. 41 & 72.

[27]Ibid. pp. 35–38.

[28]David Schweickart, *Against Capitalism.* Boulder, CO: Westview Press, 1996. pp. 180–182.

[29]Lukes, *Individualism.* pp. 150–151.

[30]Ibid. pp. 151–152.

[31]Louis Dumont, *Essays on Individualism: Modern Ideology in Anthropological Perspective.* Chicago: University of Chicago Press, 1986. pp. 25 & 117.

[32]Mike Featherstone, *Undoing Culture.* London: Sage, 1995. pp. 78–79.

[33]Lash and Urry, *End of Organized Capitalism*. p. 286.

[34]Johannes Fritsche, *Historical Destiny and National Socialism in Heidegger's Being and Time*. Berkeley, CA: University of California Press, 1999. p. 213.

[35]Ulrich Beck, 'The analysis of global inequality', in M. Kaldor *et al.* (eds) *Global Civil Society*. Oxford: Oxford University Press, 2004. pp. 45–55.

[36]Lash and Urry, *End of Organized Capitalism*. pp. 3–7.

[37]Lash and Urry, *Economies*. p. 280.

[38]Ibid. pp. 279–281.

[39]Mary Kaldor, Helmut Anheier and Marlies Glasius, 'Global civil society in an era of regressive globalization', in M. Kaldor *et al.* (eds) *Global Civil Society 2003*, pp. 3–33.

[40]Harold Meyerson, 'Plutocrats and populists', *The Washington Post*, 5 February 2004, A21.

[41]Arjun Appadurai, *Modernity at Large: Cultural Dimensions of Globalization*. Vol. 1, *Public Worlds*. Minneapolis: University of Minnesota Press, 1996; U. Hannerz, *Transnational Connections: Culture, Peoples, Places*. London: Routledge, 1996.

[42]Lash and Urry, *Economies*. p. 306.

[43]Lash and Urry, *End of Organized Capitalism*. p. 290.

[44]Ibid. pp. 312–313.

[45]Robert Brenner, *The Boom and the Bubble*. New York: Verso, 2002.

[46]Lash and Urry, *Economies*. pp. 305–313.

[47]Marc Edelman, 'Transnational peasant and farmer movements and networks', in M. Kaldor *et al.* (eds) *Global Civil Society 2003*, pp. 185–220.

[48]Lash and Urry, *Economies*. pp. 280–292.

# 6  Network Society Theory

[1]Manuel Castells, *Rise of Network Society*. Oxford: Blackwell, 1996. pp. 376–428.

[2]Ibid. p. 421.

[3]Doug Henwood, *After the New Economy*. New York: The New Press, 2003. p. 147.

[4]Manuel Castells, *The Power of Identity*. Oxford: Blackwell, 1997. p. 6.

[5]Ibid. p. 6.

[6]Ibid. p. 7.

[7]Ibid. p. 7.

[8]Castells, *Rise of Network Society*. p. 426.

[9]Ibid. p. 423, boldface is in text.

[10]Ibid. p. 425.

[11]Ibid. p. 8.

[12]Ibid. p. 8.

[13]Ibid. p. 8.

[14]Ibid. p. 9.

[15]Castells, *Power of Identity*. p. 8.

[16]Johannes Fritsche, *Historical Destiny and National Socialism in Heidegger's Being and Time*. Berkeley, CA: University of California Press, 1999.

[17]Ibid. p. 69.

[18]Castells, *Rise of Network Society*. p. 199–200.

[19]Max Weber, 'Politics as a vocation', in H.H. Gerth and C. Wright Mills (eds) *From Max Weber: Essays in Sociology*. New York: Oxford, 1958, pp. 115–28; Wolfgang J. Mommsen, 'Politics and scholarship: the two icons in Max Weber's life', in W.J. Mommsen (ed.) *The Political and Social Theory of Max Weber: Collected Essays*. Cambridge: Polity Press, 1989. pp. 3–23.

[20]Castells, *Power of Identity*. p. 9.

[21]Ibid. p. 9.

[22]Ibid. p. 8.

[23]Ibid. p. 10.

[24]Fritsche, *Historical Destiny*. p. 17ff.

[25]Castells, *Power of Identity*. p. 10.

[26]Ibid. p. 11.

[27]Ibid. p. 11.

[28]Ibid. p. 11.

[29]Ibid. p. 11, italics in original.

[30]Ibid. p. 11.

[31]Castells, *Rise of Network Society*. p. 199.

[32]Ibid. pp. 182–183.

[33]Ibid. p. 182.

[34]Ibid. p. 24.

[35]Ibid. p. 97–98.

[36]Ibid. p. 97–99.

[37]Ibid. p. 98.

[38]Ibid. p. 168.

[39]Ibid. p. 168.

[40]Ibid. p. 20.

[41]Martin Carnoy, *Sustaining the New Economy: Work, Family and Community in the Information Age*. Cambridge: MA: Harvard University Press, 2000; Manuel Castells, 'The informational economy and the new international division of labor', in M. Carnoy *et al.* (eds) *The New Global Economy in the Information Age: Reflections on Our Changing World*. University Park, PA: Pennsylvania State University Press, 1993. pp. 15–43.

[42]Carnoy *et al.*, *The New Global Economy in the Information Age*.

[43]Ibid. p. 2.

[44]Bennett Harrison, *Lean and Mean: Why Large Corporations Will Continue to Dominate the Global Economy*. New York: Guilford Press, 1994. p. 171.

[45]Ibid. pp. 125–171.

[46]Martin Carnoy, 'Multinationals in a changing world economy', in Carnoy *et al.* *The New Global Economy in the Information Age*. pp. 45–96. p. 46.

[47]Castells, 'The informational economy'. pp. 19–20.

[48]Carnoy, *Sustaining the New Economy*. pp. 60–61.

[49]Ibid. p. 62.

[50]Castells, *Rise of Network Society*. p. 173.

[51]Ibid. p. 196.

[52]Ibid. p. 151.

[53]Ibid. p. 152.

[54]Ibid. p. 156.

[55]Ibid. p. 171, boldface in original.

[56]Ibid. pp. 194–195.

[57]Ibid. p. 163.

[58]Peter Dicken, *Global Shift*. New York: Guilford Press, 2003.

[59]Ibid. p. 421, Figure 12.7.

[60]Ibid. p. 421.

[61]Scott Lash and John Urry, *Economies of Signs and Space*. London: Sage, 1994.

[62]Ronald Dore, 'Goodwill and the spirit of market capitalism'. *British Journal of Sociology* 334(4) (1983): 459–82; Ronald Dore, 'Where we are now: musings of an evolutionist', *Work, Employment & Society* 3(4) (1989): 425–46.

[63]Ronald Dore, *British Factory, Japanese Factory: The Origin of National Diversity in Industrial Relations*. Berkeley, CA: University of California Press, 1973; Ronald Dore, *Flexible Rigidities*. London: The Athlone Press, 1986; Ronald Dore, and Mari Sako, *How the Japanese Learn to Work*. London: Routledge, 1989.

[64]Dore, *British Factory-Japanese Factory*.

[65]Castells, *End of Millenium*, pp. 20–21; Castells, *Rise of Network Society* pp. 206–309; Dore, 'Where we are now'.

[66]Michael W. Howard, *Self-Management and the Crisis of Socialism: The Rose in the Fist of the Present*. New York: Rowman & Littlefield Publishers, Inc., 2000. pp. 188–193.

[67]Masahiko Aoki and Ronald Dore (eds) *The Japanese Firm: Sources of Competitive Strength*. Oxford: The Clarendon Press, 1994; Christian Berggren, *Alternatives to Lean Production: Work Organization in the Swedish Auto Industry*. Ithaca, NY: Cornell International Industrial Labour Institute, 1993.

[68]Yahia Said and Meghnad Desai, 'Trade and global civil society', in M. Kaldor *et al.* (eds) *Global Civil Society 2003*. Oxford: Oxford University Press, 2004. pp. 54–85.

# 7 'Localization' Explored

[1]Colin Leys, 'Colin Leys Replies'. *Southern African Report* 12(4) (1997).

[2]Alex Callinicos, *An Anti-Capitalist Manifesto*. Cambridge: Polity Press, 2003. pp. 67–105.

[3]W. Brus and K. Laski, *From Marx to the Market*. Oxford: Clarendon Press, 1946; J. Kornai, *Contradictions and Dilemmas*. Cambridge, MA: MIT Press, 1986; Harold Lydall, *Yugoslav Socialism: Theory and Practice*. Oxford: Oxford University Press, 1984; Alec Nove, *Economics of Feasible Socialism*. London: Unwin Hyman, 1983; Sik, *The Third Way*; P. Sutela, *Economic Thought*. Cambridge: Cambridge University Press, 1991;

[4]Howard, *Self-Management*; Sharyn Kasmir, *The Myth of Mondragon: Cooperatives, Politics, and Working Class Life in a Basque Town*. Albany: SUNY Press, 1996; William Foot Whyte and Kathleen King Whyte, *Making Mondragon: The Growth and Dynamics of the Worker Cooperative Complex*. Ithaca, NY: Cornell University Press, 1988.

[5]John Roemer, *A Future for Socialism*. Cambridge, MA: Harvard University Press, 1994; D. Schweickart, *Against Capitalism*. Boulder, CO: Westview Press, 1996.

[6]John Cavanagh (ed.) *Alternatives to Economic Globalization: A Better World Is Possible*. San Francisco: Berrett-Koehler Publishers, 2002. p. 9.

[7]Nove, *Economics of Feasible Socialism*; Sutela, *Economic Thought*; Peter C. Caldwell, 'Revisionism and orthodoxy: Stalinism and political thought in the German Democratic Republic's founding decade', in J.P. McCormick (ed.) *Confronting Mass Democracy and Industrial Technology: Political and Social Theory from Nietzsche to Habermas*. Durham, NC: Duke University Press, 2002.

[8]Franz L. Neumann, 'The change in the function of law in modern society', in W.E. Scheuerman (ed.) *The Rule of Law under Siege. Selected Essays of Franz L. Neumann and Otto Kircheimer*. Berkeley, CA: University of California Press, 1996. pp. 101–141; Otto Kircheimer, 'Legality and legitimacy', in ibid. pp. 44–63.

[9]Colin Hines, *Localization: A Global Manifesto*. London: Earthscan, 2001. p. 7.

[10]Adam Smith, *An Inquiry into the Nature and Causes of the Wealth of Nations*. Chicago: University of Chicago Press, 1976; G.W.F. Hegel, *Philosophy of Right*. New York: Oxford University Press. 1967; Karl Marx and Frederick Engels, *The German Ideology*. Moscow: Progress Publishers, 1968.

[11]John Cavanagh (ed.) *Alternatives to Economic Globalization*. San Francisco: Berrett-Koehler, 2002. p. 5.

[12]Ibid. p. 8.

[13]Martin Khor, 'Commentary: conflicting paradigms', in *Alternatives to Economic Globalization: A Better World Is Possible*, edited by John Cavanagh, Box A. San Francisco: Berrett-Koehler Publishers, Inc., 2002.

[14]Cavanagh, *Alternatives*. pp. 104–120.

[15]Ingeborg Maus, 'Sinn und Bedeutung der Volkssouveränität in der modernen Gesellschaft', *Kritische Justiz* 24(2) (1991).

[16]Cavanagh, *Alternatives*. p. 6.

[17]Bennett Harrison, *Lean and Mean*. New York: Guilford Press, 1994.

[18]Cavanagh, *Alternatives*.

[19]Saskia Sassen, *Cities in a World Economy*. Thousand Oaks, CA: Pine Forge Press, 2000.

[20]Richard Pares, '*Merchants and planters*', *Economic History Review*, Supplement 4 (1960), pp. 60–76.

[21]David Graeber, *Toward an Anthropological Theory of Value: The False Coin of Our Own Dreams*. New York: Palgrave, 2001.

[22]Hegel, *Philosophy of Right*.

[23]Ibid. p. 123.

[24]Michel Foucault, *The Order of Things*. New York: Vintage Books, 1994; Reinhart Koselleck, *Futures Past: On the Semantics of Historical Time*. Cambridge: MA: MIT Press, 1994.

[25]Inga Markovits, *Imperfect Justice: An East–West German Diary*. Oxford: Clarendon Press, 1995.

[26]Zigurdis L. Zile (ed.) *Ideas and Forces in Soviet Legal History: A Reader in the Soviet State and Law*. New York: Oxford University Press, 1992; W.K. Scheuerman. *Between the Norm and Exception*. Cambridge, MA: MIT Press, 1997.

[27]Scheuerman, *Between the Norm and Exception*.

[28]Roberto Unger, *The Critical Legal Studies Movement*. Cambridge, MA: Harvard University Press, 1975.

[29]Maus, 'Sinn und Bedeutung'.

# 8 Alternatives: A Global Approach to Anti-Globalization

[1]W. Brus and K. Laski, *From Marx to the Market.* Oxford: Clarendon Press, 1996; J. Kornai, *Contradictions and Dilemmas.* Cambridge, MA: MIT Press, 1986, J. Roemer, *A Future for Socialism.* Cambridge, MA: Harvard University Press, 1994; David Schweickart, 'Market socialism: a defense', in B. Ollman (ed.), *Market Socialism: The Debate among Socialists.* New York: Routledge, 1998, pp. 7–22; O. Sik, *The Third Way.* London: Wildwood House, 1976.

[2]G. W. F. Hegel, *Philosophy of Right.* Trans. T. M. Knox. New York: Oxford University Press, 1967.

[3]Mark Rupert and Hazel Smith (eds) '*Historical Materialism and Globalization*', in Richard Higgott, *Warwick Studies in Globalisation.* New York: Routledge, 2002.

[4]A. Nove, *The Economics of Feasible Socialism.* London: Unwin Hyman, 1983.

[5]Paul Davidson, 'The future of the international financial system', paper presented at the Conference of the Future of Economics at Cambridge University, Cambridge, 2003.

[6]M. Howard, *Self-Management and the Crisis of Socialism.* New York: Rowman & Littlefield, 2000; D. Schweickart, *After Capitalism.* New York: Rowman & Littlefield, 2002.

[7]Davidson, 'The future'.

[8]J. Fritsche, *Historical Destiny and National Socialism.* Berkeley, CA: University of California Press, 1999. p. 153.

[9]Nove, *Economics of Feasible Socialism.*

[10]Bertell Ollman, 'Market mystification in capitalist and market socialist societies', in B. Ollman (ed.) *Market Socialism: The Debate among Socialists.* New York: Routledge, 1998, pp. 81–121; David Lawler, 'Marx as market socialist', in ibid., pp. 23–52. Schweickart, *After Capitalism*; *Against Capitalism*; 'Market socialism'; H. Ticktin, 'The problem is market socialism', in B. Ollman (ed.) *Market Socialism*, pp. 55–80.

[11]Brus and Laski, *From Marx to the Market*; Kornai, *Contradictions.*

[12]Jagdish Bagwati, 'The capital myth: the difference between trade in widgets and dollars', *Foreign Affairs* 77(3) (1998): pp. 7–12.

[13]A. Callinicos, *An Anti-Capitalist Manifesto.* Cambridge: Polity, 2003.

[14]Paul Davidson, 'Are grains of sand in the wheels of international finance sufficient to do the job when boulders are often required?' *Economic Journal* 107(442) (1997): 671–86.

[15]Ibid.

[16]Phillipe Van Parijs, *Real Freedom for All: What (If Anything) Can Justify Capitalism?* Oxford: Clarendon Press, 1995.

[17]Howard, *Self-Management.* pp. 171–173 & 179–180.

[18]André Gorz, 'On the difference between society and community, and why basic income cannot by itself confer full membership of either', in P. Van Parijs (ed.) *Arguing for Basic Income.* London: Verso, 1992: p. 184.

[19]Nove, *Economics of Feasible Socialism.* pp. 133–141.

[20]Howard, *Self-Management*; S. Kasmir, *Myth of Mondragon.* Albany, NY: SUNY Press, 1996.

[21]Schweickart, *After Capitalism.*

# 9 Conclusion: The Noisy Sphere and the Hidden Abode

[1]Karl Marx, *Capital*. Trans. D. Fernbach. Vol. 1, Harmondsworth: Penguin Books, 1978. p. 167.

[2]Stuart Hall, 'The problem of ideology', in D. Morley and K.H. Chen (eds) *Stuart Hall*, New York: Routledge, 1997. p. 35.

[3]P.G. Lauren, *Power and Prejudice*. Boulder, CO: Westview Press, 1988; Laura Tabili, *We Ask for British Justice: Workers and Racial Difference in Late Imperial Britain*. Ithaca, NY: Cornell University Press, 1994.

[4]Nancy Fraser, 'From redistribution to recognition? Dilemmas of justice in a "post-socialist" age', in C. Willett (ed.) *Theorizing Multiculturalism: A Guide to the Current Debate*, Malden, MA: Blackwell Publishers, 1998, pp. 19–49; 'Rethinking Recognition', *New Left Review* 3, May–June (2000): 107–120; Charles Taylor, *Multiculturalism and 'the Politics of Recognition'*, Princeton, NJ: Princeton University Press.

[5]Gilroy, *Against Race*.

# References

Aoki, Masahiko and Dore, Ronald (eds) (1994) *The Japanese Firm: Sources of Competitive Strength*. Oxford: The Clarendon Press.

Appadurai, Arjun (1996) *Modernity at Large: Cultural Dimensions of Globalization*. Vol. 1, *Public Worlds*. Minneapolis: University of Minnesota Press.

Ashcraft, Richard (1986) *Revolutionary Politics and Locke's Two Treatises of Government*. Princeton, NJ: Princeton University Press.

Avineri, Shlomo (1988) *Hegel's Theory of the Modern State*. Cambridge: Cambridge University Press.

Bagwati, Jagdish (1998) 'The Capital Myth: The Difference between Trade in Widgets and Dollars.' *Foreign Affairs* 77(3): pp. 7–12.

Beck, Ulrich (2000) *The Brave New World of Work*. Trans. P. Camiller. Cambridge: Polity Press.

Beck, Ulrich (2004) 'The Analysis of Global Inequality: From National to Cosmopolitan Perspective.' In Mary Kaldor, Helmut Anheier and Marlies Glasius (eds) *Global Civil Society 2003*, Oxford: Oxford University Press, pp. 45–55.

Berggren, Christian (1993) *Alternatives to Lean Production: Work Organization in the Swedish Auto Industry*. Ithaca, NY: Cornell International Industrial Labour Institute.

Brenner, Robert (2002) *The Boom and the Bubble: The US In the World Economy*. New York: Verso.

Brus, Wlodzimierz and Laski, Kasimierz (1996) *From Marx to the Market: Socialism in Search of an Economic System*. Oxford: Clarendon Press.

Cain, P.J. and Hopkins, A.G. (2002) *British Imperialism, 1688–2000*. Second edn. London: Longman.

Caldwell, Peter C. (2002) 'Revisionism and orthodoxy: Stalinism and political thought in the German Democratic Republic's founding decade', in J.P. McCormick (ed.) *Confronting Mass Democracy and Industrial Technology: Political and Social Theory from Nietzsche to Habermas*. Durham, NC: Duke University Press.

Callinicos, Alex (2003) *An Anti-Capitalist Manifesto*. Cambridge: Polity Press.

Carnoy, Martin (1993) 'Multinationals in a changing world economy', in Martin Carnoy, Manuel Castells, Stephen S. Cohen and Fernando Henrique Cardoso (eds) *The New Global Economy in the Information Age: Reflections on Our Changing World*. University Park, PA: Pennsylvania State University Press, pp. 45–96.

Carnoy, Martin (2000) *Sustaining the New Economy: Work, Family and Community in the Information Age*. Cambridge, MA: Harvard University Press.

Carnoy, Martin, Castells, Manuel, Cohen, Stephen, S. and Cardoso, Fernando Henrique (eds) (1993) *The New Global Economy in the Information Age: Reflections on Our Changing World*. University Park, PA: Pennsylvania State University Press.

Castells, Manuel (1993) 'The informational economy and the new international division of labor', in M. Carnoy *et al.* (eds) *The New Global Economy in the Information Age: Reflections on Our Changing World*. University Park, PA: Pennsylvania State University Press, pp. 15–43.

Castells, Manuel (1996) *The Rise of the Network Society*. Edited by Manuel Castells. III vols. Vol. I, *The Information Age: Economy, Society and Culture*. Oxford: Blackwell Publishers.

Castells, Manuel (1997) *The Power of Identity*. Edited by Manuel Castells. III vols. Vol. II, *The Information Age: Economy, Society and Culture*. Oxford: Blackwell Publishers.

Castells, Manuel (1998) *End of Millenium*. Edited by Manuel Castells. III vols. Vol. II, *The Information Age: Economy, Society and Culture*. Oxford: Blackwell Publishers.

Cavanagh, John (ed.) (2002) *Alternatives to Economic Globalization: A Better World Is Possible*. San Francisco: Berrett-Koehler Publishers.

Cohen, Stephen F. (1980) *Bukharin and the Bolshevik Revolution: A Political Biography, 1888–1938*. New York: Oxford University Press.

Davidson, Paul (1997) 'Are grains of sand in the wheels of international finance sufficient to do the job when boulders are often required?' *Economic Journal* 107(442): 671–86.

Davidson, Paul (2003) 'The future of the international financial system', in paper presented at the Conference of the Future of Economics at Cambridge University, Cambridge.

Daye, Sharon J. (1994) *Middle Class Blacks in Britain: A Racial Fraction of a Class or a Class Fraction of a Racial Group?* London: St Martin's Press.

Dicken, Peter (2003) *Global Shift: Reshaping the Global Economic Map in the 21st Century*. Fourth edn. New York: The Guilford Press.

Dore, Ronald (1973) *British Factory, Japanese Factory: The Origin of National Diversity in Industrial Relations*. Berkeley, CA: University of California Press.

Dore, Ronald (1983) 'Goodwill and the spirit of market capitalism', *British Journal of Sociology* 34(4): 459–82.

Dore, Ronald (1986) *Flexible Rigidities*. London: The Athlone Press.

Dore, Ronald (1989) 'Where we are now: musings of an evolutionist', *Work, Employment & Society* 3(4): 425–46.

Dore, Ronald and Sako, Mari (1989) *How the Japanese Learn to Work*. London: Routledge.

Dumont, Louis (1986) *Essays on Individualism: Modern Ideology in Anthropological Perspective.* Chicago: University of Chicago Press.

Durkheim, Emile (1947) *The Division of Labor in Society.* Trans. G. Simpson. New York: Free Press.

Edelman, Marc (2004) 'Transnational peasant and farmer movements and networks', in M. Kaldor *et al.* (eds) *Global Civil Society 2003.* Oxford: Oxford University Press.

Eilperin, Juliet (2003) 'Homemade-titanium rule creates defense squabble', *The Washington Post,* 24 June.

Engels, Friedrich ([1888] 1970) *Ludwig Feuerbach and the Outcome of Classical German Philosophy.* New York: International Publishers.

Featherstone, Mike (ed.) (1990) *Global Culture: Nationalism, Globalization and Modernity.* London: Sage.

Featherstone, Mike (1995) *Undoing Culture: Globalization, Postmodernism and Identity.* London: Sage.

Feuerbach, Ludwig (1957) *The Essence of Christianity.* Trans. G. Eliot. New York: Harper Torchbooks.

Foucault, Michel (1994) *The Order of Things.* New York: Vintage Books.

Fraser, Nancy (1998) 'From redistribution to recognition? Dilemmas of justice in a "post-socialist" age', in C. Willett (ed.) *Theorizing Multiculturalism: A Guide to the Current Debate.* Malden, MA: Blackwell Publishers, pp. 19–49.

Fraser, Nancy (2000) 'Rethinking recognition', *New Left Review* 3, May–June: 107–20.

Frean, Alexandra (2000) 'Huge increase in poor families', *The Times,* 14 June.

Fritsche, Johannes (1999) *Historical Destiny and National Socialism in Heidegger's Being and Time.* Berkeley, CA: University of California Press.

Furedi, Frank (1998) *The Silent War: Imperialism and the Changing Perception of Race.* New Brunswick, NJ: Rutgers University Press.

Giddens, Anthony (1981) *A Contemporary Critique of Historical Materialism: Power, Property and the State.* 2 vols. Vol. 1. Berkeley, CA: University of California Press.

Giddens, Anthony (1994) *Beyond Left and Right: The Future of Radical Politics.* Cambridge: Polity Press.

Giddens, Anthony (1998) *The Third Way: The Renewal of Social Democracy.* Cambridge: Polity Press.

Giddens, Anthony (2000) *Runaway World: How Globalization Is Reshaping Our Lives.* New York: Routledge.

Gilroy, Paul (1970a) 'The organic crisis of British capitalism and race: the experience of the seventies', in Birmingham Centre for Contemporary Cultural Studies (eds) *The Empire Strikes Back: Race and Racism in 70s Britain.* London: Routledge.

Gilroy, Paul (1970b) 'Police and thieves', in Birmingham Centre for Contemporary Cultural Studies (eds) *The Empire Strikes Back: Race and Racism in 70s Britain.* London: Routledge, pp. 95–142.

Gilroy, Paul (1970c) 'Steppin' out of Babylon: race, class and autonomy', in Birmingham Centre for Contemporary Cultural Studies (eds) *The Empire Strikes Back: Race and Racism in 70s Britain.* London: Routledge, pp. 276–314.

Gilroy, Paul (1993) *The Black Atlantic: Modernity and Double Consciousness*. Cambridge, MA: Harvard University Press.

Gilroy, Paul (2000) *Against Race: Imagining Political Culture Beyond the Color Line*. First edn. Cambridge, MA: Harvard University Press.

Goodman, Peter S. and Pan, Philip P. (2004) 'Chinese workers pay for Wal-Mart's low prices'. *The Washington Post*, 8 February, AO1.

Gorz, André (1992) 'On the difference between society and community, and why basic income cannot by itself confer full membership of either', in P. Van Parijs (ed.) *Arguing for Basic Income*. London: Verso.

Graeber, David (2001) *Toward an Anthropological Theory of Value: The False Coin of Our Own Dreams*. New York: Palgrave.

Gray, John (1998) *False Dawn: The Delusions of Global Capitalism*. London: Granta Books.

Grossberg, Lawrence (1997) 'On postmodernism and articulation: an interview with Stuart Hall', in David Morley and Kuan-Hsing Chen (eds) *Stuart Hall: Critical Dialogues in Cultural Studies*. New York: Routledge.

Hall, Stuart (1997a) 'Gramsci's relevance for the study of race and ethnicity', in David Morley and Kuan-Hsing Chen (eds) *Stuart Hall: Critical Dialogues in Cultural Studies*. New York: Routledge, pp. 412–40.

Hall, Stuart (1997b) 'New ethnicities', in David Morley and Kuan-Hsing Chen (eds) *Stuart Hall: Critical Dialogues in Cultural Studies*. New York: Routledge.

Hall, Stuart (1997c) 'The problem of ideology: Marxism without guarantees', David Morley and Kuan-Hsing Chen (eds) *Stuart Hall: Critical Dialogues in Cultural Studies*. New York: Routledge, pp. 25–46.

Hall, Stuart (1997d) 'What is this "black" in black popular culture?', in David Morley and Kuan-Hsing Chen (eds) *Stuart Hall: Critical Dialogues in Cultural Studies*. New York: Routledge, pp. 465–75.

Hall, Stuart (2003) 'New Labour has picked up where Thatcherism left off', *The Guardian*, 6 August.

Hannerz, U. (1996) *Transnational Connections: Culture, Peoples, Places*. London and New York: Routledge.

Harrison, Bennett (1994) *Lean and Mean: Why Large Corporations Will Continue to Dominate the Global Economy*. New York: Guilford Press.

Harvey, David (2003) *The New Imperialism*. Oxford: Oxford University Press.

Hegel, G.W.F. (1967a) *The Phenomenology of Mind*. Trans. J.B. Baillie. The Academy Library edn. New York: Harper Torchbooks.

Hegel, G.W.F. (1967b) *Philosophy of Right*. Trans. T.M. Knox. New York: Oxford University Press.

Henwood, Doug (2003) *After the New Economy*. New York: The New Press.

Hilferding, Rudolf (1981) *Finance Capital: A Study of the Latest Phase of Capitalist Development*. London: Routledge & Kegan Paul.

Hill, Christopher (1997a) 'James Harrington and the people', in C. Hill (ed.) *Puritanism and Revolution: Studies in the Interpretation of the English Revolution of the 17th Century*. New York: St Martin's Press, pp. 269–81.

Hill, Christopher (1997b) 'Thomas Hobbes and the revolution in political thought', in C. Hill (ed.) *Puritanism and Revolution: Studies in the Interpretation of the English Revolution of the Seventeenth Century*. New York: St Martin's Press, pp. 248–68.

Hill, Herbert, Cayton, Horace, Bontemps, Arna and Redding, Saunders (1970) 'Reflections on Richard Wright: a symposium on an exiled native son', in D.B. Gibson (ed.) *Five Black Writers: Essays on Wright, Ellison, Baldwin, Hughes, and Leroi Jones*. New York: New York University Press, pp. 58–69.

Hines, Colin (2001) *Localization: A Global Manifesto*. London: Earthscan.

Howard, Michael W. (2000) *Self-Management and the Crisis of Socialism: The Rose in the Fist of the Present*. New York: Rowman & Littlefield Publishers, Inc.

Kaldor, Mary, Anheier, Helmut and Glasius, Marlies (2004a) 'Global civil society in an era of regressive globalization', in Mary Kaldor, Helmut Anheier and Marlies Glasius (eds) *Global Civil Society 2003*. Oxford: Oxford University Press.

Kaldor, Mary, Anheier, Helmut and Glasius, Marlies (eds) (2004b) *Global Civil Society 2003*. Oxford: Oxford University Press.

Kasmir, Sharyn (1996) *The Myth of Mondragon: Cooperatives, Politics, and Working Class Life in a Basque Town*. Albany, NY: SUNY Press.

Khor, Martin (2002) 'Commentary: conflicting paradigms', in J. Cavanagh (ed.) *Alternatives to Economic Globalization: A Better World Is Possible*. San Francisco: Berrett-Koehler Publishers, Inc.

Kircheimer, Otto (1996) 'Legality and legitimacy', in William E. Scheuerman (ed.) *The Rule of Law Under Siege: Selected Essays of Franz L. Neumann and Otto Kircheimer*. Berkeley, CA: University of California Press.

Kornai, Janos (1986) *Contradictions and Dilemmas: Studies on the Socialist Economy and Society*. Cambridge, MA: MIT Press.

Koselleck, Reinhart (1994) *Futures Past: On the Semantics of Historical Time*. Cambridge, MA: MIT Press.

Lash, Scott and Urry, John (1987) *The End of Organized Capitalism*. Madison, WI: University of Wisconsin Press.

Lash, Scott and Urry, John (1994) *Economies of Signs and Space*. London: Sage.

Lauren, Paul Gordon (1988) *Power and Prejudice: The Politics of Diplomacy and Racial Discrimination*. Boulder, CO: Westview Press.

Lawler, David (1998) 'Marx as market socialist', in B. Ollman (ed.) *Market Socialism: The Debate among Socialists*. New York: Routledge, pp. 23–52.

Le Grand, Julian and Bartlett, Will (1993) *Quasi-Markets and Social Policy*. London: Macmillan.

Lenin, Vladimir ([1916] 1987) 'Imperialism: the highest stage of capitalism', in *Essential Works of Lenin: 'What Is to Be Done?' and Other Writings*, edited by Henry M. Christman. New York: Dover Publications.

Leys, Colin (1997) 'Colin Leys replies', *Southern African Report* 12(4).

Lukács, Georg (1965) 'In search of bourgeois man', in G. Lukács (ed.) *Essays on Thomas Mann*. New York: Grosset & Dunlap.

Lukács, Georg (1976) *The Young Hegel: Studies in the Relations between Dialectics and Economics*. Trans. R. Livingstone. Cambridge, MA: MIT Press.

Lukes, Steven (1973) *Individualism: Key Concepts in the Social Sciences*. Oxford: Basil Blackwell.

Lydall, Harold (1984) *Yugoslav Socialism: Theory and Practice*. Oxford: Oxford University Press.

MacMaster, Neil (2001) *Racism in Europe: 1870–2000*. London: Palgrave.

Macpherson, C.B. (1962) *The Political Theory of Possessive Individualism: Hobbes to Locke*. Oxford: Oxford University Press.

Markovits, Inga (1995) *Imperfect Justice: An East–West German Diary*. Oxford: Clarendon Press.

Marx, Karl (1974) *Grundrisse: Foundations of the Critique of Political Economy (Rough Draft)*. Trans. M. Nicolaus. Ed. Quintin Hoare. Harmondsworth: Penguin Books.

Marx, Karl (1978) *Capital*. Trans. D. Fernbach. 3 vols. Vol. 1. Harmondsworth: Penguin Books.

Marx, Karl and Engels, Frederick (1968) *The German Ideology*. Moscow: Progress Publishers.

Maus, Ingeborg (1991) 'Sinn und Bedeutung der Volkssouveranität in der Modernen Gesellschaft', *Kritische Justiz* 24(2).

Meyerson, Harold (2004) 'Plutocrats and populists', *The Washington Post*, Thursday, February 5, A21.

Mommsen, Hans (1989) *The Rise and Fall of Weimar Democracy*. Trans. E. Forster and L.E. Jones. Chapel Hill, NC: The University of North Carolina Press.

Mommsen, Wolfgang J. (1989a) 'The antinomical structure of Max Weber's political thought', in W.J. Mommsen (ed.) *The Political and Social Theory of Max Weber: Collected Essays*. Cambridge: Polity Press, pp. 24–43.

Mommsen, Wolfgang J. (1989b) 'Capitalism and socialism: Weber's dialogue with Marx', in W.J. Mommsen (ed.) *The Political and Social Theory of Max Weber: Collected Essays*. Cambridge: Polity Press, pp. 53–73.

Mommsen, Wolfgang J. (1989c) *The Political and Social Theory of Max Weber: Collected Essays*. Cambridge: Polity Press.

Mommsen, Wolfgang J. (1989d) 'Politics and scholarship: the two icons in Max Weber's life', in W.J. Mommsen (ed.) *The Political and Social Theory of Max Weber: Collected Essays*. Cambridge: Polity Press, pp. 3–23.

Monbiot, George (2001) *Captive State: The Corporate Takeover of Britain*. New York: Pan Books.

Moses, Wilson Jeremiah (ed.) (1996) *Classical Black Nationalism: From the American Revolution to Marcus Garvey*. New York: New York University Press.

Moses, Wilson Jeremiah (1998) *Afrotopia: The Roots of African American Popular History*. Cambridge: Cambridge University Press.

Neumann, Franz (1944) *Behemoth: The Structure and Practice of National Socialism 1933–1944*. Second edn. New York: Oxford University Press.

Neumann, Franz (1996) 'The change in the function of law in modern society', in W.E. Scheuerman (ed.) *The Rule of Law under Siege: Selected Essays of Franz L. Neumann and Otto Kircheimer*. Berkeley, CA: University of California Press.

Nove, Alec (1983) *The Economics of Feasible Socialism*. London: Unwin Hyman.

Ollman, Bertell (1998) 'Market mystification in capitalist and market socialist societies', in B. Ollman (ed.) *Market Socialism: The Debate among Socialists*. New York: Routledge, pp. 81–121.

Pares, Richard (1960) 'Merchants and planters', *Economic History Review* Supplement 4.

Parijs, Phillipe Van (1995) *Real Freedom for All: What (If Anything) Can Justify Capitalism?* Oxford: Clarendon Press.

Riddell, Peter (2000) 'Labour fails to bridge the class divide', *The Times*, 29 June, 1.

Robotham, Don (1980) 'Pluralism as an ideology', *Social and Economic Studies* 29(1): 69–89.

Robotham, Don (1989) 'The development of a black ethnicity in Jamaica', in R. Lewis and P. Bryan (eds) *Garvey: His Work and Impact*. Kingston: ISER, University of the West Indies, pp. 23–38.

Robotham, Don (2000) 'Blackening the Jamaican nation: the travails of a black bourgeoisie in a globalizing world', *Identities: Global Studies of Culture and Power* 7(1).

Roemer, John (1994) *A Future for Socialism*. Cambridge, MA: Harvard University Press.

Rupert, Mark and Smith, Hazel (eds) (2002) *Historical Materialism and Globalization*. New York: Routledge.

Said, Yahia and Desai, Meghnad (2004) 'Trade and global civil society: the anti-capitalist movement revisited', in Mary Kaldor, Helmut Anheier and Marlies Glasius (eds) *Global Civil Society 2003*. Oxford: Oxford University Press, pp. 59–85.

Samuelson, Robert J. (2003) 'The creaky job machine', *The Washington Post*, 17 September, A27.

Sassen, Saskia (2000) *Cities in a World Economy*. Thousand Oaks, CA: Pine Forge Press.

Sassoon, Anne Showstack (1987) *Gramsci's Politics*. Second edn. Minneapolis: University of Minnesota Press.

Scheuerman, William E. (1997) *Between the Norm and the Exception: The Frankfurt School and the Rule of Law*. Cambridge, MA: The MIT Press.

Scheuerman, William E. (1999) *Carl Schmitt: The End of Law*. Lanham, MD: Rowman & Littlefield Publishers.

Schmitt, Carl (1976) *The Concept of the Political*. Trans. George Schwab. New Brunswick, NJ: Rutgers University Press.

Schmitt, Carl (1985) *The Crisis of Parliamentary Democracy*. Trans. E. Kennedy. Cambridge, MA: MIT Press.

Schweickart, David (1996) *Against Capitalism*. Boulder, CO: Westview Press.

Schweickart, David (1998) 'Market socialism: a defense', in B. Ollman (ed.) *Market Socialism: The Debate among Socialists*. New York: Routledge, pp. 7–22.

Schweickart, David (2002) *After Capitalism*. New York: Rowman & Littlefield Publishers, Inc.

Sik, Ota (1976) *The Third Way: Marxist-Leninist Theory and Modern Industrial Society*. London: Wildwood House International Arts and Sciences.

Smith, Adam (1976) *An Inquiry into the Nature and Causes of the Wealth of Nations*. Chicago: University of Chicago Press.

Sparks, Colin (1997) 'Stuart Hall, cultural studies and Marxism', in D. Morley and K.-H. Chen (eds) *Stuart Hall: Critical Dialogues in Cultural Studies*. New York: Routledge.

Sutela, Pekka (1991) *Economic Thought and Economic Reform in the Soviet Union*. Cambridge: Cambridge University Press.

Tabili, Laura (1994) *We Ask for British Justice: Workers and Racial Difference in Late Imperial Britain*. Ithaca, NY: Cornell University Press.

Taylor, Charles (1992) *Multiculturalism and 'the Politics of Recognition'*. Princeton, NJ: Princeton University Press.

Ticktin, Hillel (1998) 'The problem is market socialism', in B. Ollman (ed.) *Market Socialism: The Debate among Socialists*. New York: Routledge, pp. 55–80.

Unger, Roberto (1975) *The Critical Legal Studies Movement*. Cambridge, MA: Harvard University Press.

Wade, Robert (1996) 'Globalization and its limits: reports of the death of the national economy are greatly exaggerated', in Suzanne Berger and Ronald Dore (eds) *National Diversity and Global Capitalism*. Ithaca, NY: Cornell University Press, pp. 60–88.

Walker, David (2000) 'Brown's beneficence', *The Guardian*, 17 July.

Wayne, Leslie (2003) 'Butting heads with the Pentagon', *The New York Times*, 23 July.

Weber, Max (1958) 'Politics as a vocation', in H.H. Gerth and C. Wright Mills (eds) *From Max Weber: Essays in Sociology*. New York: Oxford, pp. 115–28.

Whyte, William Foot and Whyte, Kathleen King (1988) *Making Mondragon: The Growth and Dynamics of the Worker Cooperative Complex*. Ithaca, NY: Cornell University Press.

Wintour, Patrick (2000) 'Class-riven UK exposed in new study', *The Guardian*, 12 July.

Zile, Zigurdis L. (ed.) (1992) *Ideas and Forces in Soviet Legal History: A Reader in the Soviet State and Law*. New York: Oxford University Press.

# Index